Advan 

MW01004031

Holy Bleep! That Was NOT a Coincidence

"This book is a beautiful and down-to-earth expression of something we all experience... but often lack the confidence in believing! Michelle shares her personal accounts of these "Godincidences," reminding us all of how present and involved this power of The Universe is in our everyday life, if only we took the time to notice. Her authenticity and genuine desire to help others feel the connection to God is heart-warming and uplifting, while her practical advice for doing so enables anyone to begin recognizing these signs with ease in their own lives."

-Ashley Kay Andy, author of *Empaths at the Edge*

As a believer, I grapple with my scientific mind running amok to rationalize and try to explain all of the magical moments, the signs, the beautiful gifts that God sends each day. I dismiss serendipitous moments as coincidental, even though the small, patient voice is consistently there, reminding me that my communiques, my miracles are all around me, ready for me to embrace.

People always remark that "seeing is believing." While we can all understand the tangibility of this saying, what we neglect is another, even more profound statement. "Believing is seeing." Michelle reminds me that as a believer, God is communicating with me every single day and through so many venues. The magic, the mystery, the beautiful messages are there. Always there. When I am in touch with the Almighty, I am truly blessed with His gifts. I believe, and I can see. I am open to receive. Thank you, Michelle, for being His vessel and reminding us all to embrace His precious glory and wonders that are around us every day.

-Wendy Valentine, Professor of Psychology

It is the perfect mix of light and profound. Whether you're a lifelong believer or don't quite know what to believe, there is something to be learned in Michelle Prohaska's *Holy Bleep*. You'll feel like you're chatting with your best friend over coffee or a cocktail. You'll laugh, you'll cry, you'll feel inspired, you'll feel loved.

-Chris Gruhn, Secondary Educator

A powerful message of hope at a time when so many need it. In *Holy Bleep*, Michelle shares how her grief was transformed into the evidence of God. She shares an invitation to see God in a new way and teaches us practical tools, so we too can see Godincidences in our lives regardless of our circumstances.

-Aby Garvey

If you're looking for inspiration, joy, and even magic, this is the book for you! Michelle Moine Prohaska shares from her life and from her heart to help others see what's possible. This book teaches you how to become connected, at peace, and optimistic no matter what's happening around you.

- Dawn Mattera, Author of Amazon #1 New Release
The Italian Art of Living

This is a "how to" book about one woman's journey of losing her father and how that experience shaped her view of what God means to her. Through this new view, she stepped into a place of positivity, joy, laughter, and gratitude like she's never felt before. Now, she is sharing this journey with others in the hopes that they, too, will learn how to lean into another part of themselves and create all these things into their own life.

-Traci Lynn, Life Coach at Traci Lynn Life Coaching

The book gave me a bold realization of what the world can look like if I just open my mind to the daily presence of the universe's power and how I can tap into this power and experience life in a way I have been missing for years.

-Larry Prohaska, business owner

"Would you like to be happier, more satisfied with your life? Spending a few hours with Michelle and *Holy Bleep* will arm you with the tools of a happier daily life. Michelle's insights and experiences have helped me love my life...just. as. it. is."

-Andrea Bell

This book invites you to discover a life filled with new perspective, new discoveries and gives insight and revelation to the spiritual realm that we all live in. The experiences she writes about will awaken an awareness of "Godincidences" that surround our everyday lives. An inspiring read!

-Amy Wienands, Real Estate Broker/Owner

Reading Michelle's book and therefore being introduced to her world and her viewpoint is a lot like meeting her in person. I have had the privilege of both. To me, her book is a natural extension of the heart and passion she radiates for God and is a forever testimony to the place and importance her faith is. How divine interactions should not be a surprise or something to fear; but instead be sought out like buried treasure and cherished when you have them. I leave from this place excited and (in) awe and wondering when I should expect my next encounter with a God who loves and is crazy about me and wants to be involved in every part of my life so that He can bless and overfill every area He is part of.

-Martyn Wood, Business Owner

"I am fortunate to call Michelle my friend. After you read this book, you will understand the wisdom, wit, and most of all, the love that she brings to life. This book got me reconnected, re-centered, and re-invigorated. I highly recommend it!"

-Bill Bass, business owner

It's hard to believe in coincidences, but it's even harder to believe in anything else. Michelle does a fantastic job of explaining your ability to open your mind and accept the fact that coincidences are much more than mere coincidences. They are connected, related mini-stories in this thing called life. In fact, I would say that becoming friends with Michelle years ago, through mutual friends, was now much more than just a coincidence... It was meant to be!

-Sue Thuringer

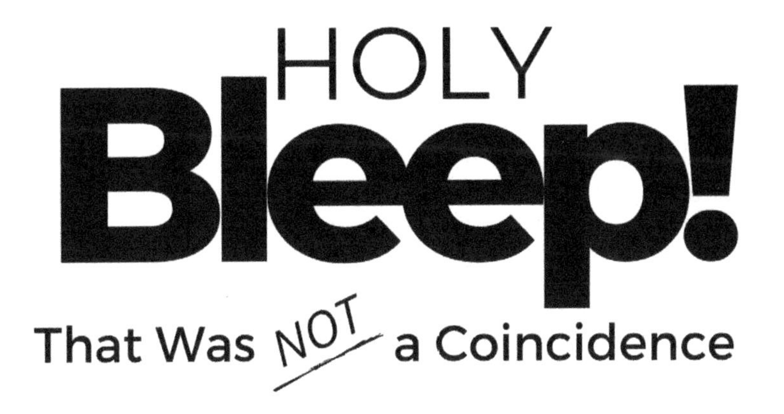

MICHELLE MOINE PROHASKA

Published by Nudged Media

Identifiers:
Library of Congress Control Number: 2021900631
ISBN: 978-0-578-84011-6 (paperback)
ISBN: 978-0-578-84012-3 (hardback)
ISBN: 978-0-578-84013-0 (ebook)

Available in paperback, hardback, e-book, and audiobook

Edited by Jill Ellis
Cover Design by Klassic Designs

Dedication

I dedicate *Holy Bleep! That Was NOT a Coincidence* to:

All who have yet to discover the AWEsomeness
of this life we are living.

My Dad, the life of the party, who is missed greatly every day.

Photo credit – P. Cerwinske

"The more you praise and celebrate your life,
the more there is in life to celebrate."
— Oprah Winfrey

Contents

Part I: My Story

Part II: God is...

Part III: How to...

Part IV: You. Are. Being. Nudged.

INTRODUCTION

This book is about my discovery of our connection to a magical, mysterious power. Some call this power God. Others call it The Universe, Higher Power, Spirit, The Law of Attraction. Call it what you want (I like to mix it up!); it's real, powerful, and just waiting for us to connect to it. Once we make this true connection, we will realize we are not going through this thing called life alone.

Many people are suffering from grief, loss, or lack (all of any kind). We feel all alone. Like it's us against the world. We feel deserted or abandoned.

But I'm here to tell you...We are not alone! There's a force of love so powerful and strong, with such a synchronized connection to all of creation, that once we learn to see it, we'll never feel alone again.

This book is *not* about religion. It's about *God*. There's a difference.

In this book, I'll ask you to be open. Be open to this Higher Love. Be open to its existence. Be open to connecting with it. Be open to laughing until you cry with it.

Really! This is crazy fun stuff, and I think life can be crazy fun if we let it.

We've all heard it.

Life can change in the blink of an eye.

You may experience an unexpected loss of a job, a financial hardship, a disheartening medical diagnosis, or the loss of a loved one.

Has this ever happened to you?

How did it affect you? What did you take away from it? Were you able to see the good in it? Were you able to see things to be grateful for? Were you able to see the many gifts in it?

In June 2008, my life changed forever, in one really bad way but also in many, many good ways. What happened at that time was just the beginning of my journey of viewing the world in a whole new, magical way.

PART I

My Story

This is my story, but I didn't write it; God did, and it's beautifully magical.

1

The Blinking Light

The little blinking light on an answering machine...

There are endless possibilities that could lie behind that little blinking light.

It could be a message from a long, lost friend.

It could be someone inviting you to a party.

It could be someone informing you of a massive windfall with *your* name on it. The Publisher's Clearing House, maybe?

Or, it could be your sister-in-law informing you of the worst news of your life.

Flashing lights flash to get your attention. They usually have a meaning of caution behind them. They're telling you to look and to pay attention.

I had *no* idea how this small, blinking, red light would forever change my life. What I wouldn't give to go back to that day, Father's Day in 2008, and have that little light *not* be blinking. But pushing that play button was the beginning of the most incredible growing experience of my life.

My husband Larry, my daughters, Holly and Brooke, who were twelve and nine years old at the time, and I were getting ready to go to church. After getting myself to an acceptable appearance, I walked out into our great room to see that little red light on our answering machine blinking.

It was my sister-in-law, Amy.

"Michelle, Honey..."

Honey! Honey! Why was she calling me Honey? We really like each other and all, but...HONEY? We do *not* address each other as Honey. Unless she was going to "set me straight" in one of our jovial discussions as to the way she sees it—"Oh Honey, let me tell you..."—she does not call me "Honey."

Either she's starting to celebrate Father's Day a little early, or something is up. And by up, I mean very wrong.

"Your mom wanted me to call to tell you that your dad isn't feeling well, so they've taken him to the hospital by ambulance."

Wait! Did she just say ambulance? Ambulance? Ambulance! This could not *be good. Why would they need an ambulance if he's just "not feeling well"?*

Ambulances are only used in emergencies. You don't use an ambulance when you're just not feeling well!

Maybe they were just being extra cautious.

He has to be ok. He was just here at our house...what was it... like ten or eleven hours ago? He was fine then. He had a very hoarse voice, but I even asked him if he felt ok. He told me he felt fine. I can still hear him in my head:

"I feel fine. I just can't talk."

The last I knew, being hoarse did *not* constitute a ride in an ambulance.

What could've happened in those twelve hours to go from fine to an ambulance?

Why did I suddenly feel like my heart and stomach had switched places? I wasn't sure what was where. But something was stuck in my throat. I suddenly thought, "Now, *I'm* not feeling very well."

A hospital. That was not at all how I'd imagined celebrating Father's Day with Dad.

2

Frog Legs and Ice Cream

The day before the worst-Father's-Day-ever was a busy day. First, we had a birthday party for my grandma, my dad's mom. When I called to ask Dad where we were supposed to meet for the party, he could hardly get the word "hello" out.

"What's wrong with you?" I asked.

"Oh, I had frog legs for supper last night."

That was Dad. Always being a jokester. Sometimes corny. Sometimes funny. All the while, thinking he was hilarious. No matter how bad his jokes were, you couldn't help but laugh. He proceeded to use the frog legs line many times that day. Every time I heard it, I just smiled and shook my head.

We had a great turnout for Grandma's party. Lots of family and friends gathered, all sharing their stories and memories of Grandma.

Dad told stories—with what little voice he had—of growing up on the farm with his brothers.

Larry, the girls, and I left the party a little early to go home and get Brooke ready for her dance recital. The recital was fantastic. Afterward, we had almost twenty of our extended family members at our house to eat supper and have ice cream sundaes.

Although I don't think I heard it that night, I can almost guarantee Dad said, "There's always room for ice cream."

Dad had lots of sayings he would use frequently. I'm sure anyone who knew Dad well has heard several of them often. His reasoning behind, "There's always room for ice cream," was that when you ate ice cream, it would just melt and go into the cracks between the food that was already in your stomach.

I'm sure digestive research would dispute this argument, but we affectionately went along with Dad's reasoning.

After everyone had their bellies sufficiently full, even the cracks, everyone was preparing to leave our house and venture out into the night, all heading to their different destinations. Several of us were standing in the front entryway, saying our goodbyes. I can still hear Dad say to Larry's dad, "Take care, Bob. And... Live it up while you're young." This was one of his classic Bernie lines.

Live it up while you're young.

Live it up while you're young.

He didn't just preach this line. He practiced it. He would deliver this line to anyone of *any* age. I'm willing to bet he even said it to his eighty-eight-year-old mom earlier that same day at her birthday party.

It was his philosophy. Live it up! Enjoy life. You just never know...

I had no idea the meaning behind that line of his was about to change forever.

3

Flood Waters

2008 was the year of the 500-year flood in Iowa. The flood caused a lot of damage and destruction throughout Iowa, including at my parents' cottage. The cottage was where we'd spend most of our summer weekends on the lake; well, it's actually a dammed-up river. Just two weekends before the worst-Father's-Day-ever, we were at the cottage watching it rain all day. Maybe a better way of wording it would be pour. Dump buckets. Rain cats and dogs. Well, no, not cats and dogs, but the sights were rather entertaining. The water on the river was very high and continuing to rise. There were flood warnings out. We watched large clumps of trees and debris floating down the river towards the dam.

We saw a huge chunk of land with foliage float by. It looked like a little island just drifting down the river. There was even wildlife on the island. A bird sat perched on a branch, just watching the world go by.

It was quite a sight.

Dad had the great idea that we should quickly go to the dam and watch the island careen over the edge. Luckily, at this point, the rain had let up because he probably still would have thought it'd be a good idea, even if it was still pouring rain.

All of us jumped into our vehicle and drove to the dam to watch this exciting spectacle.

Or not.

The water level was so high on the other side of the dam that there was hardly any fall at all.

It was very anticlimactic.

We laughed at ourselves and the ways we were seeking entertainment. I mean, really...all of us hurriedly running to the vehicle to beat "the island" to the dam to watch it fall over. Who does that? We do.

Later that day, the water had risen into the yards along Lake Shore Drive and gone over the road. We heard they wanted volunteers to go to the Volunteer Fire Department building to help fill sandbags. So, Dad, Larry, Holly Ann, and I went to help.

I had the job of tying bags shut with twine. Easy enough job. This was great. I was making a difference one knot at a time.

I should've worn gloves.

I very quickly developed blisters, which ripped open soon after forming. Youch! Within a matter of twenty minutes, I had managed to purge the skin right off of my fingers. I felt like such a wimp. Someone gave me Band-aids to put on my wounds. I tried to continue tying but to no avail. The tying motion just ripped the Band-aids off. I felt like a failure. Some help I was. I couldn't do anything without using my hands.

I felt useless.

I looked over at Dad and Larry. They were doing the heavy work of lifting the full sandbags. I saw Holly Ann. She was right there in the action, holding bags open and helping with the tying, happy as could be.

Amazing.

All of those people—most of them residents of the town, most of them strangers to me—working together to help others.

That's what it's all about.

It wasn't much longer until they ran out of sand, and the operation was halted. Well, now, *no one* could do anything. I have to admit; it made me feel a little better.

4

Basement Wall is Falling Down

Being the service-minded people that they are, Larry and Dad continued to find ways to help. They had gone over to an elderly lady's house who lived on the lake to help carry stuff out of her basement. Later that day, the volunteer firefighters were going around telling people about the flood warning. One of them told Larry and me they didn't want people down in the basements because of all the hydraulic pressure against the basement walls. If a wall were to give, the person would have no time to get out.

On Monday, Dad left to go back home for work. He had to go a very roundabout way north and west to get south because of all the closed bridges and roads. It took him four times longer than usual to get home.

Mom, Larry, the girls, and I stayed to keep an eye on things at the cottage.

Very soon after Dad left, Lakeshore Drive was underwater, and no traffic was allowed through. That meant we weren't driving anywhere. Mom and Dad's friends from a few doors down, Dick and Chris, had to leave their house because it was surrounded by floodwaters on all four sides. So Chris came to the cottage.

Chris, Mom, and I were sitting and chatting in the TV area. I was telling Mom and Chris about what the firefighter had said about not being in the basements. Just then, we heard what sounded like very heavy furniture being dragged across a concrete floor, and all the walls of the cottage started creaking and moving.

We felt a rush of panic wash over us and ran toward the front door. We yelled upstairs to the three kids and told them to come quickly. Grandma (my mom) threw the kids in the car and started backing out. I stood with my hands on my hips in the driveway, looking at her and laughing. Where did she think she was going to go? The only road out was under a couple of feet of water and closed.

I thought, "Wait a minute. Where was Mom's concern for *my* well-being?" Chris and I stood there dumbfounded while she attempted to back out of the driveway. Obviously, the grandkids trumped me.

I shook my head and approached the car window. She turned and looked at me with panic on her face. I smiled as I motioned for her to roll down the window.

Laughing, I said, "And where do you think you're going?" raising my eyebrows in anticipation of her response.

"I don't know. We've got to get out of here."

"Well, you can't get anywhere...remember? The road is flooded. And where's your concern for us, by the way?" I questioned as I motioned to Chris and me.

She laughed, "I guess you're on your own."

"I guess I know where I stand now." I laughed. I told Mom to put the car in park and relax; she couldn't go anywhere.

I tried to call Larry, who was off helping people sandbag their homes, but got his voice mail.

We didn't know what had happened, but the cottage was still standing. Since we didn't know how stable things were, we decided it would be best to stay outside until we knew more. So, we grabbed some lawn chairs out of the garage and set up camp in the driveway.

I went wading around the house to see if I could see anything. The water had come up under the deck, so it was hard to see if there was any damage. I couldn't see anything. Let's just say the Cedar River is not the clearest water in the world. It's murky and brown, not Caribbean clear blue.

Then I opened the outside storm cellar type doors to the basement. The walk-in door was closed, but the water had filled up the steps leading down into the basement.

Once Larry got there, he figured out the basement wall had split open and pushed in like a double gate opening up.

The rest of us didn't want to go back into the cottage. Understandable, right? But he assured us the water pressure was holding the walls in place at this point because the basement was totally full of water.

"It's fine," he said.

Yeah, right. We were leery, but we reluctantly went back into the cottage.

Larry said he'd been down in the basement just forty-five minutes earlier, checking on the sump pump. We were so thankful he wasn't down there when the wall broke because the rush of water slammed the door shut; there were only a few inches of breathing space between the water and the ceiling.

Eventually, as the hours passed, the road opened back up, and we were all able to return to our own homes an hour away.

5

Perspective

A few days after the cottage basement wall broke open, Dad and Larry ventured back to the cottage to work on hauling out all the mud that had filled up the basement.

The route they had to take to get there was an even more roundabout way than the way we had to take home because several additional roads had been closed due to flooding. They ended up having to drive ten miles to the west before they could go north. This different route took them through Parkersburg, which had an F5 tornado tear through the town just a couple of weeks before the flood. The tornado totally flattened a large portion of the town. I remember Larry describing to me the destruction. I thought to myself how lucky we were with the amount of damage to the cottage compared to those people who had lost all of their possessions.

It was good for us to see and recognize this perspective, to be thankful for the size of our loss compared to others.

6

The Ditches were Full

When I called my sister-in-law, Amy, back on the morning of the worst-Father's-Day-ever, she said Mom was very adamant we all come to the hospital.

Adamant? If Mom was adamant, that must mean Dad was not ok.

I had to get to Dad. I had to see that he was ok, and then we could go on with our day as scheduled.

Instead of going to church, we each packed a small bag and started heading north about forty-five minutes to the hospital. Because it was Father's Day, we planned to head up to my parents' cottage and spend the day with my family, like we usually do on Father's Day. We had some flood cleanup to do, but we were going to make time to relax and have some fun, too. Because that's what we do at the cottage.

So, in my mind, I was thinking that after he was feeling better than "not well," we'd all head back to the cottage, have a couple of cocktails, and lots of laughs. I really wanted to laugh.

It was about a forty-five-minute drive to the hospital, although I knew it would seem a lot longer. You know, like when you're watching the sand go through an hourglass, and it feels like the sand at the top keeps multiplying. There are times when you want it to slow down and times when it can't go fast enough. What's with that? Maybe it's because we focus on where the sand is coming from and where it is going, rather than watch each grain of sand flow through. I just wanted to get there and get there fast. Little did I know there'd soon be a time I'd wish the sand to start falling up as though time was rewinding.

I needed to get there to see Dad, to see and hear he was fine, that all this was nothing, and everything was going to be ok. Ok, as in the same—all is well. Nothing had changed. That all was great, in fact. It couldn't be better. Normal. I just wanted my normal.

I was so thankful as we were driving that they reopened the roads. Earlier that week, many roads, including the one we were driving on, were closed to traffic. The ditches and land surrounding the highway were still filled with floodwaters, but the road was open.

Just then, out of the corner of my eye, I saw a car approaching us very rapidly on the gravel crossroad to our left. It hit the railroad tracks that paralleled the highway at an alarming speed and flew through a stop sign. It was headed right toward us!

By the time I could even comprehend what was happening, the car uncontrollably made a sharp right-hand turn, as if trying to make a perfect ninety-degree angle. It turned before the median and onto the road heading south, joining the flow with the southbound traffic. My heart, still reeling from the news of the day, increased in rate even more.

I quickly turned my head to see the car over-steer right into the ditch...full of water!

I hurriedly explained to Larry what had happened and said, “We have to go back and make sure they’re alright.”

At the next possible opportunity, we turned around. I added, “If they’re alright, we’ve got to keep moving.”

As we neared the spot where the car had gone into the ditch, we noticed there were already three cars that had stopped to assist. One person had a cell phone to their ear.

I said, “They’re covered. We’ve got to keep moving.” We turned around and began driving north again.

I still don’t know what happened with that driver. I pray that all was well. But I believe if that car hadn’t made that sudden right turn, it would’ve crashed right into our vehicle.

7

Driving in Circles

In route, I called my mom to find out if they had learned anything. She said they planned to transfer Dad to a hospital closer to our home, and we should just meet them there. So, I told Larry to turn around yet again.

We started heading toward hospital number two. As we were approaching the hospital, I was talking to my mom on the phone again. She informed me they thought Dad might've had a stroke, and he was unresponsive.

A stroke? How could that be? My dad's healthy. He's the life of the party. A stroke would change everything.

Suddenly, it felt like someone had turned the thermostat to my bloodstream down to ice cold. My hands and feet began to tingle, but yet they were sweating profusely.

Unresponsive? How are we going to resume our normal Father's Day festivities if he's unresponsive?

They were still trying to find out if there would be a neurologist available at hospital number two. They hadn't even begun the transport process, and it was a forty-five-minute drive. But, if there wasn't a neurologist available, they might send him to the Mayo Clinic in Rochester, Minnesota. So, we decided to head back home and wait until we knew where and when to go.

If not for the seriousness of the whole situation, an aerial view of our driving route that morning would've been rather comical. We had literally been driving in circles for about an hour, and we ended up right back where we started. If only we could go back to the night before when everything was as it should be.

Ever since my husband, girls, and I had moved back into their area about seven years earlier, my parents had become some of our best friends. We did everything together. All of our good friends knew my parents and were also friends with them. They were part of our everyday lives, and we loved it. Not everyone can say that, and I felt very blessed we had this special bond.

Once home, we repacked our bags. We might be heading to Rochester, and who knew for how long.

One phrase kept running through my head over and over.

"Things will never be the same...Things will never be the same."

8

Would You Like Some Mayo With That?

We finally got word that they were flying Dad by helicopter to the Mayo Clinic. I felt a sense of relief. Although we wouldn't be close to our home, I knew the prestige the Mayo Clinic name carried. At that point, all I wanted was for Dad to get better and be healthy, so we all could move on with business as usual.

On the way, we stopped to get gas and take a restroom break. While in the convenience store, the purse packs of tissues caught my eye. Although I hadn't really shed many tears yet, I had a feeling there would be waterfalls in my future. I grabbed a pack of tissues but reassured myself I wouldn't actually need them. Everything was going to be ok. I wanted the tissues to be a reassurance of that. You know, like taking an umbrella to ensure that it won't rain.

Once we made it to the emergency room at the Mayo Clinic, we went in and told them who we were there to see. The lady behind the desk took a quick assessing glance at my family and asked that I, and only I, follow her, leaving my family behind. I wasn't sure of the reasoning behind this request. She must've thought my girls were too young to see what I was about to see.

What am I going to see? What am I going to learn? What condition is my dad in? Is he going to be ok? If it's bad news, I don't want to know. I can't do this by myself.

Deep down, I really felt like a scared little girl.

I recall feeling empty and lonely. I had no idea what I was about to encounter, but I felt like I had to do it as the grown thirty-eight-year-old woman I was. Deep down, I really felt like a scared little girl.

After we were out of earshot of my young girls, the lady explained she thought I should assess the situation first before letting my girls see him with a breathing tube. Instantly, it felt like someone inside me was tugging on a chord that was tightly stretched from my heart to my chin. No matter what tactic I would've tried, I wouldn't have been able to keep my chin from quivering and my heart from aching.

As we rounded the corner into a large, curtained triage area, I quickly and continually scanned my surroundings for the sight I was dreading to see. But I didn't see Dad. Where was he? My chaperone informed a couple of people in the room who I was and who I was there to see. As they made eye contact with me, I can't even imagine what the fear in my eyes looked like. It must've been pretty bad because they immediately guided me to a nearby chair. The first thing I thought of was the scene we've all seen in the movies when someone is about to deliver some terrible news, and they advise the recipient to sit down.

Is he dead? Is this it? Is my life changed forever?

The two people—I'm not sure what title they held—one male and one female, started telling me with calm, matter-of-fact faces the situation with my dad. I honestly can't recall a single word they said. I just remember sifting through each word as it was thrown at me, trying to identify any of them as a confirmation of my fears.

The lady who had led me to the room disappeared and returned with my husband and girls. Larry looked at me, searching my face for some type of answers—answers that I still was not sure I'd received. Finally, someone let us know they took him upstairs. A sense of relief—though slight—washed over me.

Upstairs. Upstairs. I'm pretty sure when someone dies, they do not *take them upstairs.*

They told us they would get someone to take us up to where he was.

Upstairs is good! Yes! Let's go upstairs. Upstairs, people get better. Upstairs has to be so much better than going downstairs.

I don't remember the walk. I have no idea how long it took. Our usher guided us to the neurology department. When one nurse was about to take us back to the room Dad was in, another nurse said we needed to go to the family waiting room first; they were prepping him for surgery. These additional "circles" were adding to my dizziness. I'm reasonably certain I was walking upright and straight. Normal. But I felt like I was walking like a middle-aged person who did not fare well with spinning and had just stepped off the Tilt-a-Whirl.

9

The Waiting Room

When we arrived at the family waiting room for the neurosurgery intensive care unit, Mom, my brother, Mark, and my sister-in-law, Amy, were there. When you see strangers in a waiting room, you have no idea what their situation is or why they are there. You don't know what emotions are flowing through their hearts. When I saw Mom, Mark, and Amy, I knew. I knew why we were there, and I knew how I was feeling.

I didn't like it.

I immediately went to Mom and hugged her. Then, we all exchanged embraces. They *all* looked like they were boding better than I.

My mom took a deep breath as she sat back down, sighed out loud, and said, "I didn't think I'd have to deal with something like this, this soon." None of us did. The day's surreal feeling still didn't have me convinced we were actually dealing with it then. Dad was only sixty-three. There was a day, probably decades earlier, that I would have thought sixty-three was old. That sixty-three meant you had lived a nice, long life. But now, now I felt very differently. Sixty-three was much too young for a life to end. For *my dad's* life to end.

The family waiting room was a large room with two big seating areas connected by a small kitchenette with a microwave and coffee maker. I didn't realize how fortunate we'd been that day to have the whole space to ourselves. That first day we were there was the only day this was the case. To have that space to ourselves while we acquainted ourselves with our new situation was a gift. We were free to be silent. Free to be in the silence.

We needed that space.

Then I thought about it. Of course, no one else was there. Not only was it a Sunday, but it was Father's Day. Of course, there were no scheduled surgeries that day.

It was Father's Day.

Why?

Why did this have to happen on Father's Day?

Why would God allow this to happen on Father's Day?

10

Of Course, Father's Day

I believe before we begin our lives here on this wonderfully mysterious earth, we are in the space that I—and many other people—refer to as heaven. Our souls are there. Our souls that always have been and always will be. I believe it's a distinct possibility our souls are in heaven, conspiring with God and the other souls about our life path. Who will be involved, major life events, and possibly even our death.

As I sat there, I pictured Dad's jovial soul conspiring. I could just imagine him saying as he giggled, "Yeah. Father's Day. I want to go out on Father's Day."

And then he'd giggle some more. "That'll be good."

If you knew my dad, I'm sure you could imagine this right along with me. He was quite the jokester. Although I'm sure some of you can't see the humor in it...

Bernie could.

Although I still don't find any humor in the situation and how horrible I felt that day and the days to follow, I still, to this day, get a smile on my face, thinking of Dad giggling as he conspired.

11

The Sigh

Someone came to lead us to him so we could see him briefly before they took him into surgery. We met the gurney in the hall just outside of the neurological ICU. There, my dad laid looking lifeless, with his eyes closed, and the breathing tube coming out of his mouth. My chin immediately resumed the quivering that had also spread to my voice. I told him I loved him (something my family has never been very verbal about), and we were praying for him. I wanted to pray him right off that gurney and back to the cottage where we were supposed to be enjoying the lake and the sunshine and celebrating Father's Day. This was the absolute *worst* way to spend Father's Day with my dad that I could possibly imagine.

We all took turns expressing our loving words and then returned to the family waiting room.

Now, what do we do? Just sit here and wait? Sit here with our fears?

We were asked if we would like to have a chaplain come and talk to us. We all agreed it would be good. We could use all the prayer power we could get.

After some time, the door to the waiting room opened. My stomach dropped.

Is this someone bearing news about my dad?

We were the only ones in the waiting room, so I knew this person was coming to speak to us. The kind-looking lady approached us and asked if we were the Moine family. We said we were, and she introduced herself as one of the chaplains on staff at the hospital. I felt a soothing sense of relief. I was mostly relieved she wasn't there to convey some bad news about my dad's condition.

She asked about the details surrounding why we were there. We told her what little we knew. She spoke with us for a while. I don't recall most of what she said, but I very vividly remember her opening up her bible and reading:

> *Likewise, the Spirit helps us in our weakness; for we do not know how to pray as we ought, but that very Spirit intercedes with sighs too deep for words.* Romans 8:26

I saw her mouth moving. I knew she had to be speaking actual words, but all I heard was "Whaa whaa whaa whaa," like in the Charlie Brown TV shows. The sound that depicted grownups talking.

She then explained the scripture by saying when we are too distraught to even know how to pray for what we want, the Holy Spirit steps in for us. When all we can do is sigh, that is when the Holy Spirit is taking over and praying for us.

I'd heard this scripture many times before but never really knew what it meant.

This passage now and will forever have a whole new meaning to me. During the several days that followed, I was amazed at the number of sighs I heard in the family waiting room. There were so many people with incredibly devastating and stressful situations who were so overwhelmed with emotion that all they could do was sigh. Spirit is very busy in a place like this.

The next time you're in such a place, take notice of the sighs. Find peace in hearing them, knowing the Spirit of pure Love is at work.

12

The Sign

After a few hours of nervously waiting, the doctor entered the family waiting room and spoke with us. He told us Dad had had a brain aneurism, which created a very large blood clot to form in his brain, causing a stroke. It happened on the left side of his brain. He explained they repaired the aneurysm and removed a large portion of the clot but had to remove part of his skull on that side to allow the brain to swell.

The doctor asked if he was right or left-handed. We said right. He explained the left side of the brain controls movement on the right side of the body.

So, our bad news continued to get worse. The doctor continued to say the next seventy-two hours would be critical, and we just needed to wait and see.

Once again, this was so not what I wanted to be doing on Father's Day. This was the suckiest Father's Day EVER!

A while later, we all went into his room in the neurological ICU. It was so hard to see him lying there hooked up to so many machines. I pictured in my mind his smiling face and heard his cackle of a laugh. That's who my dad was. Not that seemingly lifeless body on the bed in front of me.

I hurt. Everywhere. My heart actually hurt, right smack dab in the middle of my chest. It made me just want to leave. I didn't want to be in that room. It just brought reality to the situation. I had to look at him. I had to look at him not looking like himself.

Taped to the I.V. pole above his head, a computer printed page said in bold letters:

NO
SKULL
FLAP
LEFT SIDE

It was in very bold letters. You couldn't miss it. You couldn't *not* look at it. *I* couldn't not look at it. I looked at the sign and then at the large c-shaped scar that had been closed up with staples. It just made Dad and the whole situation seem so vulnerable...and fragile.

I felt so helpless. The sign was posted there, so the hospital staff knew to be careful and protect the left side of Dad's head when they came in contact with him. His brain, the thing that controls his entire body, was just right there, under his skin that was now being held in place with staples.

Staples. Our head is not supposed to be held together with staples!

The doctor explained to us the piece of skull was left out to allow for swelling. Vulnerable. His brain had been through so much trauma that it was *expected* to swell. Vulnerable. Not just him, but me. I felt so incredibly vulnerable. Seeing all of this made me feel like I could just shatter at the simplest touch. It hurt. It hurt. It hurt!

I don't like to hurt.

Where's the rewind button?!

This sucks! This sucks! This sucks!

I don't like it when situations suck.

Being in Dad's ICU room hurt so much. It was the last place I wanted to be, which is what made it so hard. And not wanting to be in that room made me feel horrible. I wanted to be there for Dad; let him know I loved him and would do anything for him. But it hurt too much.

Why is it so hard? What kind of daughter am I? I don't even want to stand watch by the bedside of my vulnerable dad. What's wrong with me? Who doesn't stand vigil at the bedside of their loved one?

Luckily for me, we only would go in three or four times a day for only about 10-15 minutes at a time. I couldn't handle any more than that. My body couldn't handle it. My aching head couldn't. My heart couldn't.

What's wrong with me?

We were each taking turns holding his left hand, rubbing it, and talking to him. We wanted him to know we were there. We wanted him to feel our love and comfort.

I felt sick. I felt like the acid in my stomach was doubling by the second. *We should not be here*! Just twenty-four hours prior, we were all at Brooke's dance recital.

What was fair about this? What's happy about this Father's Day?

As we held his hand, he would rub our hand with his thumb, like holding hands with someone to offer them comfort. Like *he* was trying to comfort *us*!

When the nurse came to talk to us, she very kindly and compassionately answered all of our questions. I recall asking what was best for his recovery, to talk to him or to be quiet to let his brain rest and heal. I don't remember a lot of what she said to us, but one thing I will never forget is when one of us wasn't holding his hand, he would lift it slightly and continue to move his thumb in a back and forth motion. The nurse said, "He's looking for another hand to hold." It makes my eyes sting, and my heart ache thinking about it. It's like he was saying, "I love you," without words.

I remember Larry saying, "I can't imagine what must be going on in his mind, not being able to move or open his eyes." I can't even describe how hard it was to be in that room. When I was in that room, all I could hear running through my head was, "Things will never be the same." I wanted more than anything for things to be the same.

13

Hands

While holding his hand, I wondered if it was the same hand he had stitches in as a kid.

Just the night before, when we were at our house after the dance recital, people were hanging out in the kitchen and chatting. I was standing by the kitchen island talking with Dad and a couple of other family members. Dad was telling the story, very animatedly, I might add, about when he was growing up on the farm. He and his brothers were helping his dad. The details are fuzzy, but I remember something about hay and a barbed-wire fence.

He said when he went to free the wire from the hay, it let loose and sliced his fingers. He showed us his scar on his right hand.

After all those years, I'm guessing at least forty-five, he still had a scar and a story. Some things stick with you, and others don't.

I looked down at the palm side of my right hand and rubbed my scar. It's right above where my thumb meets my wrist. My hand is still numb there. It happened a couple of years earlier at the cottage when trying to dock the pontoon. We had a group of people there to celebrate our friend Jen's birthday. It was Memorial Day weekend, and it was fabulous weather. It was sunny and warm, which was amazing. (The weather on Memorial Day is always a crapshoot.)

It was a very windy day, and the wind kept pushing us out away from the dock. I was at the front of the pontoon in position to grab the dock post while Dad was driving. As we neared the dock and saw we were at the mercy of the wind, I leaned over even farther to try and catch the post. I wasn't too concerned about leaning too far because the water was only about chest high at the end of the dock. Just as I was leaning a bit too far to be stable, Dad decided to back up and come at it again.

I'm sure you can picture it: the boat's sudden direction change combined with my excessive leaning caused me to plop right into the water. Everything would have been fine, but unfortunately, I accomplished my goal of reaching the post. As I plopped into the lake, my hand slid down the dock post and over the bolt that was sticking out from a bracket on the end of the dock.

I felt the tug.

I knew it wasn't good.

I looked down at my hand and saw blood and a large section of my skin flapping back and forth in the murky lake water. I quickly pressed down the flap of skin with my other thumb.

I started stating rather loudly, "I need to go to the hospital."

One of the guys on the boat with us jumped into the water to see if I was ok. Of course, he wanted to look at my hand. I did not—I repeat—I did *not* want to let go.

I'm not a big fan of seeing blood. My blood. Anyone else's. It doesn't really matter. Blood is not my thing.

Finally, he convinced me to let go. I only released my thumb from the flap of skin for approximately 1.2 seconds. As soon as I let go, it laid right back open as if that was its natural state. I quickly returned pressure on it, pressing so hard that maybe it would just go right back together to the way it was just a few short minutes before.

"Ewww!" he said.

"Exactly."

I stood there in the muck at the bottom of the river, looking at the dock that was above my eye level, thinking, "Now what? How the heck am I going to get up there, because I know there is *no* way I'm going to release my thumb again. How will I ever be able to hoist myself up?"

Larry pulled up in the other boat and immediately jumped into the water. The two of them quickly and easily lifted me onto the dock.

I was *not* going to let go of my hand.

That was until a few minutes later, when my sister-in-law, Amy, convinced me I needed to flush it out with clean water. I figured she was thinking more rationally than I.

Dad apologized multiple times. He felt responsible, but I knew it wasn't his fault.

It was quite a feat to get my wet swimsuit off and my dry clothes on in preparation for going to the hospital, but somehow we managed.

I ended up getting multiple stitches and was rendered rather useless for several days.

The scars were just one of the ways that my and Dad's hands were similar.

Standing in the ICU room, I looked at the age spots on Dad's hands. I'd never really noticed or thought about the similarity, but when I looked at the back of my hands, I saw the same speckling of spots—some larger than others. When I was younger, I'd always thought I had my mom's hands. But over the years— after rearing two babies through what seemed like millions of diaper changes followed by millions of hand washings—my hands had changed. Until that point, I didn't like to look at or acknowledge those spots. But on that day, when I looked at those spots, I felt a kindred connection with my dad.

My eyes were a bit more similar to his than anyone else's in our family. Both Mom and Mark have green eyes. Dad's eyes were varying shades of blue and squinted up at the outer corners when he smiled. My once-blue eyes also squint when I smile. The color has changed over the years. Sometimes, they still appeared blue; other times, they have a green hue, but most of the time, they look steel grey.

I looked down at his legs that were covered by a sheet. They looked as skinny as ever. He's always had very long, lanky legs, too thin for the rest of his body. Not that he was large on top or anything. They were just bony, knobby-kneed legs. Not like mine. I've never had knobby knees. As a baby, I had what I call rubber band legs and arms. You know, those chubby rolls that look like they are caused by tight rubber bands.

I moved my gaze down to his feet. Those wonderfully goofy feet. He had the trait of having his second toe longer than any of his other toes. There's another similarity, one that I was not particularly fond of. My second toe also is slightly longer than my other toes. But only slightly. *His* second toe was exceptionally longer than the rest. I smiled in my mind. It required too much effort to have it reach my face. Mom would always tease Dad about how his second toe was so long it wrapped up and around his big toe, which is not exactly on the small side, either.

I noticed Dad's left foot was sticking out from under the end of the sheet. His feet were in some kind of waffle-weave, toe-less socks the hospital staff had put on him. How many steps had these feet made throughout his lifetime? How many more would they take...if any?

In my mind, I reached out and massaged his foot in a nurturing way.

In my body, I just stood there with my hands to myself.

I looked back up towards his all too skinny legs and flashed back to 1988. I was a senior in high school. Several of us were standing around my grandpa's (Dad's dad) hospital bed. He was in the final stages of lung cancer, and we had gotten the call that it was not going to be much longer. My mom had taken me out of school early. It was my grandma, two sets of my aunts and uncles, a couple who were close friends with my grandparents, my parents, and I gathered by Grandpa's side. I was the only one of his seven grandchildren there.

Being there was a gift.

I remember my dad standing beside the bed, looking down at his dad. He reached out and rubbed Grandpa's leg. It wasn't a soft, gentle rub, but rather a brisk, deliberate rub. I wished I knew what he was thinking. It was as though Dad was saying, "You did a good job. Life well lived. Thank you."

Thinking back to that brought me to the vision of the numerous times my girls had hugged Mom and Dad goodbye in our entryway. I could see Dad bending down and picking little Brookie up in a hug, embracing and rubbing her back in the same brisk fashion, saying, "You're a good girly."

That day in Grandpa's room, it was so hard to look at him. His breathing was so labored. It looked like it hurt him to take each breath. The sight hurt me. I was uncomfortable.

I tried to picture him laughing and saying "jess" instead of the word "yes." I remembered him teaching me, at about age six, that "possum" actually started with the letter o. I was shocked when I found the opossum picture in the O volume and not the P volume of our encyclopedia set. Yes, that's right, encyclopedia. I'm that old. For those of you who don't know what an encyclopedia is, Google© it.

I pictured him holding on to my hands as I would flip through his arms.

I pictured handing my very own shiny quarter to my brother to hold on to when Grandpa bet me a quarter that Santa was going to come to our house that afternoon.

In the afternoon? We all know Santa only comes at night when everyone was asleep.

Grandpa said we needed a neutral party to hold the money. I'm not sure I knew what a neutral party meant, but I wasn't getting a "neutral" vibe from my brother. He was teasing me left and right that I was going to lose my precious money. (I think he'd been tipped off.)

I'm sure you've guessed; I lost the bet. Santa did show up at our house that afternoon! Did you know when there is no snow, Santa drives a green four-door sedan?

He was an awesome grandpa, and now, so was my dad.

"You're a good girly."

Oh, man! I can't believe how much this hurts! I don't want my girls to lose their grandpa this early in their life.

I looked at Holly Ann—she looked how I felt—and suddenly, my hurt was amplified tenfold. I could see the pain in her eyes. She was only twelve years old, but she was wise beyond her years. What thoughts were going through her head? What was she feeling in her heart? How was this affecting her and her sister, Brooke?

This is not *fair!*

Why do my girls have to learn this kind of life lesson now?

This sucks! SUCKS!

I am so *not good at this.*

I flashed back to 1988 again. Shortly after my dad was rubbing Grandpa's leg, one of my uncles asked me if I wanted to go with him to get a snack. I don't think I was actually hungry for a snack, but it hurt so much to see Grandpa in that condition that I welcomed the reprieve. Could my uncle sense my discomfort? Was he uncomfortable, too?

When we returned from the convenience store, we saw a family friend standing in the hall outside Grandpa's room. She looked at us with a sad expression and shook her head. My uncle stopped walking and said, "Oh no. He's gone."

Was that just a coincidence that Grandpa passed while I was gone? I don't think so.

I rode home with Mom that night. Even though I was a senior in high school and about to turn eighteen in a few weeks, I curled up like a little child on the floor of the front seat of Mom's car. I laid my head on the seat, and I could *not* hold back the tears.

Even though it was dark, Mom could tell I was crying. Maybe she could hear me. I don't know.

She asked, "What's wrong?"

I choked out between sobs, "I never got to tell him that I love him..."

She said, "He's a grandpa. He already knows."

My attention came back to Dad's room. I looked at Holly Ann again. She loved him. He loved her. He might never be able to hug her and call her "Holly Babes" ever again.

I remembered back to the day when Mom and Dad walked into the hospital room the day after Holly Ann was born. They were beaming with joy. So excited. Their love could be seen and felt.

I remembered about a year before Holly's birth when Larry and I called Mom and Dad to tell them we had a miscarriage. I will never forget hearing the pain in Dad's voice.

Dad had so much love to give.

It can't be over now.

I can not *do this.*

I really suck at this.

I need out of here!

Luckily, it wasn't much longer, and we all decided to leave to get something to eat.

I didn't feel like eating in the least bit, but I thought I would be better at that than staying in the room any longer.

The realization of that made me feel like a terrible person—a horrible daughter.

14

Dad's Cell Phone Beeping

That night, I was lying in the hotel bed...not sleeping. I kept hearing Dad's cell phone beep. Mom had thought clearly enough to bring it along with her to the hospital. Because Dad was a realtor, he was on his phone morning and night, seven days a week. Some would even call it his lifeline. The irony fell short of humorous.

Mom had given Dad's phone to Larry to retrieve messages and contact the people and inform them of the situation. So, Dad's phone was in our hotel room bathroom, periodically beeping. I went in there to go to the bathroom, not because I needed to, but rather because I wasn't sleeping. I was restless. All I wanted to do was sleep. Sleep and wake up and have this all just be a terrible dream. I couldn't will myself to sleep. I looked at the phone that continued to beep. The display read, "3 new voice-mails". Three new messages for Dad. Three people who were expecting a call back from Dad. Three people who wanted to talk to Dad. Make that plus one. I wanted to talk to Dad. With Dad. I wanted him to tell me everything was going to be ok.

It's rather comical thinking back to some of the amazing feats Dad would accomplish and the things he would hurdle in his attempt to get to his phone before it would stop ringing. I can still picture him dashing to his phone and then attempting to answer it as if he was casually answering it. I can still hear his voice that would often sound squeaky and would crack, "This is Bernie."I had no idea who the three messages were from. Whether they were new customers or people who knew him well, they expected to hear that same familiar salutation.

It struck me.
These people didn't know.

It struck me.

These people didn't know.

These people have no idea what had happened.

These people may be wondering why he hasn't called them back.

These people don't know he's *unable* to call them back.

And I didn't know...if he'd ever...be able to.

15

Telling Dad to Get Better

The next day, we went to visit Dad. It was so achingly clear I wanted to do most anything but be in that room, looking at his helpless body lying there with all the wires and tubes connected to him. I relayed a message to Dad from our good friend Brady. Chris and Brady are our good friends who we always tailgated with for UNI (University of Northern Iowa) football games. Who *we* tailgated with. *We* being Mom, Dad, Larry, and I. *Would we ever get to tailgate all together again*? I told Dad that Brady said he had to get better so he could help break in Brady's new tailgating grill.

That should be motivation enough, right? Using a grill at a tailgate, it would be fun! We'd be making more memories.

Dad loved getting together with our tailgating group. In just a couple of months, we'd be resuming our UNI Panther Football tailgates. In just a few short months, we were going to be breaking in Brady's new tailgating grill... PLEASE!

Please let us all be a part of the breaking in of the grill. ALL of us. All laughing, smiling, standing, eating. Eating the food we are going to be grilling on Brady's new grill.

Please.

All.

Of.

Us.

It just wouldn't be the same without Dad.

Could I even go if he wasn't there? What if he was in a wheelchair? What if he couldn't eat the burgers that we'd be grilling on Brady's new grill? What if he couldn't talk with all of our friends and tell yet another cheesy joke that would make everyone laugh?

He had to *get better.*

I wanted nothing less than the whole miracle. My heart needed the whole miracle.

16

Talking on the Phone

Once the word started getting out about Dad, encouraging messages began flooding in by e-mail, CarePage message, text, and voicemail. I was overwhelmed by all of the support. Every time I read the posts left by so many people, my eyes would well up, and my heart would swell. I was floored by the amount of support we were getting. Each message was like a caring, heartfelt hug. And with each hug would come my tears. Each tear was flowing with love. Love for Dad. Love for each and every one of our friends and family. Love for all the memories. And love, pleading love, for the future.

Most of us know at least one person who never really shows any emotion. You know the ones. The ones you're quite convinced that even as a baby or a small child, they never had a tear run down their cheek. How can they do that? Why don't they show any emotion? It's like that emotion never existed in them. Where did their emotion go?

To me.

I got it.

I got their share of emotion in addition to my own. I'm one of those people who can cry at the drop of a hat. To say I'm a very emotional person is an understatement. I cry at commercials, for Pete's sake. There are times when I can't *not* cry. I have no control over it. It comes from a part of me that is so deep that something other than me is in control of it.

So, stick me in a personal, highly emotional situation, and you get tears.

Lots of them.

I was getting rather tired of crying. I didn't want to cry, damn it! I was trying really hard to hold it in and that just made matters worse. I felt like my head was going to explode. With each wave of emotion, the pressure continued to build. Plus, the tissues in the family waiting room sucked. As Larry would say, 'Like fifty-grit sandpaper.' My nose was becoming raw. I needed my Puffs Plus.

I had already depleted my little purse pack I'd bought on the drive up. I knew I'd cry, but I grossly underestimated how much. I'm quite sure there weren't enough tissues in that gas station to suffice.

I was so thankful I had picked up the Puffs Plus and didn't have to use the sandpaper the entire time. I made a mental note to add this to my gratitude list.

I am thankful for Puffs Plus waiting for me at home.

The entire time we were up at Mayo, I continued to have these well-defined moments of gratitude. It was an unusually beautiful thing that was happening to me. I'd definitely have to say it happened *to* me rather than stating it was something of my doing. Or maybe I'd even say something amazing happened *through* me.

I kept having these thoughts about things I was seeing, learning, and experiencing. And these were all tied to a sincere sense of gratitude. Even though I was going through one of, if not the most terrible experience of my life, I was continually being shown things to be grateful for.

I've always been a fairly positive person, but not one of those over-the-top positive people who make you want to gag. But what I am about to tell you is sort of one of those things that might make you want to gag...or at least think, "Well gee...Isn't that just so flippin' dandy for you?"

The thing is...it didn't come from me. It came from something much greater than me.

Have you ever had the experience when a "thought" popped into your head, and you think, "Where in the heck did that come from?" because your line of thought was nowhere near this. You know it came from somewhere else.

Let's call it an impression. The thoughts were not created by me but rather impressed upon me—upon my heart. It was felt, rather than thought.

Throughout my stay and all the experiences while at the Mayo Clinic, I kept having these "thoughts," these impressions, and I knew I needed to make a point to remember them.

The outpouring of support was so touching; I couldn't help but cry. So, this made talking on the phone to people when they called out of the question. Just feeling the love and support come through the phone was so comforting and painful at the same time. It hurt. It hurt to be in that situation.

In every tear I shed was love. Love for Dad. Love for all of my friends and family who were showing us all their love and support. Their love and support made me love them even more than I already did, which led to more tears.

Tears for love, but also for fear. Fear of this love possibly being taken away from me. From us. From our family. There wouldn't have been the fear without the love. The fear was actually love being threatened. My heart and my head needed this love to stay intact.

Every time I had a call coming in, I had to let it go to voicemail and then reply with a text or e-mail. I felt terrible about it, but really...I needed to save my head from exploding.

Any addition to the emotion welling up in me would exponentially increase the pressure in my head. I just wanted to get back to life the way it had been. I wanted normalcy, and I wanted it now. I wanted to breathe normally again. Deeply. Calmly. Maybe it was all the shallow breathing that caused all the sighs. The Spirit.

I needed to...just breathe.

17

Perfectly Straight

Amazing how on Father's Day, the waiting room had been empty except for us.

The next day, I stepped out of the now crowded waiting room to take a phone call. As I attempted to talk without crying, I paced back and forth. I noticed several neatly, identically framed documents hanging on the wall. They were all perfectly straight. Perfectly spaced. After ending my call, with my head still intact, I took a closer look. They all looked like the exact same document. The only difference was the year on each one. On the top of each one in bold letters was:

#1 Neurosurgery Hospital in America

I went back to the first one on the left. I focused in on the year. I moved to the next one. And the next. Each year was sequential. No year was missing. It continued. There was one for each year right up to the present.

Wow!

I immediately felt such a sense of relief. I was relieved knowing Dad was getting the best care possible. Of all the hospitals in the U.S., the one I was standing in right then, the one that my Dad was life-flighted to, was the best of the best. We were in the best place to be. Well...actually, the best place would be back in Iowa at the cottage laughing and smiling like usual. But the best place we could be considering these very sucky circumstances into which we'd been thrown. Thrown into and punched.

This sucks.

This sucks.

This sucks!

But I was very thankful.

Very thankful. As much as I needed to feel any sense of relief, those perfectly straight frames on the wall brought a sense of relief. They removed any doubt that we were where we needed to be.

Note to self: I am thankful.

I added this to a list in my head.

18

Tinkle in the Night

On that Monday night, Larry and my sister-in-law, Amy, had gone home with our kids to get them all settled in with grandparents on the other side of the family. So, my brother, Mark, stayed in my hotel room that night.

When was the last time we slept in the same room together? It was probably in a hotel room while we were on vacation when I was in high school, and he would've been in college. Prior to that, it would've been in our pop-up camper when I was in elementary school. Those were the days.

Sometimes, we'd have our Aunt Ruby and Uncle Holly along with us. Six people sleeping in the same small camper. Three beds with two people in each bed. How did we ever get any sleep?

I remember one trip to the Smokey Mountains in Tennessee. In the middle of the night, Mark decided there was too much snoring going on in the camper, so he was going to sleep in the car. After climbing over me and our aunt and uncle, he went to open the door of the camper. Mom asked what he was doing. After saying he was going to sleep in the car, Mom said she just heard a bear outside. He obviously decided that snoring wasn't as bad as a face to face confrontation with a bear. Mark did an about-face and returned to bed next to me.

Thankfully, in the hotel room across from the hospital, we didn't have to share a bed. But just like the previous night, I had trouble sleeping. In my sleeplessness and tossing and turning, I found myself visiting the bathroom frequently. My first trip in there could have been a doozy. I was navigating my home-away-from-home with the lights off to spare my eyes any added strain. Luckily, with my groping to find the toilet and making sure I was properly centered, I discovered Mark had left the seat up before I sat down. Thank goodness! That could've been bad. Believe me, I was VERY thankful!

19

Thankful for Technology and Those Who Make It Work

On Tuesday morning, I set up a CarePage for Dad. I'd never heard of CarePages. After reading a little about it, I learned it was a website people can use as a tool to keep friends and family up to date on a patient. This was before Facebook was widely used. I would be able to keep anyone who wanted to be in the loop updated. I could send out the link to people I knew and ask them to forward the link to others who may be interested. I'd just have to write the updates and not have to keep track of e-mail addresses and not have to worry about whether I was bothering someone with all the updates. If someone wanted updates, they could control whether they got the email notifications. When I decided to use this as a tool to help facilitate updates, I had no idea what a fabulous emotional therapy tool it would be.

When we packed up that Father's Day morning to head to Mayo, I grabbed my handicapped laptop computer. I say handicapped because just earlier that week, the screen had gone out. I couldn't see anything. It goes without saying that this was very inconvenient. I had to connect it to the monitor of our desktop computer at home to use it.

There was a computer in the Family Waiting Room for people to use, so I got smart.

Luckily, I've been the social organizer for several things we were involved in. So, I would often send out group e-mails to people to organize our next event. Because I was unable to physically talk on the phone without crying, I texted a couple of people and asked them to text me their e-mail address. I then logged into my web e-mail (that I did not have my contacts stored in it because I use Outlook for that) and sent them an e-mail. I asked them to forward me my last group e-mail I had sent out to our various "social groups," such as our small group from church, our couples BUNKO group, and our tailgating group.

Once they sent me those, I had a large number of e-mail addresses I could add to my contacts on my webmail. Then I started going through my contacts on my phone—this was before smartphones—and texting people, asking them to text me their e-mail address. It was a lot of work, but eventually, I collected a sizeable number of e-mail addresses.

Whew.

It was a lot of busywork, but it was worth it to be able to contact our support system at home. Luckily for me, I didn't have to continue using the computer in the family waiting room the whole time we were at Mayo. Dell came to my rescue. We had an extended warranty with Dell. That next morning, I met a Dell tech in the lobby of our hotel, and thirty minutes later, I had a working computer screen. Halleluiah! Oh, so *very* thankful!

I made a note of gratitude in my mind.

20

Dancing on the Barstools

One of the times we went into Dad's ICU room, I thought about how lifeless he looked, how much he didn't look like himself.

This reality felt so awkward. So unnatural. This seemingly life-less man was not him. How he was. This was not us. How we were. We laughed. We smiled. We joked around.

A LOT!

We could be and were serious when conditions warranted it, but this had been going on for too long. Much too long. It was high time for Dad to sit up and tell a joke. Make us laugh.

My sister-in-law had an awesome idea. She brought up a poster board and filled it with pictures of Dad and all of us—all of us laughing and smiling the way we usually were. The way we should be. She said it helped the nurses connect with the patient. That way, they could see the frail man was not who he usually was. He was lively and the life of the party.

Would he ever be the life of the party again?

Would he have life?

Would he ever be the life of the party again?

I thought back a few years to a fun gathering we had at our house with some of our close friends, which of course, included my family. We had our mix of entertaining party music playing. It included everything from KC and the Sunshine Band, to Buckwheat Zydeco, to Jimmy Buffet. We had a house rule: when the theme song to Hawaii Five-O came on, everyone had to stand on a piece of furniture and dance as cued. (Don't try this at home. We're practiced, trained professionals.) When the song came on, everyone jumped up on a couch, chair, or barstool, and we'd "surf," "swim," "paddle," basically doing whatever "the announcer" shouted out. It was always a lot of fun. There was never a face that wasn't smiling.

Smiling. THAT'S *what we do!*

That particular night, Dad was surfing on the love seat. I was on a barstool. Mom was on the barstool beside me. Dad thought he'd be funny and throw a koozie at me. I didn't see the throw. I just saw an object hurtling towards me out of the corner of my eye. I quickly did a balance check and threw my arms out to the side to ensure I would stay upright on the barstool. In the process, my arm flew over and ever-so-slightly nudged Mom, sending her careening off her barstool and onto the floor. Oops!

She was ok. She was laughing. I don't know if it was a genuine happy laugh, but she was laughing, and she was ok, so we all joined in the laughter.

Ah...laughing.

Careening makes me think of another story. When I was in college, Mom, Dad, my brother Mark, and Larry were helping me move from one apartment to another. Dad had borrowed a pickup truck, and we had pretty much everything I called mine in the back end of it.

Dad and Mark were in the bed of the truck, lifting my dresser. As Dad backed up to give Mark space to move parallel to him, the back of his legs hit the sidewall of the truck bed with too much momentum. The next thing we knew, Dad toppled over the side of the truck and landed smack dab on the top of his head on the side of the street.

Mom, who was watching this from the curb, had a delayed, reflexive reaction. She tried to reach out to try to help him but stepped off the extra tall curb that was obviously a bigger drop than anticipated. She ended up splayed out on the street where Dad had fallen. He was no longer there, though, because he'd popped right up, almost as if his head was made of rubber, and had bounced up to his feet. That could've been a horrible situation, but once we saw they were both ok, it was hilarious! All of us laughed and have continued to laugh at it over the years.

Humor. Laughing. It was something we were good at. Oh, how I wanted to be right back there, all laughing together. Instead, I felt like my head was about to explode from all the tension and repressed tears I was bottling up behind my eyebrows.

21

Low Blow

On that Tuesday afternoon, we were dealt a devastating blow. The neurosurgeon came to talk to us with the news none of us wanted to hear. There was no improvement. They did an MRI on Dad's brain, which confirmed what they'd initially thought. There was extensive damage to the left side of the brain in the area that controls speech, communication, and the movement of the right side of his body. We were told that even in the best-case scenario, if he *did* regain consciousness, he would have split plane vision with no vision on his right side. He also wouldn't be able to talk, read, or even comprehend spoken words. He would hear noise but not be able to understand any words. He likely wouldn't be able to feed himself, either.

This is the best-case scenario? Where are the good and the better?

We knew from day one this was probably the case, but we were holding on to faith he'd fully recover. We wanted Dad back the way we all knew him. We knew this diagnosis was nothing close to the real Bernie. Nothing close to the fun-loving, joke-telling guy who we all knew and loved. We knew he wouldn't want to go on this way. And we wouldn't want to see him this way. The doctor confirmed he would be in a state we knew he wouldn't want. We were still asking for the miracle, but we wanted the full miracle, not the "best-case scenario" they were spelling out for us.

Dad was right-handed. That meant that even with this best-case scenario, Dad would never be able to communicate with us again. Not even write us a note. Never again would he be able to jot down a quick note in his hard to decipher "chicken scratch."

In my head, I could picture the notes that he and Mom would leave for Mark and me when we were kids, listing the chores that we were to do before they got home from work. Mom's messages were always in her pretty, loopy handwriting. But Dad's handwriting...well, sometimes, we weren't quite certain about what we were supposed to do.

Never talk again? That meant he'd never be able to tell another one of his corny jokes. Never be able to greet me as "Missy Lee." Never be able to say to my girls they were good girls, and he loved them.

No!

I believed this was a knowledgeable and talented doctor, but no*! There is no way he could be talking about* my *dad!*

No way! Not Bernie!

The doctor was still talking—something about not being able to feed or take care of himself.

I wanted to scream, "But, Doctor! You don't understand! You can't be talking about *my* dad."

"Don't you know...he's the life of the party."

"He loves to dance!"

"He would spin me around in circles as a little girl until the clouds would all blur together."

"He's not a vegetable!"

"Please tell me you have him mixed up with another patient."

That has to be it. He thinks my dad is someone else. Someone else who won't be able to talk. My *dad is going to be fine...* soon. *And we will be able to put this all behind us.*

"My dad doesn't fit that description. You *can't* be talking about *my* dad."

I felt numb. I felt tired.

I wanted to wake up.

I had seen the staples on the left side of his head.

I saw the sign in *his* room that said, "No left-brain flap."

I knew it fit.

What he was saying *was* about *my* dad.

I was numb.

No tears.

No sobbing.

I didn't know how to process it. *Am I really hearing this right now?*

Numb.

22

The Doctor with the Huge Heart

I was always thoroughly impressed with all of the staff at the Mayo Clinic. Every doctor, nurse, chaplain; they were all fabulous.

But Gloria, she was one of my favorites. She was a P.A. who spoke with us a few times. And I emphasize *with* us, not to us. Not only was she an informative medical professional, but Gloria was a comforting counselor. She was a major source of reassurance and spoke to us from her heart like we were people with breaking hearts, not just another medical case. She told us how she was once in our shoes with her mom. She was thousands of miles away and got a call about her mother being in a very similar situation as Dad was.

When you're in these situations, the doctor often gives you the facts and tells you, frankly, your options. I didn't want to hear facts. I didn't want to hear statistical odds. I believe in miracles. I do. I wanted to hear, facts aside, what the best thing was for us to do. I really don't know how doctors in the medical world can give a percentage to the chance of survival. How did this practice ever start anyway? Because people need things spelled out? I didn't want my brain spoken to; I wanted my heart spoken to.

You often hear of people asking the doctor, "So, if it was your dad, what would you do?"

I didn't want my brain spoken to; I wanted my heart spoken to.

I wonder if the doctors' answers in these instances are what they'd really do if it was their heart, love, and emotions on the line. It seems like it would be easy to *say* you'd do one thing, but once you're really there...

It was a gift that Gloria had been there. I actually knew what Gloria...the doctor...the neuro P.A. with a huge heart, would do. I had an honest answer, and that gave me comfort.

23

Chaplain in the Family Room

After we'd been dealt the low blow—the news that had split open our hearts and could change our image of the future forever—we met with a chaplain. She ushered Mom, my brother Mark, his wife, Amy, their son, Drew, my aunt Ruby, my uncle Holly, and I into the small family room next to the large waiting room. Larry came a little later. He had driven our girls home so they could try to go about their normal activities and also so Holly Ann could attend a week-long day camp. Larry's mom volunteered to stay at our home to juggle their chaotic schedule.

The chaplain was a very sweet, young woman with a tender voice and a comforting presence. You could sense her heart was full of love and compassion.

We all talked, laughed, and cried. We reminisced and told stories, most of them funny. Uncle Holly told a story about when they stopped at a convenience store during a road trip, and Dad made him buy a pair of the "ugliest gloves he'd ever seen." Dad could sell you anything. Mom shared the story of when he was first in real estate, and he was showing a couple the house across the street from ours; he ended up selling them our home.

Laughing felt good, but I felt so hurt and worn inside. It almost felt wrong to laugh. It felt like a great release, but it felt wrong not to have Dad laughing with us. His body was lying down the hall, unable to laugh. Would we ever hear his infectious laugh again?

I said, "All I can think about is how he won't be at my girls' weddings."

My girls were only twelve and nine at the time, but that was the thought in my head. I always pictured him dancing with them in their wedding dresses, gliding across the dance floor, probably to "Could I have this dance…for the rest of my life." It was one of his favorite songs. It was the song I danced to with him on my wedding day.

The rest of his life…

Now, those dances were very likely never going to happen. It was like my dream was being taken away. *How can this be?*

So many dreams and future memories would never happen. I thought of all the jokes Dad would never get to tell. Of all the laughs we'd never get to have. Of all the holidays he wouldn't be sitting at the table with us. Nothing would ever be the same.

Pain. Heart aching pain. Those of you who have experienced it know the pain that radiates from the center of your heart into the core of your soul.

That hour or so we spent talking with the chaplain in the small family room was such a therapeutic time for all of us.

We were embracing what we'd had.

It was the beginning of the healing of our broken hearts.

24

Taking the Ditch

The next morning, Larry, yet again, had gone to meet his mom partway to get the girls and bring them back up to the hospital so they could say goodbye to Grandpa. We'd called them the night before, after Larry had returned. We, or I should say Larry, explained to them their grandpa—the man they would run to screaming, "GRANDPA!" whenever he stopped by—was probably going to die.

I couldn't feel myself in my life at that moment.

This can't be my life right now!

I didn't want my life to include having to tell my young girls one of their most favorite people in the world was probably going to die.

Whose life was this? I wanted to kindly hand it back and say, "No, thank you. I'd like my rosy, happy, little life back, please."

"Go Fish."

Find someone else to deal this to.

I pass.

No thanks.

But...

This was my life.

The next morning, Larry went home to bring the girls up to see Grandpa one last time. As they were driving back to the hospital, Larry saw an on-coming vehicle cross the center line into his lane. It was headed straight towards them at highway speed!

When sharing the details of the event, Larry told me he thought, "Oh no! What do I do? They always say not to go over into the other lane because the driver will realize where they are and swerve back."

The driver continued drifting across the lane until he was all the way over on Larry's shoulder of the road, and he wasn't wavering. He was still headed directly at them. Larry knew he couldn't take *his* ditch because he would hit the guy. So, Larry did what he had to do; he moved over into the other lane. Sure enough, just as he did, the other guy noticed where he was and swerved back into his proper lane.

By that time, it was too late for Larry to go back into his lane because they were sure to collide. So, Larry did the only thing he could, and he took the ditch on the opposite side of the road from where he started. Luckily, right at that spot, the ditches weren't very deep, and he was able to keep the car under control and just drive right back out.

The sudden dip and change of terrain startled the girls, and they started screaming, "Daddy, what are you doing?!"

The driver of the other car turned around and came back. It turned out his prosthetic leg had come unsnapped. He was trying to put it back on as he crossed the center line and almost took out my entire family—my whole world—in one fell swoop.

Larry called me and told me what had happened. My heart sank. My already broken, hurting heart hurt even more than I thought possible. Dad was just down the hall, barely hanging on to life, and I came within seconds of losing my husband and two children.

What kind of test is this?

How much does God think I can handle?

Dude! (I wanted to say to God.) *I'm not* THAT *strong!*

Ease up already!

I felt drained. I didn't feel like being strong. I just wanted to curl up in a ball, close my eyes, then wake up to my *normal* life.

I posted a message on CarePages asking the question, "How much does God think I can handle?" A friend replied, "God won't give you more than you can handle."

We've all heard it before, but I was convinced God had more confidence in me than I did.

Now, more than a decade later, I don't believe that's how God works. He's not up in the sky dealing out situations for us to handle. We just need to have faith in the love that is there and not worry. Isn't that the part we really suck at? The not worrying part. Most of us, some more than others, worry or expect the worst all the time. We aren't supposed to do that!

After that day, I was able to see that that *was* the blessing. They were ok, and nothing happened to any of them. I'm sure many guardian angels were guiding them through that ditch. I just needed to give thanks for that and move forward.

25

Talking About Comfort Care with Gloria

We were at the point when we knew we needed to make a decision. I felt tired and worn and just wanted things to be however they were going to be. I didn't want to wait around through the agonizing part. I just wanted to fast forward to whatever was going to be. If Dad was going to be fine, let's just celebrate and move on. If he was going to die, then let's figure out our new normal. It would suck worse than anything had ever sucked in my life, but I didn't like our current place. It hurt to hope because I wasn't sure if there was any hope to hope for.

Was I impatient?

I'm not sure what to call it.

Exhausted. That's what it was. I was exhausted.

My body felt physically exhausted, even though the only activity I'd done was walk from the hospital to our hotel across the street a couple of times a day. We'd walk to get something to eat. Other than that, I'd done nothing but sat on my butt—sat on my butt and hurt. My head hurt. My heart hurt. My heart hurt badly. Being worried and broken-hearted hurt. It was exhausting.

Even though I'd only sat on my butt, my body felt like I'd been through a battle. I wanted to rest. I wanted whatever was to be, to hurry up and just be.

If Dad wasn't going to make it, however much I didn't want that to be the outcome, I just wanted to move on with moving on.

I think many people would say, "How could you just give up? Why wouldn't you hold out for all hope?"

My answer...

I don't know.

I think I knew he was already gone. I think I knew he was never coming back to us.

It hurt being stuck in that place, and I so wanted to move on. I wanted to feel better. I wanted to heal. If it wasn't going to be Dad healing, then I wanted me to heal. I just wanted my heart to stop hurting and heal.

We asked to meet with Gloria again. She was so fantastic at talking with us like we were hurting people who had deep emotions about a real person with a big personality. She didn't treat us like we were just another family mourning yet another patient who was inevitably going to die.

She took us to a large conference room with a long, dark wood table surrounded by chairs in the middle of the room.

We all sat at the table: Mom, Mark, Amy, Larry, and I. I felt like we were there to strike a deal. To barter and haggle until we all walked away, somewhat satisfied with what we were going to get.

I think we got screwed.

Is that where the term "This is not what I bargained for" originated?

Gloria again told us she'd been in a similar situation with her mom. As a daughter with medical knowledge, she knew the best thing to do was to let her mom go.

Let go.

The hardest thing we'd ever have to do, but knowing that Gloria knew helped me know.

I can't tell you how comforting it was to talk with Gloria. She was so compassionate and understanding of our feelings. She knew it was a difficult decision and explained it in a loving, caring, down to earth, knowledgeable way.

Let go... Let go, and let God.

She explained about comfort care. It was how they would do everything possible to keep Dad comfortable, remove his breathing tube, and then let God and the natural processes of the body take over.

Let go... Let go, and let God.

It was an uncomfortable thought, but yet I knew it was the right one.

I truly believed if Dad was supposed to live and be with us again, a miracle would happen.

I believed it to my core.

Sometimes, you just need to let go and let God.

26

Chaplain in the Meeting Room

A chaplain, one we hadn't previously met, joined us in the conference room. He was a gray-haired gentleman with a quiet demeanor. He sat with us while we explained everything that had happened over the previous four days.

I think he wondered if we just wanted him to pray with us or what it was we wanted. He knew we were struggling with making the decision. He reaffirmed what Gloria had said about leaving it up to God and the body's natural processes.

Mom talked about when they had gone to visit their friend, Bill.

Just a couple of months prior, Mom and Dad had visited a very close family friend who was in a care center in the end stages of Parkinson's disease. After seeing Bill and how he couldn't get around or do things for himself, it broke Dad's heart.

Dad said to Mom, "I'd never want to live like that."

And there we were, just three months later, in the very unlikely place that if Dad pulled through, he would very likely be "like that."

All of us already knew Dad would never want to be in a state where he couldn't care for himself.

Or talk.

No talking!

He wouldn't be Dad. He wouldn't be the life of the party. No more laughing or joking.

We already knew what Dad would want, but knowing he had said this to Mom, meant we knew we didn't have to second guess ourselves.

It was a gift.

To me, that was our answer. In not choosing comfort care, we would be keeping Dad in his vegetative state. And we knew, even without Mom telling us what Dad had said, exactly how he felt.

We knew it was ok to put it in God's hands.

So, we met with Gloria again. We told her we'd like to proceed with comfort care and the removal of Dad's breathing tube. She assured us we could feel good about that decision. She told us to get something to eat, and the hospital would give us a call when he was gone.

Gloria knew.

27

Welcome Home Party

That night, Larry and I called the girls to tell them Grandpa would be going to Heaven. I wasn't really sure how a twelve-year-old and a nine-year-old would comprehend this. They were staying at our friends, Chris and Brady's home, just a couple of streets over from ours. Aunt Ruby and Uncle Holly had driven the girls to their house. Chris and Brady picked them up from there and took them to their home.

Later, Chris told me that when they were getting ready to go to bed that night, she prayed with our girls and her two girls. After saying their usual prayer, Chris asked the girls if they had anything they wanted to add. I can just picture their young, innocent faces. Holly asked God to have a big welcome home party for Grandpa.

Just writing this now, many years later, brings me to tears.

Chris went on to tell them Heaven *was* like a big party with lots of beautiful music and happiness. At the time, she was reading a book about a man who had a near-death experience. In the book, he described how beautiful and wonderful Heaven is.

I'm so blessed to have a friend like Chris, who would pray with and comfort my kids in the saddest time of their lives.

And what an AWEsome "coincidence" she was reading a book about Heaven at that time. She and the book she was reading were right where we needed them to be.

Every time I think about Chris doing this for me, for my girls, for us, I get tears in my eyes and get all choked up (if not a full-out cry, resulting in multiple well-used tissues). I love feeling God's Love reveal itself in so many different ways.

What a gift.

28

The Call

I was sound asleep. Soundly. Asleep. Not just a light, restless sleep like I'd been having the previous three nights, but sound asleep.

I was awoken by Larry gently shaking my shoulder.

I opened my eyes. I looked at him. I looked around.

Where was I? I knew I wasn't at home. I wasn't at the cottage. Where was I?

Then, recognizing the surroundings of our hotel room in Rochester, I realized, once again, it wasn't just a bad dream. It was my reality—a reality that was about to get worse.

Larry said gently, "He's gone."

"What?"

"He's gone."

Larry hugged me.

He's gone? Really? What about my miracle?

I didn't get my miracle.

I wanted my miracle. I really wanted my miracle.

I feel different. I feel hollow, yet that hollowness hurts.

I feel changed.

Forever. Things would never be the same. But I like same. I liked and loved our fun, same, predictable life.

I asked him how he knew. What happened when I was actually asleep?

Larry explained Mark had called. The hospital had called Mark.

What? There was a phone call? Larry answered it? Larry was talking in the room right next to me?

And I didn't hear any of it? How? How did I not hear any of this?

I'd hardly slept all week, and now I had not just been asleep, but I, the light sleeper, had been totally out in a deep sleep.

I looked at the clock. It was only twelve-something.

I hadn't even been in bed very long. I hadn't been lying there tossing and turning for hours.

It made me wonder if there was any synchronicity between the time Dad died and the time I fell asleep.

My thankful list. It wouldn't rest. I fetched my fixed (Thank You!) laptop and sat there on the bed and typed up the CarePage update I had really hoped I'd never have to write.

My actual CarePage entry:

Posted Jun 19, 2008, 8:17 am by Michelle

The Lord has called him home.

It happened shortly after midnight.

It makes me wonder what time I fell asleep. Last night (Tuesday night), I literally only slept 1/2 hour. I was wide awake the rest of the night. This did not make yesterday any easier. I was dizzy from lack of sleep. When I went to bed tonight, I laid there and had the same sleepless feeling and was afraid that the same thing was going to happen again tonight. Larry woke me at 12:30. I had actually finally fallen asleep, and I know I had not been asleep for very long. I probably fell asleep shortly after midnight...

I am writing this at about 1:00 a.m. but will not post it until morning so that we can call family and notify them first.

I have learned that...
I am thankful for...

I have learned that...we have the best, most supportive friends in the world!
I am thankful for...each and every one of you and for the support that you've given us.

I have learned that...Mayo has been ranked #1 neurosurgery hospital in America for the past 16 years.
I am thankful for...the fact that Dad was brought here so that we know he got the best possible care.

I learned that...Mayo Clinic has some of the most fabulous and warmhearted doctors and nurses!
I am thankful for...the gifts that God has given to these wonderful people.

I have learned that...Mayo Clinic also has many incredible chaplains on staff that are available 24/7.
I am thankful for...their gift of comfort that comes through them directly from God.

I am thankful for...the fact that the Courtyard Hotel has very comfortable beds.
I have learned that...comfortable beds and Advil pm do not ensure a good night's sleep.

I have learned that...Mayo Clinic needs better Kleenex.
I am thankful for...the fact that I have Puffs Plus waiting for me when I get home.

I have learned that...when you have an extended warranty with Dell, they will come to wherever you are to fix your computer.
I am thankful that...someone came and replaced my screen on my laptop so that I could access my address book.

I learned that...my brother leaves the toilet seat up in the middle of the night.
I am thankful that...I figured it out BEFORE I sat down!

I have learned that...Dad knew a lot of people. (I actually already knew that)
I am thankful for...the fact that so many people love Bernie and are praying for him and for us. We feel your prayers. THANKS!

29

The Message in the Mirror

Later that morning, after trying to get some much-needed sleep, I went into the bathroom to take a shower. We would be going home that day—going home without Dad. I tried to let the spray of the water calm my tense, tired, weary body.

The last four and a half days had been draining. Now I was trying to wash the stress down the drain.

I was looking forward to going home. Sleeping in my bed. Hugging my girls.

As I was getting out of the shower, something caught my eye. In the steam on the full-length mirror on the back of the bathroom door, there was writing. My eyes continued to move past the mirror and quickly moved back. In the steam was written something that looked like:

Hi!
Dad
☺ I Love You! ☺

My heart jumped. *Was I seeing things?*

That morning wasn't the first time I had showered in that bathroom. It was the fourth time! The three previous mornings, I hadn't noticed anything.

Now, I'm not trying to make this sound like I saw the words being written as I stood there, like in the movie *Ghost*, but it was enough to have my breath sucked right out of me. My dad had just breathed his last breath only hours before, and I was staring, heart racing, at these words on the mirror. I rubbed my eyes like you see in old black and white movies. I looked again. The words were still there.

Without diverting my eyes, for fear the words might disappear, I called for Larry to come in to make sure he could see it, too, and to prove I wasn't just seeing things. He saw it also.

Oh good. I'm not going crazy. I'm not just delirious from lack of sleep. The words are there. The words are real.

My common sense told me someone probably wrote it days, maybe even weeks earlier. But the fact remains there are thousands of hotel rooms in Rochester, Minnesota, and I got the one that had <u>*this*</u> message on the mirror.

Coincidence? I think not.

I maybe used to believe in coincidences, but I don't anymore.

I truly believe I was supposed to see that message. That message, however it got there, whenever it was put there, was meant for me.

What an AWEsome world we live in.

30

Do You Like My Outfit?

After Larry and I had finished getting ready, we joined Mom, Mark, and Amy for breakfast. It was once again a beautiful day, and we were sitting at an outside table on the patio. We felt rather numb, but we ate the food that I'm sure was delicious but still tasted bland to me. After breakfast, we would pack and drive back to the cottage and then to Mom and Dad's home. Mom and Dad's home. We were going to Mom and Dad's home without Dad. It was a stab.

As we were silently finishing up, not in any big hurry to do anything, Amy broke the silence. She was sitting directly across the table from me.

She had planned on going home two days earlier but decided to stay once we were dealt the low blow and knew things were not good. Because she hadn't planned on staying overnight, it was the third day of her wearing the same outfit. It was a very pretty peach hoodie and shorts.

She broke the silence by saying, while slouched back in her chair and pointing to her clothes with both pointer fingers from top to bottom, "So...you like my outfit?"

Mom, immediately with her usual wit, replied, "Well, obviously *you* do."

We all burst out into hysterical laughter.

It felt *so* good to laugh. It felt so right to *finally* laugh again. Genuinely laugh.

I still snicker when I think of them delivering their lines. It couldn't have been scripted better.

Laughter. It's so therapeutic.

It really was the best medicine.

31

Driving Home

We packed up and left the hospital to drive home.

All of us, but Dad.

We were driving back to a hurting, forever-changed home.

A home that was now missing a big part of what made it home.

Things will never be the same.

Things will never be the same.

When we were driving into town to get Dad's car and some of Mom's things from the cottage, my cell phone rang. I let it go to voicemail, as I had done so many times that week. I was just too drained to put any energy into a phone conversation I knew would lead to tears and a worsening headache.

Once my phone beeped again, indicating I had a new voicemail, I looked and saw it was from my friend Aby. Aby was my best friend from when we lived near St. Louis. We had remained in touch and visited each other several times over the seven years we'd been gone. Jay and Aby are the kind of friends who, even though we don't see each other for years, it's like we've never missed a day.

Jay and Aby weren't just friends who lived two doors down; they were the people we got together with two or three times a week. We went through pregnancies together, raised babies together, shopped together, scrapbooked together, and drank wine together.

They were a significant part of our life. And whenever we had family come to visit, Jay and Aby were there too.

So, of course, she knew Dad.

I listened to her message. I remember hearing her attempting to talk but getting choked up. She said, "I don't even know if I can talk." I could feel her emotion, and tears welled up in my eyes.

I was moved.

It felt eerie walking into the cottage. Just a few days prior, Dad was there. He was fine.

He brushed his teeth for the last time.

He went to bed for the last time.

He was fine.

That afternoon, a good friend of Dad's who lived just down the street from the cottage stopped by to drop off a proof copy of an article for the local newspaper about Dad. He wanted us to look it over.

We took that opportunity to ask him if he would be one of Dad's pallbearers. He said he would be honored, but he'd rather be doing it in another thirty years or so.

That struck a chord with all of us. It made me think of all the years of life he wouldn't get to live, that we wouldn't get to share with him. All the memories we wouldn't get to create. All the laughs we wouldn't get to laugh.

Dad was too young to die.

Where was the discard pile? I was dealt a card I didn't want. It didn't fit in with all my other cards.

No death... Go fish.

Afterward, Mom and I drove the forty-minute drive from the cottage to Mom and Dad's house. It was now, I guess, just Mom's house. We stopped and picked up some sandwiches for lunch. When we got to the house, we had to sit at the formal dining room table because the kitchen table was covered with Dad's real estate papers. We sat at the table where we'd sit for our family gatherings: Christmas, Easter, and Sunday dinner. We'd never share these with Dad ever again.

Just as we took our first bites, the back doorbell rang.

When we opened the door, it was two gals from Dad's office—two gals and a van *full* of stuff. They said, "Oh, good! You're here! We have some supplies for you." They started bringing in enough food for the Walton's. They'd gone to Sam's Club, so nothing was in small portions. They brought in cold meat, cheese, buns, plates, napkins, cups, paper towels, and Kleenex. They continued to bring in toilet paper, salads, water bottles, beer, rum, and whiskey. And God bless them, they brought Diet Pepsi!

Trip after trip, they kept coming in with more and more *stuff*. It was rather comical. We were like, "Holy Cow! We're going to be using this stuff for months." It was like we were stocking a nuclear war shelter.

I still kind of chuckle when I think about the volumes of stuff they kept bringing in. The funniest part...we went through almost all of it in a matter of five days. All except some of the paper products. It was an amazing outpouring of support. It was heartfelt knowing people were willing to give us anything we needed to comfort us in any way.

So many people brought us food, others mowed Mom and Dad's lawn. Everyone we talked to offered to help in some way or another. It was such a humbling feeling.

I found it rather comical how many people brought toilet paper. I didn't know it was a thing to bring mourners toilet paper. I mean, I get it—a house full of people for days. The last thing you want to do is run out of toilet paper. No one wants to go to the store during a time like this. It'd be horrible to run out, but I'd just never really thought about it. It makes me smile. The love we felt from everyone, in every gesture, makes me smile.

It's the kind of love that swells in your chest so much that you think it might pop.

It was a gift.

32

My New Normal

Later that day, when I was back in town, I went to pick Holly Ann up from her week-long day camp program. I felt so different. I was very numb. It seemed like everyone around me was moving in slow motion.

I parked and began walking toward the front doors of the school.

I looked around at all the people. All the parents were greeting their children. It was a sunny day and not too hot or humid. It was a perfect day. A perfect day except...

I flashed back to the many times Dad would come over on a Friday after work. I'd let him in, and he'd hold out his arms for a hug, smiling, and say, "Missy Lee!"

I would never get to have that embrace again.

I remember looking at people's expressions. So many smiles. Parents happy to see their children. Children happy to see their parents. I would never get to see one of my parents ever again...until Heaven.

Surrounded by smiles...and all I wanted to do was cry.

These people look so happy, but don't they know the world is now a different place?

A lesser place.

It was a place without my dad. The world was now a place without the sound of Dad's laugh.

Everyone was going about their normal lives. They still had *their* normal.

How could I? How could I go about *my* normal? Nothing about my normal was the same. Everything was intertwined with Dad.

My life was no longer the normal I was used to. My normal was forever changed.

It was now time for me to discover my new normal.

33

The Things People Do

Half-Staff

After picking up Holly Ann, we were going to go back over to Mom and Dad's house, but first, I needed to stop by Chris and Brady's (our close friends with the new tailgating grill) to pick up some food she had for us.

Dad was a huge UNI Panther fan, and so is Brady. You could say UNI brought us all together.

As we approached their house, we noticed Brady had his UNI flag out—the flag he proudly flew every game day.

But it was the middle of June. No games were being played. He's a big enough fan, though, to fly his flag anytime, but it stood out to us.

Then we noticed.

He had the flag fastened only halfway up the pole.

He had the UNI flag flying at half-staff.

At half-staff for Bernie. Now that's a friend.

Tears poured down my face.

Yard Cleanup

During that whole time, when we were at Mayo and after we came home, we had a lot of people saying, "If there's anything we can do to help, just let us know." People would just show up on their lawnmower and mow the yard. Food, food, and more food kept showing up. People kept asking what they could do.

"What can we do? No, really. What can we do?"

So...we came up with something.

The yard at the cottage was full of debris from the flood. My cousins offered to clean up the yard, so I posted one of my cousin's contact info on CarePages and said if anyone was willing and able to help clean up the yard, contact her.

It was great. A group of people showed up—mostly my cousins and some close friends. And they all worked together to help. They didn't all know each other, but they worked together, just like Dad had done for others just a couple of weeks earlier during the flood.

The next time we went to the cottage, it was all cleaned up. The difference was night and day.

That gesture, and all the others, was like a warm hug. It reinforced the fact people loved Dad...and us.

Love Big as Billboards

Mark and Amy came to Mom and Dad's house to meet with the pastor and work on sorting through photos to use on picture boards and a slide show for the visitation.

When they showed up at the house, Mark said as they were driving into town, they saw a marquee at a local business that read:

Bernie Moine

R.I.P. Huge UNI Fan

They did a double-take, turned around, and went back to take a picture of it.

More support. It was amazing.

It was very touching. We'd always known Dad knew a lot of people, but it was amazing the support we were getting from people who seemed to be total strangers. But to Dad, they were obviously so much more.

Someone from the local newspaper emailed me a copy of the article they were going to run.

Not just an obituary write-up, but an article.

I could almost hear Dad saying, "It must've been a slow news day."

It's amazing what you can learn about someone *after* they die.

Even your own father.

The article contained several quotes from a few people who had worked with him over the years:

"It's very difficult to think about anything else; it's so untimely. Everybody liked Bernie. He was the consummate good guy. A great sense of humor. Always there when you needed a hand."

"I knew him for thirty years in the real estate business. I felt he was one of the most decent people I ever met."

"...trustworthiness..."

"...positive and friendly attitude..."

"The one word is honest..."

"...he did so much for so many people that no one ever knew about."

That. That last one there. Dad did so much...that no one ever knew about.

That made me think back to when I was in elementary school, and Dad hired a guy to help with a landscaping project in our yard. I don't know what this man's back story was, but I do know Dad giving him that opportunity helped this man more than it was helping us.

"...he did so much for so many people that no one ever knew about."

This. This was why people were showing us so much kindness and love.

34

Tearless Talk

The time came when we had to sit down and talk with the pastor officiating the funeral. He was a new pastor to the church and didn't know Dad or our family at all.

He came to Mom and Dad's house, and we all sat around the living room. I remember feeling like I was just slumped into the chair, like if you were trying to prop up a sleeping child. I was drained. We all were. Drained and cried out.

The pastor was a very friendly and pleasant guy, and he asked all the right questions... So that was great and very helpful since we didn't feel like doing anything, let alone drum up conversation. Very emotional conversation.

The problem was, we had already been asked the same questions and did our reminiscing with the chaplain at Mayo in the small family room. We had laughed and cried. We had shared our fears and disappointments. We shared story after story.

We drew that chaplain into our family and our memories. It was all raw emotion.

But on that day in Mom and Dad's living room, we sat dry-eyed, straight-faced, spewing out just a few facts and short stories. And they weren't even the best stories. We were cried out...for the moment. We didn't do the prep work justice.

If only this pastor had been present a few days earlier. *Then* he would have gotten the whole story with all the raw emotions and well-used tissues. *Then* he would have seen how much we loved and would miss Dad. *Then* he would have felt our pain and known this would not be just another funeral to him. He would have felt like he knew Dad by the time we were done.

But instead, we were dry.

We were duds.

We showed almost no emotion. I felt like this guy had no idea how much we loved Dad and how hurt we were. He had no idea we are a very tight-knit family. We did about as good of a job telling him about Dad as a bunch of strangers would off the street.

I even at one time thought, "This isn't right. We should be crying." I tried to come up with a tear. You know, one of those huge crocodile tears that slowly runs down your cheek.

Nothing.

35

Prayer Bank

We spent hours upon hours looking through pictures to use at the visitation. Laughing and reminiscing. We started sorting our photos by making separate piles. Family. Friends. Grandkids. Work. Organizations. The piles continued to grow—so many memories.

I had been on a picture-taking streak for the previous decade. Luckily, I had all the printed pictures chronologically organized in envelopes with the event and date printed on them. I was so thankful. That made it so much easier to sift through all my pictures.

My digital pictures weren't quite so organized.

I spent hours trying not to get sidetracked while going through four and a half years of digital pictures.

I selected some of the pictures to upload and get prints made—others we made into a slide show.

All in all, I think we ended up with a few hundred pictures.

So many memories.

So many blessings.

Another step in our therapy.

While sorting pictures, we had several visitors stop by the house. Most of them didn't stay long. Many just dropped things off. One was a former work colleague of Dad's who our family had known for many years. He stayed for quite a while talking about Dad.

I felt terrible that I was multitasking and appeared to be uninterested in what he was saying. I was listening while searching for pictures on my computer's hard drive, but I was listening. I was listening, *and* I will never forget one of the things he told us.

...your prayer bank is overflowing ... it will never be depleted.

He said, "You have so many people saying so many prayers for you right now that your prayer bank is overflowing. It's so full of love and support that it will never be depleted. So even years down the road, whenever you need to, you can make a withdrawal from this prayer bank and find comfort."

What an awesome analogy.

I knew people were praying for us. I could feel it. I could feel a sense of comfort and peace amongst all the discomfort and pain. I could actually visualize a cup overflowing and continually overflowing because so many were working to fill it.

So often, immediately after a loved one dies, the family is surrounded by love and support. Sometimes, despite the genuine love and support, the pain and emptiness can far exceed the supportive company. These grieving people need to realize that days, weeks, months, and years down the road, they're still not alone. That love and support are still there.

I still feel this when Dad's name comes up, or I meet yet another person who knew Dad. It's been amazing over the years when I've met someone who knew Dad—he knew a lot of people. When I tell them he's my dad, so many of them say, "Oh, I have a funny story about Bernie." It's rather incredible just how often I've heard those exact words. More people than not have said this, or they say, "Oh! We know Bernie. We love Bernie." Or, "We think the world of Bernie." And then they go into some story they can't tell without laughing and smiling. You wouldn't believe the number of people who told me one of their funny Bernie stories. It's those stories and the laughing and smiling that warms my heart.

It's all part of our prayer bank overflowing.

I think because our prayer bank was so full, that's why we were able to find moments when we could laugh. Truly laugh.

36

I Have a Dick?

While we were sitting outside on Mom and Dad's patio, Amy was going to tell us something about my parents' good friend Dick. Only in the moment, she couldn't come up with his last name, so she just said, "Dick."

Mom said, "Dick...?" They have a couple of friends named Dick. She was trying to get out of Amy which Dick she was referring to.

Amy said, "You know... OUR Dick."

Mom said, "I have a Dick?!"

We all burst out laughing. It was funny in so many ways and laughing felt so good that we just kept laughing.

More therapy. Laughter therapy.

Typing this now, many years later, I still have to smile. We retell this story from time to time, and it still brings up the same response. Not just because of the humor it holds, but because I think we remember how that original outburst of laughter felt.

Laughter *is* good medicine.

37

Friends Cry Too

The visitation was amazing.

We had hundreds of pictures displayed on picture boards and many more in a slideshow.

We had the letters to Grandpa from each of the three grandchildren displayed.

Dad looked good. He even had a little more hair than usual. (They had to add more hair to cover the scar on his head.)

He was wearing his sport coat with the UNI lining.

In his casket was a little drawer where mementos could be kept. We put the grandchildren's letters in there, a couple of UNI items, and a small airplane-sized bottle of Bacardi. It was only fitting. (We hid the bottle further back in the drawer so no one could see it.)

The crowd was unbelievably huge. I couldn't get over the unending line of people. There were many of our friends and extended family I hadn't seen in ages, a lot of Dad's work colleagues—some of them I knew, and others I didn't—and, of course, there were many close friends. Friends who had always been there for us. The line was so long that the funeral director had to tell us a few times to keep it moving. Evidently, it wound through the funeral home and out the door. Dad knew a *lot* of people.

I'll never forget my friend Jenny coming through the line. I'm not sure I'd ever seen her cry before. I'd definitely never seen her sob. That day I saw her sob. She was trying hard not to—I could tell. She had a forced smile on her face, but the tears and the gasps of air gave her away. Between gasps, she asked how we were doing and if we were ok. I hugged her and said, "We're doing ok. How are *you* doing?"

Mark and Jenny were some of those friends who really knew Dad. Jenny was one of Dad's favorites. Mom and Dad would go out of their way to stop over when they knew Mark and Jenny were in town. We'd had a lot of laughs and fun times together.

It both broke my heart and warmed it at the same time to see Jenny as...well...such a wreck. I knew she hurt for us, but I knew this was a loss for them too.

People kept filing into the funeral home. There were familiar faces and others who one might call total strangers, but were they? Although we had never met before, we were connected. We were connected through Dad.

38

The Funeral

After we had time with our extended family in the chapel before the service, it was time for the family procession down the aisle—the same aisle that Dad walked me down almost fifteen years earlier on my wedding day. But on our wedding day, when I was about to walk through the same doors with hundreds of people waiting, I was standing there *with* Dad. On the day of the funeral, I was standing there *for* Dad. On that day, Dad was only in my heart—my compound-fractured heart.

Our wedding day was a very hot, stormy day in July, fifteen years earlier, and the church was full beyond capacity. Extra chairs were set up in the back of the church. Larry and I both valued all the special friends and family in our lives. Plus, we loved any excuse for a party. We still do. We wanted all those people there to celebrate with us and to share in the joyous day. And celebrate we did.

Some of our guests had difficulty getting to our wedding because of some major flooding that year. 1993 was known as the "year of the floods" in our part of the country. There were many closed roads.

Fast forward fifteen years, 2008 was also known as the "year of the floods." There I stood in the same church, about to walk down the same aisle, with many of the same people in attendance. Again, I had butterflies in my stomach and felt a quivering in my chin, but these were very different butterflies and quiverings. Fifteen years earlier, they were of excitement, joy, and happiness. On the day of the funeral, they were of heartache, grief, and loss.

On both of those days, all the emotions I was feeling existed because of love. One was a blossoming love, and one was a loss of love—love that had nowhere to go.

We entered the sanctuary. I kept my eyes low; I couldn't make eye contact with anyone. I didn't want to see that sad, sympathetic look on everyone's faces. As we turned to go down the center aisle, I quickly glanced out of the corner of my eye and noticed the entire overflow area was full, and there were even people *standing* in the back.

Wow!

The outpouring of support was AWEsome.

The service was beautiful.

It started with the three grandchildren walking in together to light the altar candles.

My sister-in-law, Amy, led the singing. Larry and Holly Ann read scripture. I was amazed at how composed they were. I was a blubbering mess. There is no way I could speak in front of all those people. I couldn't even *look* at them! And considering

I'm no Whitney Houston, I obviously couldn't sing in front of all of them, either. All those people who cared about Dad and about us. It was an incredible gift of their time.

Amy led the congregation in singing "How Great Thou Art." She started by saying we had chosen that song because I could remember singing it at Grandpa's (Dad's dad) funeral. She instructed everyone to sing loud no matter how well people sang (we Moine's are not known for our beautiful singing) so Bernie would hear us. I'm not sure how Amy could sing so beautifully at that moment, but she did a fabulous job. I, on the other hand, lost it. I'd stood beside Dad so many times, "singing" that song.

Everyone was singing. Well, actually, I couldn't even attempt to sing. My chin was quivering so badly; there was no way my voice was going to come out. So, while trying to mouth the words with tears streaming down my cheeks, I swear I heard Dad singing along with us. I could hear it in my right ear. His voice was louder than any other. Instantly, goose-bumps covered my arms and neck. I turned my head slightly and peered over my shoulder to see if I could figure out who was sounding like my dad.

I didn't want to turn too far. I knew I probably looked like a swollen-eyed mess, and I didn't want to make eye contact with anyone. That would only make me cry more and make matters worse.

I took a quick look, but I couldn't come up with a logical source. The only two people I could see in my swift glance were women.

But I heard Dad.

I heard him singing in his sometimes decent, sometimes a bit squeaky and off-tune voice. It has always been a family joke that none of us can sing. Not a lick. But we do it anyway. We've always wondered how scarred some other people would be if they heard us singing along with Mitch Miller at Christmas time. I'm telling you, it's never been pretty.

But we sing anyway.

I had heard Dad sing many times throughout my life. I remember when I was a little girl in church and hearing him sing next to me at church. His singing voice always stood out to me. It didn't really sound like his speaking voice. It was so much lower.

Hearing Dad that day took me back to ten days earlier, just two days before Dad's aneurysm...

I had gone to the funeral of my aunt's mother with Mom and Dad. I sat between them. I can't recall for sure, but I think we sang that same song, "How Great Thou Art." I remember actually listening to Dad sing, not just hearing him.

But listening.

That day, Dad and I stood side by side, singing that song.

Only on that day, he stood to my left.

And on the day of his funeral, I heard him on my right.

Larry read the poem "The Dash" by Linda Ellis. His cousin had posted it on Dad's CarePage shortly after his passing. (You can read the poem online at http://thedashpoem.com.)

The poem spoke volumes to me. I think it was the epitome of Dad's life. He lived the dash well.

That very service, which hundreds of people chose to take part in, reflected what the dash was in Dad's life. He took the time for people. He smiled. He laughed. He made people's days brighter. I'm sure most everyone there was recalling their memories of Dad and the way he lived out his dash.

For you never know how much time is left... With Dad leaving us so suddenly, boy, isn't that the truth. It really has changed how Larry and I look at things and has affected how we make decisions. Is there something hanging over you that you need or want to do? Don't say, "There's always tomorrow," because you know what? There's not. There isn't always tomorrow for the things that really matter. Some of us know when the end of the dash is coming, but some don't.

The dash. Dad lived it right and lived it well.

He didn't just always say it...

He modeled it...

He lived it up while he was young.

The pastor tied Dad's well-used line of, "There's always room for ice cream" into an amazing story of Dad. He talked about how Dad always made time ("room") for others. I'm not sure how the pastor was able to take what little we gave him on that day in Mom and Dad's living room, showing little to no emotion, and turn it into an incredible message that embodied Dad so well.

For the "grand finale," everyone sang "Lord of the Dance." We chose this song because Dad loved to dance, and we wanted to end on an upbeat note. Dad was not a doom-and-gloom kind of person, and we wanted to go out of this celebration of life to feel like we were actually celebrating.

As Amy started to lead us in singing, she also led the three grandchildren in a dance in front of the altar. The three of them continued to hold hands and dance in a circle until the end of the song. Everyone in the pews started clapping. The ones who could see what was going on, that is.

We had a friend tell us later that he had no idea what was going on when he heard the applause. Then he looked at his wife, and she was sobbing. He had to be told what had happened.

It was all so beautiful. Now, I wish we had it on video. You wouldn't think that a funeral would be something you'd like to watch over and over, but it truly was an amazing service.

39

The "Fun"eral

I think it's funny, not in a ha-ha kind of way, but in an "isn't that a weird coincidence" kind of way, that funerals begin with the word "fun." That is not the word most people would use to describe a funeral. And I wouldn't say that that is the first word I would think of to describe the day of Dad's funeral. But I might consider it to be a close second.

Once the actual funeral service was over and everyone went downstairs for the luncheon, there were a lot of fun parts. My favorite was after we ate, we went to talk to some of our local friends. So that was several couples. Then our friends who used to be local but moved an hour away joined us. Then our best friends and neighbors from where we used to live near St. Louis came over. Then a couple of my best friends from high school joined the crowd.

Not everyone knew each other, but all of these people had a common bond...me. Dad and me. All of these people—some of my favorite people in the world—were there to support me. Wow. What an awesome feeling. I was actually giddy to be surrounded by so many of the people who I'd been closest to over the years, all from different times in my life.

Something else for my list.

Something else for my list. My now ongoing "I'm Thankful For" list.

I've learned my friends are willing to take time out of their day, miss work, dress up, even drive for hours just for me. I am thankful to call such a great group of so many people friends.

And all of those people knew and were friends with Dad, too. Because Mom and Dad did so much with all of us, my friends were their friends. Of course, they were there to support me, but they all actually knew Dad and were doing their own grieving.

Blessed.

An overwhelming feeling of being blessed is how I felt.

To be surrounded by so many friends who truly cared about me, all standing around, laughing and smiling. That's my idea of fun.

So yeah, funerals *can* be fun.

40

Going Pell Mell

After the "fun"eral meal, everyone loaded up in their vehicles to drive to the cemetery for the burial.

It was a beautiful day; it was sunny, and the temperature was just right. Not too hot and not too cold. It would have been the perfect day if it weren't the day of Dad's funeral.

Once we got to the highway, it was a four-lane road to where the burial would be. It was an easy drive, a drive we had driven hundreds of times. It was usually a fun drive, a drive that led to boating and fun family times.

We had several cars in our caravan. We were in our car. Mark, Amy, Drew, and Mom were in Mark's car. Then there were all the relatives. I have no idea, but I would guess at least 15-20 vehicles full of people were making the forty-five-minute drive to the cemetery. Or should I say the drive that *usually* takes about forty-five minutes.

Not that day.

You think of funeral processions as moving slowly. Almost a visible sign of the grief. The dread of the event that lies ahead.

But in Bernie fashion, we were speeding right on down the highway. The pace was set by the hearse. We were going much faster than I would normally drive on the highway, which is usually a bit over the speed limit.

Larry and I started laughing.

"Holy Cow!" Are you kidding me? Is this really happening? Are we really speeding (extra fast) just to keep up with the hearse?

Once again, our drive during this whole ordeal was quite comical.

I could just picture Dad saying, "Yeee haaa!"

After speeding to the cemetery, we had a beautiful ceremony at the burial site. Many people were there. I distinctly remember the director guiding us to sit in the chairs under the canopy.

It struck me.

We were the ones sitting in the chairs. I had been to numerous funerals and burials. It was always someone *else* sitting in the chairs. But now, we were the special guests of honor. I didn't want to be this special. I wanted to be someone standing in the back. Someone who was maybe just an acquaintance. Someone who wasn't very closely connected to the person in the casket. But I accepted my position. My role. I felt it. My body was tired. I didn't want to stand. I just wanted to lie down and take a nap. So, yes, yes, I'll take a seat. I'll accept any reprieve I can get. Thank you for the chairs.

The chairs were very cushy and comfy, which was nice. I guess they know you're going through so much *dis*comfort that a comfortable chair would be appreciated if it was even noticed.

I noticed.

I noticed the chairs. I noticed the blue sky. I noticed the perfect weather.

It was a gorgeous day for mid-to-late June. It wasn't hot. There was a nice breeze. The sun was shining. The birds were singing.

I glanced over at the top of the vault. We'd selected one with a beautiful lakeside scene etched into the bronze top. It was perfect. Perfect for Dad. Perfect for us.

As we sat there, the pastor said some more beautiful words. More words I don't remember, but I wish I did. He read a beautiful poem that I also don't remember anything about, but I wish I did.

I don't remember the words, but I will *never*, ever, ever forget what happened while those wonderful words were being said.

I was sitting on my comfy chair next to Mom. We were surrounded by friends and family who loved us and loved Dad. I remember Mom was sitting on my left. I don't know if anyone was sitting on my right.

I stared blankly, looking straight ahead at the edge of the vault. My eyes weren't focused on anything in particular.

Suddenly, a small, yellow butterfly landed on the edge of the vault. My heart jumped.

I remember thinking the bright, cheery color of yellow made the butterfly appear to be happy.

I kept staring at this wondrous visitor expecting it to flit off at any second.

But it didn't.

I stared more intently. I watched as it stood still—as time stood still. I was entranced.

Then, my mysterious visitor started to move. At first, slowly, then faster—it began dancing! I kid you not! This little yellow winged visitor started to dance.

It was actually picking each leg up in a varying pattern as if dancing to the rhythm of the words, moving slightly forward and back.

The butterfly was dancing! It really *was* happy.

I continued looking at it. Wide-eyed now. No longer a blurred stare.

I had bated breath, just waiting to see what it was going to do next. I knew in the heart of my soul this was not just a random butterfly that just happened to have landed in front of us.

This butterfly was dancing for me. For us.

I never wanted it to leave.

Then, as if it knew what I was thinking, it quickly took off in flight and swooped right towards Mom and me. It came within inches of our faces before it flew off into the bright blue sky.

I knew Dad was ok...happy...dancing.

Dad shared one last dance with us.

41

Just the Beginning

Seeing the butterfly on the day of Dad's burial was just the beginning of my amazing journey of viewing God, Spirit, The Universe, and the world we live in differently. I started seeing the world in a magical new way.

I've always had a belief in God. I don't ever remember a time when I didn't believe in a loving God. And I really don't think this belief just stems from being raised going to church and Sunday school.

I'd always believed in God and prayers and miracles and an eternal soul.

I was more than grateful for my beliefs when I was going through the horrible, grief-stricken time at the Mayo Clinic. I couldn't imagine going through all of that without them. I couldn't imagine the grief being stronger or the pain being greater because I know without my beliefs, they would've been.

I'm not sure if you had asked me back then to spell out in specific words my definition of God, what my answer would've been, but I know it would've been different than it is today. Back then, my description would've had no depth, or confidence, or personal connection. I would've said God was something "out there." That "He" listened to all of our prayers, but "He" didn't necessarily answer them. I would've said I hadn't ever heard God speak, nor would I have believed I had the ability to hear "Him." I would have said I sometimes felt close to God, but then again, not really or very often, at least.

Back then, I had no idea what I was capable of seeing and hearing and feeling. I had no idea of just how connected I could be to this AWEsome power. I had no idea the loving Universe was communicating with me all the time. I had no idea there could be a glorious connection, a conversation that could occur...all day...every day.

The writing in the mirror at the hotel and that beautiful yellow butterfly at the burial were just the beginning of a very beautiful relationship, a conversation that has changed the way I look at life forever.

Over the years, the plethora of signs and synchronicities have blown me away, taken my breath away, and occasionally made me blurt out an expletive or two. I was asked to attend a conference with my girls as a favor for a high school classmate. Long story short, this led me to a book, which led me to dozens of more books and a whole new way to look at how the force of love and belief works. Each leading was wrapped in a "coincidence" or synchronicity that just reinforced my new beliefs. The signs have been varied, but the butterflies have been plentiful.

42

Birthday Butterflies

It was Labor Day weekend 2010, which meant it was Dad's birthday weekend. We were at the cottage, as usual. That Sunday was the actual day of his birthday. Even though we were staying at the cottage that weekend, we had to drive back to Cedar Falls to go to our church because Larry was scheduled to do the reading. When we were about to leave, we noticed Holly was standing by the sliding glass door, looking out at the lake, with tears running down her cheeks.

We put our arms around her and asked her what was wrong.

She said, "Today is Grandpa's birthday."

And the tear flow increased.

It broke my heart. To see Holly hurting made me hurt even more.

What a much different day it would have been if only...

Larry hugged her and said, "Yeah, I miss him too."

Then we all were standing there, hugging each other with tears streaming down our cheeks. Tears filled with love and hurt. The hurt for the memories that would no longer be made.

We eventually composed ourselves and loaded up in our vehicle for the thirty-plus minute drive.

I'd been thinking for a long time about writing this book. I needed to tell this story. I'd had sign after sign, but it felt like such a scary and daunting task. I don't know why, but it did. Maybe it wasn't really my idea. Even though the thoughts were running through *my* head, they didn't seem to be there by *my* doing. Something much bigger than me had put them there. I think that's why it seemed so...terrifying.

And with fear comes doubts.

I doubted myself to write a book, wondering why anyone would want to read *my* story. What is so special about *me*?

Then I saw one of the most beautiful, unreal, unbelievable sights I'd ever seen.

Monarchs.

Everywhere!

Not just a few.

Thousands!

I am not exaggerating.

There were thousands of monarch butterflies. Everywhere I looked. Over all the fields for as far as the eye could see.

They were migrating to Mexico.

It was like a scene from a movie. One of those scenes you think could never happen in real life. It felt like it could only be done with computer animation.

Was I dreaming?

It was breathtaking.

Breathtakingly beautiful.

One minute, I was full of doubt and fear, and the next minute...

God gave me butterflies.

That was no coincidence.

God and this fantastic Universe put an exclamation point on Dad's birthday and my fears with... thousands of beautiful butterflies.

43

Mysterious Visitors

Just over three years after Dad died, my oldest daughter, Holly, started having pain in her abdominal area. Over time, it continued to worsen so much so that she couldn't sleep. Any time she was sitting or lying down, the pain would intensify. It was affecting every part of her life. Just the lack of sleep alone was making her feel even worse by the day.

We spent many months going to doctor after doctor. Specialist. Therapist. We couldn't find any answers.

Then, one very cold January night, the doorbell rang. I went to the door, and there were about four or five, what appeared to be college-aged students, standing on my porch, each one of them smiling from ear to ear. They introduced themselves as a group of students from some church or organization. I really don't remember. Heck, I don't even remember how many of them there were.

The one doing the introduction went on to say, "We're here to see if there is anything we can pray for you about."

Wow! Really?

First of all, I thought how brave these young people were to just go around door to door, asking people if they can pray for them. But with the way they carried themselves and were smiling, they didn't seem to think there was any reason to be daunted by their task.

I said (I'm sure with eyebrows raised), "Actually, there is."

Their glowing faces got even brighter. They had a taker!

"My daughter has been having a mysterious pain for months."

Their faces all shifted to a caring, concerned look.

I went on to give a brief description of what had been going on.

Then the girl asked, "Is she here?"

The others all nodded and continued smiling.

I paused, not really sure how to process what was going on.

"Yes..."

"We would love for her to join us so we can pray for her."

"Ok..." I looked at them out of the corner of my eye, I'm sure with a questioning, furrowed brow.

I quickly gave each of them an assessing look right in their sparkling eyes. I swear they were all sparkling.

It was cold out. Very, very cold out. So, I thought, I can't be cold-hearted and make these sparkling eyed prayer-warriors wait outside while I fetch Holly, so I invited them into our entryway to wait.

They gladly accepted the invitation.

I went to the staircase and hollered up to Holly to come down.

Of course, the sixteen-year-old had to reply with, "Why?"

"Just come here...*now*."

I glanced back toward the entryway, probably to make sure all of our mystery visitors were staying put. Holly started coming down the stairs, staring at me with a questioning look.

I said, "There are some people here who want to pray for you."

The questioning look multiplied by ten as she reached the bottom of the stairs. I placed my hand on the back of her arm and nudged her toward the entryway.

As Holly and I rounded the corner, the praying gang's faces lit up even more. How was that even possible?

The girl acting as spokesperson spoke up and said while smiling (of course), "We'd like to pray for you."

"Ok..." Holly said with an even more questioning look on her face.

The correlation of the increasing joy of the pray-ers' faces and the questioning look on Holly's and my faces was rather funny.

They gathered around and placed their hands on Holly. In unison, they all bowed their heads. Holly and I subtly glanced at each other as we both joined them in bowing our heads.

It's not that praying was such a foreign concept to us; we'd been pray-ers all of our lives, but this...this showing up of total strangers whose sole purpose at this moment was to pray for us... This was foreign.

The girl prayer-warrior spoke what I'm sure was a very lovely prayer. I don't remember a single word she said, but she prayed for doctors and Holly's healing.

"Words. Words. Words... Amen."

We all added our amens and slowly raised our heads. All of the prayer-warriors smiled at Holly and then at me. We all exchanged smiles and nods.

I said, "Thank you."

Holly said, "Thank you."

They said, "Yes! God Bless!"

Then they all turned toward the door and exited out into the dark, cold, cold night.

I closed the door behind them and turned to look at Holly. We exchanged puzzled looks.

"What was that?" she asked.

"I have *no* idea, but it was very nice. "

Holly turned to go back upstairs. I started to return to the family room, but after a few steps, I turned back around and went to the front door. I unlocked it, opened it, and stuck my head out into the fridged air. I looked to the driveway. Nothing. I looked toward the neighbors' houses on either side of us. Nothing. I scanned down the street on both sides.

Nothing.

No car.

No people.

Nothing.

They couldn't have gotten that far. They'd just left.

Thank you, God, for our prayer-warriors.

The following week, we had an appointment out of town with a urologist. We were checking off all the possible boxes. The doctor was very kind and thorough. He said he didn't think Holly's issue was urology-related, but he thought we should have a full-body MRI (not just the lower abdomen) with contrast.

The next week, Holly had a full body MRI with contrast. When we returned home, a message was waiting for us on the answering machine.

That same blinking light...this time with a most wonderful message. It was our family doctor saying, "I think we have an answer."

Wait! What? We just *left the MRI. We only live about ten minutes away! How can we have an answer?*

I called our doctor back.

He sounded very positive. "The MRI showed a tumor on her spinal cord."

Tumor? I thought, *How can that be good?* Using the words good and tumor in the same sentence seemed like an oxymoron.

But...it was good! We had an answer—an answer to our many prayers. There was now something we could do to give Holly some relief. But with this sense of relief was also a large dose of worry. My "baby girl" was going to have spinal cord surgery. They were going to remove part of her spine, cut into the spinal cord sac, and remove an inch-long tumor attached to her spinal cord.

What mother wouldn't be worried?

I did a lot of praying. We had a lot of people praying for us.

We anxiously waited, but finally, about six long weeks later, we found ourselves back at the Mayo Clinic. The Mayo Clinic...the same place where my life changed forever.

Just four years earlier, I lost Dad, the first man I ever loved, at this amazing, prestigious place. Now we were going back, and once again praying for a miracle and a favor.

44

Surgery Day

I asked God for a favor.

On the morning of Holly's surgery, I asked God to show me a butterfly before the surgery to let me know everything was going to be alright. Over the years, I had been shown so many butterflies at very meaningful times. I didn't think my request was odd at all.

Now, I realized it was March in Minnesota, and the likelihood of this happening outside with a real live butterfly was rather unlikely. Still, it was unseasonably warm that year, and just the week before, I'd seen two butterflies dancing while they flew above me in Cedar Falls—only two hours south.

Plus, God is God.

All things are possible.

When we walked across the street from the hotel toward the hospital, my eyes were darting in search of my reassuring butterfly.

My hug from God.

The closer we got to that door with no butterfly in sight, the slower I walked, giving God a little more time to show me "our sign."

Door.

Nothing.

We entered the hospital. I reminded myself to breathe.

Just breathe.

We had quite a walk through the halls to get to the check-in desk. We wound around the maze of hallways. We entered the last hall before the desk, and I heard Larry say, "Wow, Holl! Look at that."

I looked to my left; in a display case, I saw a t-shirt covered with butterflies.

I felt a lump of joy form in my throat. There's my sign—dozens of little butterflies.

Thank you!

Then I heard Holly say, "Oh, wow!"

And I realized their attention was not being directed into the display case but to the wall on the other side of the hall.

I turned around.

On the wall were about two dozen large canvases. Each one was about three feet by three feet.

On each one was a huge...

Beautiful...

Painted...

Butterfly!

It took my breath away.

I had received my sign.

This wall may have been beautiful to anyone...

But to me, it was the most beautiful wall in the world!

I had received my sign.

After they wheeled Holly back for surgery, Larry and I went to the cafeteria. It was the same cafeteria that almost four years prior, I could hardly choke down half of a salad.

And I ate a giant omelet.

God is good!

That was no coincidence!

45

What If

What if I was supposed to learn how to view the world with these new rose-colored glasses? To see things to be grateful for in situations that aren't so rosy? To see the wonders of this magnificent world? To see that God is on my side and see all the ways that "He" communicates to me. Each way is an additional exclamation point at the end of the statement, "Love is everywhere!"

If you just look for it.

And better yet… What if I was supposed to learn this so I can teach you how to do it, too?

What are *you* looking for?

What do you see?

Do you see Love everywhere?

How hard are you trying? How aware are you? Are you taking the time to look around you? Notice the world. There are God signs everywhere; you just need to notice them. See them as being these amazing coincidences that aren't actually coincidences. They are little (and big) hugs of Love from this amazing universe we live in. That God created. That Love created.

Holy BLEEP! That was NOT a Coincidence

Discussion Questions

***This is a partial list of questions.
Make your discussion even better!
Go to https://www.michelleprohaska.com/free-resources/
for the full, downloadable, printable list.

Part I

1. Have you ever lost a loved one unexpectedly?

   Who was it?

   How did it affect you?

   What was different about holidays or other events after they passed?

2. While Michelle's dad was at Mayo Clinic, she kept noticing things to add to her gratitude list.

   Have you ever been able to see the good in a very unpleasant situation? What did you notice?

3. Michelle can now look at the spots on her hands with a softer heart than before her dad died.

   Are there things that you appreciate after a loved one has passed that you did not appreciate before?

4. One of Michelle's most recurring "signs" are butterflies.

   Do you have a predominant "Godincidence" sign?

5. Michelle believes that we are eternal spiritual beings having a temporary human experience.

   Do you believe we have eternal souls/spirits?

   Have you ever thought otherwise?

PART II

God is...

1

In a Box... Not in a Box

What's in a name?

This book isn't about religion. It is about God. There's a difference.

My publisher told us to define our ideal reader. I really wanted to say everyone, because my point is to make EVERYONE look at God/The Universe/Spirit/the world differently. It's not important if you've never stepped foot in a church or religiously go to church every day. If there is any chance you have God in a box of any sort and are definitive on how you view "Him," I want to show you how to be more open-minded about the subject.

Let me emphasize I don't care what you call God because I know what it's like to be turned off by someone's message because of the verbiage they use. This message should feel loving, open-minded, and inclusive. If you have God in a box of any size, I invite you to open your mind and don't get caught up in rules and preconceived notions and explore the ways we're connected with the power of Love.

I want to make clear the kind of person I am and the message I carry. I am familiar with the Bible, but I'm not a biblical scholar, nor do I want to be. When I knew I was supposed to write this book, I thought, "Ummm...no, thank you." Do you know what I think of when I think of an author of a book about God? I think of Dana Carvey's Church Lady character from Saturday Night Live.

Some of you are probably too young to know what I'm talking about. It was a recurring Saturday Night Live skit from back in the late '80s. Google it.

The Church Lady was the very judgy type of person who was usually scowling or had pursed lips. I'm *so* not anything like the Church Lady. I'm the one who is not afraid to go out on the dance floor and dance...all by myself. I've even been known to dance on top of furniture. I'm no stranger to a shot of Fireball. Fun is the name of the game, and if you like fun too, well, you could very well be a friend of mine. The stereotypical Church Lady mold definitely doesn't fit me.

I've been a member of and involved with Christian churches all my life, but let me tell you, my beliefs, morals, and values do not line up with those of many "Christians" I know. (Some people who claim to be Christian make me very uncomfortable.)

All this to say, I felt like writing a book about God would:

1. Personally be a very uncomfortable endeavor
2. Set me up for a lot of ridicule

So, I just wanted to point this out to you, the reader, to be transparent about myself and the nature of my message.

Carrying on.

Whether you believe there's a God in this world or not, we've all at least heard of the concept. We've all heard people reference "God." Some people might call God by a different name. Some of the many names include:

God	Source	Most High
The Universe	Source Energy	Yahweh
Higher Power	Allah	Jehovah
Spirit	Nature	Love
The Force	Divine Intelligence	Big Magic
The Power	I Am	Bob
Creator	Father	
The Divine	Abba	

The list could go on and on. The first thing I want to do is encourage you not to get caught up in what other people call God. Please pick a name that most resonates with you and substitute it for the word I or others use. I mean, really, what's in a name? The name of something or what you call something is not as important as what you think about it.

If I were to set a glass of milk in front of you and ask you what was in the glass, would you be wrong if you said anything other than milk? My answer is no. Now, hear me out. If someone spoke Spanish, their response might be leche. Leche is the Spanish word for milk. It's the same stuff in the glass, but we're not wrong whether we say milk or leche. It's just another word that exists in the world to label the white, cloudy liquid that comes out of a mammal to feed their young. Using a different word than you do does *not* make someone wrong.

Speaking of Spanish, I have to tell a funny story.

A few years ago, Larry and I went to Chile in South America to visit our daughter, Holly, who was studying there for a semester. One of the days, we went on a vineyard tour. Our tour guide was multilingual and was giving the tour in both English and Portuguese. Her native language was Spanish.

In Spanish, when you make a toast, the common phrase used is "Salud," which means "to health." Salud is also the phrase said to someone who has just sneezed.

Near the end of our tour, Holly sneezed, and our tour guide said, "Cheers!"

We thought this was hilarious because it's not the proper use of "cheers." It isn't what we say when someone sneezes. To her, though, I'm sure it made perfect sense. The reasoning was there.

My point is people say things differently, and that's ok. Don't be judgy, people.

I use several different words when I'm referring to what many call God. My top two are God and The Universe. Let me tell you why these are my two favorites.

God is the name most used among the people I'm around most often. If I say "God," the people I'm talking to know what I'm talking about. They may or may not have the same beliefs as I do about God, but they at least know in general what I'm talking about.

I actually prefer to use the name The Universe. I bet some of you may have just audibly gasped. Blasphemy! So, let me explain why. Many people have a fear associated with the name God. They have someone in their past who has put the fear of God in them. They've had people use it as a manipulation tool. They disagree with other people's definitions of God. These other people may have caused the person to develop a resentment of God.

Let's face it; some people have sucked all the fun out of God. They can be very stuffy about the topic. They think they have God all figured out, but they don't have a true relationship with God. Some people believe God is a vengeful God and only fear this power. I don't believe this. I believe God is loving and kind, and sometimes hilarious. "He" wants only the best for us. The key is we have to also want that for ourselves.

Let's face it; some people have sucked all the fun out of God.

When some people hear someone use the name God, they assume they know how that person would define God. I think that's a very slippery slope. There are probably as many different definitions of God as there are people.

When the name of God is used, we immediately jump to what our or someone else's definition of God is. We have the name of God defined. But to define a thing is to limit it. I believe that for us to grasp the possible totality of God, we shouldn't limit our definition of God. The name The Universe, to me, shows the expansiveness of God. The limitlessness of God. It says God is so big and so many things that no one can define all that God is.

I've always had this very deep-rooted sense in me that I'm a spiritual being with no end. It's been my belief for as long as I can remember. I was brought up going to church and taught about God, but I don't think this sense of knowing resulted from what church taught me. I believe it was just a connection to something within me—something that just is and not something that's a result of being taught. I feel some of the things churches teach only cause confusion.

This is especially true when talking about God. Somewhere along the way, all of us who believe in God were fed this image of an old man with a white beard sitting on a throne perched up in the sky somewhere so far away that we can't actually see "Him."

Now I'm not saying it's wrong to think of God this way. If it brings you comfort to think of God as a kind, loving father or grandfatherly figure, then, by all means, do that. Just don't let it define your beliefs of God. Don't let it restrict your thinking that God is a human with only human abilities.

This kind of belief puts too many limits on God.

When it says in the Bible that man was made in the image of God, I don't believe it means God has a body with two arms, two legs, two eyes, a nose, a mouth, etc. I think it means we're creative beings, and we're capable of creating great things. But this is a topic for another time.

God is so much more than that.

God is the love you see everywhere.

God is the rainbow you see in the sky.

God is what I heard when Brooke was a baby, laughing hysterically at a stuffed duck.

God is what took my breath away when I first peeked over the rim of the Grand Canyon.

God is within you.

Let's talk about what God is *not*. God is not an old man who lives in the clouds. "He" isn't angry and vengeful. "He" is not a *he*. God isn't a person, so "He" has no gender.

God is not a man. God is not a woman. However, I *do* love in the book *The Shack*, God is portrayed as a woman—a large, black woman at that. I love that because it contests the widespread belief that God is an old, bearded, Caucasian man. It's very limiting to think of God as a human. We might fall into the belief that “He” is only capable of the things that human beings are capable of. (Which is way more than we believe we are, by the way. I’ll talk more about this in Part IV.) God can do so much more than we can. That’s to say, God can do so much more than we can do...than we can do without God.

I don’t mind when people use the pronoun “He” when talking about God. It’s our vernacular. It’s commonplace. It’s the language used in the Bible. Don’t let this little word limit your beliefs in God, what “He” is, and what “He” can do.

So many of us are trying to shove God into a box. If you have God in a box, take him out! If you have limiting beliefs about God, it will limit how you can experience God and this world we live in. Take “Him” out of whatever limiting belief box you have “Him” in. No box is big enough to contain God. The box would have to be bigger than The Universe (which is just another name for God), and that’s impossible. So, take God out of the box you have “Him” in. We shan’t be trying to shove “Him” into anything.

You’re probably wondering what’s with all the quotation marks around “He” and “Him” when I just got done saying I don’t have a problem with people using these pronouns. I’m going to continue using quotation marks throughout this book to reiterate this message of not limiting your beliefs of God.

God is so many things, and we will continue to see all these different things if we remain open to “Him” continually showing face in an infinite number of ways. Some people define God as Love. Others think of God as something we should fear. I once learned the Hebrew word we translate as “fear” also means awe and reverence. The more things I see that I believe to be God, the more I’m in awe and a state of joy.

So, I invite you to consider being open in your journey of seeking this magical force in the world. Let God continually show you how *"He"* defines "Himself." When trying to define God, we don't need to explain "Him" definitively. Don't put limits on this magical power. And don't get caught up in the name. If someone uses a different name than you use, just change it in your mind to whatever name you prefer. Throughout this book, I will continually be changing up the name that I use. I'll mostly be using God or The Universe. Call this amazing thing whatever you want. Call it Bob if you wish. Won't bother me. Just be open to believing there *is* such a force, *what* it is, and *how* it can appear.

God cannot be contained in a one-sentence definition, a paragraph, or even a whole book. God is continually showing "Himself" in new ways every day.

2

Coinciдence... or Godincidence

"That's too coincidental to be a coincidence."

-Yogi Berra[1]

What is a coincidence? According to Merriam-Webster[2], it means:

1: the act or condition of coinciding: CORRESPONDENCE

2: the occurrence of events that happen at the same time by accident but seem to have some connection

By accident? Hmmm. I'm not buying it.

Since Dad died, I've experienced so many coincidences that I no longer believe these things and their timing are happening by accident. I think they're synchronicities orchestrated by God and this amazing Universe. Or I should say this AWEsome

Universe. I write the word AWEsome with a capitalized A, W, and E on purpose. These occurrences and coincidences are truly moments of awe, that feeling you know to the core of your being that something didn't just happen by chance but was orchestrated by something much greater than yourself.

Awesome is one of those words that gets overused. People are always using this word when something is good or even great. But for something to be really awesome, it's something, when witnessing it, puts you in a state of awe. Like wow! Holy cow! Holy bleep! I can't believe it! You're picking your jaw up off the floor. OMG! It's ok to say it. By all means, give God a shout out and say, "Oh my God!"

When I see coincidences that spark that "wow" within me, those moments when I think, *Wow! That's too odd not to be God*, I give God all the credit for that occurrence. I've started sometimes calling these happenings "Godincidences."

When I came to view these things as The Universe communicating with me, it changed the way I look at the world. I started noticing magic everywhere. Believing in the magic makes the magic appear more. It's not the belief that makes the magic happen. It's happening whether we notice it or not. When we're willing to see what's right in front of us, we tap into and connect with it.

God shows up in so many different ways. We've all heard of miracles, and some of us have even witnessed them firsthand. When something happens, and there's no scientific explanation for it, we call it a miracle. It's an unexpected—by scientific terms—and very welcomed outcome.

I totally believe in miracles, and I believe they are acts of God. Many people seem to have very little hope or belief that something can happen in their favor. I've told many people over the years that having faith is not just believing there is a God, but it's believing in what God can and will do for you. It's the belief and faith in what God can and will do that actually brings the miracle to fruition.

Unwavering faith is not easy to come by. We have voices in our heads and the voices of people around us who interfere with our belief in what God can do.

I challenge you to believe in miracles and believe the coincidences you notice around you are not just accidents. We didn't get the miracle of Dad's healing back in 2008, but since then, I have repeatedly experienced and noticed miracles in the Godincidences.

It all started with the writing in the mirror at the hotel. Next, it was the captivating, little, yellow butterfly that was dancing at Dad's burial. No part of me thinks those were just simple coincidences. The butterflies have continued to show up over and over, and the timing of some of these appearances have been jaw-dropping. These amazing little creatures have become my "sign" with God.

What's your sign?
Do you have one?

What's your sign? Do you have one? I'm not talking zodiac sign, but a repeated Godincidence sign that continues to show up time and time again. God is often described as patient, and "His" patience sometimes comes off as persistence. You may experience a variety of signs from God, but you might see the same type repeatedly. Have you caught on to anything like this?

The Universe sometimes patiently shows us the same thing repeatedly to give us time to catch on and notice.

My cat, Rudy, loves to cuddle. Every night when I go to bed and read for a while, Rudy jumps up to get in his nightly cuddle. When I'm ready to go to sleep, I get up to go to the bathroom. When I come back into the room, Rudy knows it's time for him to skedaddle, and he jumps off the bed and leaves the room. Over time, it was just something he caught onto.

You, too, can catch on to what is happening around you. It's actually amusing to see and discover more ways The Universe is sending you love. The more you consider the possibility these coincidences are actually Godincidences, the more things you will see.

It's been said that once a new thought or idea stretches a mind, it can't ever go back to the way it was before. Oliver Wendell Holmes explained it as, "Man's mind, once stretched by a new idea, never regains its original dimensions[3]." So, once you entertain this idea of magic being all around you, you'll never see the world the same way again.

3

Felt... Not Taught

Many people think their beliefs are the things they've been taught by their parents, their church, and their elders, but our true beliefs, the things we hold deep down in our soul, are something different. We can be taught something, but that doesn't mean it becomes our belief.

If I've learned anything about beliefs, it's they can't be taught. You can be introduced to them, but you can't be taught beliefs. When you're taught something, you either believe it, or you don't. Sometimes, you may think you believe something because you think you're supposed to believe it. Your parents believe it. Your grandparents believed it. It makes sense you're supposed to believe it, too, right? But that isn't the same thing as genuinely believing something. Your true belief is what's still there when you remove all of the supposed to's.

Beliefs can change because something shifts inside of you, but true beliefs can't be taught. When we're introduced to an idea or presented with a concept, we absorb the information. Whether we know it or not, this info then goes through our internal filtering system. It's determined at that time whether the concept moves into our belief system. Does it jive with all our other beliefs? Does this puzzle piece fit into your puzzle entitled "My Belief Set"?

Beliefs are tied to our feelings. There's a tie between our beliefs and feelings that can't be severed. Both are a part of you. And when it comes to God, those feelings should be ones of joy and love. Some people think of religion when they think of beliefs or God. While God and Love are the founding reasons for all the different religions, interpretations and views have divided people over the centuries. I've found there can be as many different views and interpretations of things as there are people.

We could all benefit greatly by focusing on Love and what we have in common rather than our differences. I am in no way bashing religion. Religion has always been a part of my life. But if your religion requires you to hate someone, you need a new religion.

How I see the connection between religion and God is God can stand without religion, but religion cannot stand without God. Although religions do their darndest, no one religion nor any one person, for that matter, can definitively define God. It's like I said before, God is continually defining "Himself" differently every day.

4

God is Love... Love is God

So, what is God? What is Love? There are so many different kinds of love, and there are so many different ways God shows "Himself." In the Greek language, there are several words for love. There's romantic love and the love you have for your child. There's also the love you have for a particular type of food or an object, a friend's love, the love and respect you have for nature, the love you have for God... I personally think the list could go on and on. My point is there are so many different types of love, and God resides in each and every one of them.

God is Love. The chapter could end here, but I don't think it would do justice to this fabulous topic of Love. God is *real* Love. God is all Love. God is the epitome of unconditional Love. Not like the love you may have for chocolate, or wine, or your kitty cat. Or even the love you have for drinking wine while eating chocolate with your kitty cat purring on your lap. Not even the love you have for your child.

That probably struck a chord with many of you. I know many of you love your child unconditionally. You would literally do anything—even die—for your child. But can you imagine a Love even greater, one that doesn't waver even a little bit? One that is totally and completely patient. Think about that. Being totally patient would mean not letting your frustration move you to a state of raised blood pressure and maybe even a little yelling.

I'm sure I'm not the only parent out there who has used the line,

"Now I know why some animals eat their young."

Am I right?

So, even if you're a saint and have never said or thought anything disparaging about your child, the Love I'm talking about is a million times stronger.

Just try to imagine it. Try to feel it. Have you ever felt a Love in you that has brought you to tears? Like I said before, I'm a crier. Any other criers in the house? It's an awesome feeling. No, really. Tears of love and joy are fantastic! I've traveled to this state many times ever since I've been on the hunt for God's Love. For the Love of this expansive universe. It is ginormous, people. And even if you feel just a small fraction of this Love, you'll understand what I'm talking about.

We live in a loving Universe.

We live in a loving Universe. Some people could argue differently, but it's important to open our eyes and hearts into seeing it as such. We can choose to see Love. The loving language of the universe is God. Or we could say the language of

The Universe is Love. That shows this Love is actually everywhere. God is the universal language. The language of Love. It's like what they say about a smile or laughter; they're our universal language. No matter where they are from or what spoken language they speak, everyone can understand laughter and a smile. That's the intent. The message of Love doesn't need to be caught up in words.

God is how the earth is hardwired. "He" is the electricity, the power—the magical power—who makes miraculous, amazing things happen. The life-force. The Force from Star Wars. Ha! Seriously. May the Force be with you. God transcends all religions. This force is so much more. It can't be contained. It's the telecommunications system that connects you to the most powerful energy of the universe.

This powerful energy is everywhere. It's *in* every one of us. We just have to seek connection with this part of ourselves, and then we'll connect better with each other and tap into God's magical power that fuels the universe.

The more we seek to see, the more we see. It doesn't matter which side of the fence you're on. If you think there is Love, you'll see Love. If you think it's all just fear and hate, well then, that's what you'll see. Believe and see.

5

Belief is Seeing... Not Seeing

Be Willing to Believe

We've all heard the saying, "I'll believe it when I see it." Maybe you have said this yourself. But what is believing? When it's tied to God, does it mean we have to see proof before we can believe there is a God? Or is it the other way around? Which came first, the chicken or the egg? God doesn't care how you come into believing. "He" will show you proof of "His" existence, whether you believe or not. You just have to be willing to see the evidence. "He'll" show it to you, so you believe, *and* if you believe, "He'll" show you even more. Accepting the opportunity to believe and strengthen your beliefs makes The Universe excited to show you even more

"There are only two ways to live your life.
One is as though nothing is a miracle.
The other is as though everything is a miracle."
- Albert Einstein[4]

When I think about this quote, I want to be in the camp who believes everything's a miracle. First of all, it's way more fun! Second, think of all you'd miss out on in life.

Bold Faith

Have you ever had the belief that something was going to happen before it happened? One morning—well, it was what I would call the middle of the night—I was sound asleep, and I was awoken by the birds singing. It was 4:20 a.m. and still pitch-black outside! The sun wasn't going to rise for almost two hours. Amazingly, instead of getting angry and putting the pillow over my head in an attempt to go back to sleep, I thought, "Wow! That's what you call faith." The birds were singing songs of praise and gratitude for a sunrise they knew would happen even though they were still sitting in the darkness. Think about that.

I'm sure some of you may be thinking, "So what? The sun rises every day." Exactly. The sun rises every day, just like God shows his face every day. We need to have faith and believe The Universe will show us its love every day, even when we're sitting in the dark.

God is like the sun. It is always there whether you can see it or not. Sometimes, it is nighttime, or clouds are blocking our view, making it seem as though "He" isn't there, but all it takes is a small break in those clouds or some patience for some time to pass, and you can see "Him." Just like the sun, that small break in the clouds gives you the proof it's still there. We know that about the sun. We know it's always there. We just need to adopt that same belief about God.

Have you ever taken off in an airplane on a cloudy, rainy day? It's dark. It's dreary. Then you rise into the clouds, and you can't see anything outside. The clouds are right up against your window. You can't see where you are going. But then you rise above the clouds, and there it is—the bright, shining sun. Now you can see it.

Those clouds are like our doubts. Did you know your doubts just lead to more doubts, and a simple shift to "It's possible" can change your world? I'm not just talking about the beliefs or doubts about what you can do or accomplish. We'll get to that later. I'm just talking about the world. There's so much about the world we think we're so sure of.

Willing to Think Differently

I think one of the greatest characteristics a person can have is their willingness to admit they don't know everything. Wouldn't you agree? Nobody likes a know-it-all.

Early in our marriage, I was on a committee at church who oversaw designing some new banners for the sanctuary. I'm not an art major or professional designer by any means, but I am very creative and have a good eye for spatial design. I don't remember for sure, but there were about five of us on this committee. One of the ladies—I have no idea what her name was, so I'll call her Gert—either had a design degree or at least thought she did.

We were discussing some possibilities since we were starting from scratch. At one point, I started to describe an idea I had. And by started, I mean, I hardly got two words out before Gert shook her head and boldly stated, "No."

I hadn't even said a word that would've given her any idea of what my idea was! She was just so sure her way was the only way that she didn't want to hear anyone else's opinion.

After I picked my jaw up off the floor, I piped in and said, "Will you at least listen to the words I have to say before you shut me down?"

I'm pretty sure my face was bright red.

We need to not be like Gert. We need to be open to possibilities.

You know, it was a standard belief thousands of years ago that the world was flat. Now when we hear that, we find that statement ridiculous because we have reasons to believe otherwise. We can now get on a plane and travel around this ball that we live on. We can see it is, in fact, a sphere.

The earth is supposedly over 4.5 billion years old. There have been anatomically modern *Homo sapiens* or people on this earth for over a few hundred thousand years. The first people probably didn't even have a clue they were actually standing on something.

Let's see...a few hundred thousand years minus thousands of years and adding in the oblivious factor... Ok, well, let's just say it was a very, very long time people thought the Earth was flat.

Then one day, scientists like Pythagoras, Aristotle, and others adopted the belief that the Earth was round. Such rebels! Supposedly, mariners—the smart ones anyway—had always known the Earth wasn't flat. My point is not who thought what when; it's that people can have very different thoughts about things and believe they're correct.

You know what's most definitely impossible? Taking a large metal structure that weighs tens to hundreds of thousands of pounds and filling it full of people and stuff, then having this very weighty object fly over an ocean and land safely on the ground a dozen hours later. That! That there! That is impossible! Right? It has to be. Sounds impossible.

Oh. Wait a tick. I think that's what we call an airplane. Airplanes do this every single day. There was a time that this was impossible. Not the physics of it; the physics were there all along. But science-minded people didn't grasp the physics of this until relatively recently, and now, most of us don't even think twice about it. Many of us look forward to getting on a plane and ending up somewhere hundreds of miles away in a matter of only a couple of hours.

That took being able to think outside the box, thinking differently than they maybe previously thought.

Thinking differently is what some of us need to do about God.

Are your beliefs still what they were years or even decades ago? Allow yourself to continue to grow. Knowledge continues to evolve. I challenge you to seek God in a new way every day. Be open to seeing God in all the things around you. God is loving and kind, and as long as what you see falls into this category, try to let yourself see this as God. A communication with God.

See Differently

Challenge your mind in the way it sees things. It's like the viral internet sensation that went on several years ago, the black and blue dress vs. the white and gold dress. Do you remember that? I remember how it continued to come up on my Facebook feed, so I clicked on it. I clearly saw the dress as black and blue, but as I was reading my friends' comments, there were people who saw it both ways! What? They're crazy! How could anyone possibly see it as white and gold? That is so totally different than black and blue. It is clearly black and blue. But these contrary comments were from people I actually knew. And from what I know about them, they're not crazy, well, at least not totally crazy.

So, I decided to ask my daughter what colors she saw. I walked into Brooke's room with my phone in hand and started to ask her if she'd seen the photo. When I glanced down at my phone (which I hadn't touched since I last saw the black and blue dress), the dress appeared white and gold! What? OMG! How did that happen? I was flabbergasted!

Now, I know there are scientific explanations about why people see two different things, but really? I was dumbfounded. There have been other similar things out there. Yanny vs. Laurel. Which did you hear? Just like the dress, I eventually heard it both ways.

And more recently, there was a picture of a pair of shoes. Were they grey and mint, or were they pink and white? This totally freaked me out. When I first looked at the picture, they were clearly grey and mint. But I kept looking at it. Without moving or changing position, I closed my eyes for a second. When I opened them again, the shoes were pink and white. Wow! And even more wow was I then sat there not moving and not closing my eyes, and I could get it to change back and forth from seeing it one way and then the other. I just focused and thought about seeing them the opposite way, and it would change. Whoa.

Why am I going on and on about this? To show we can change the way we see and hear things. We can see things we thought weren't there before, but then it's there, or it changes. It's like Eve 6 sings in the song "Inside Out"—swallow your doubt and "find nothing but faith in nothing."

Can you believe in things before you see them?

Can you find your faith in nothing? Can you believe in things before you see them? It may seem crazy, but it's true. We can see and hear things we didn't think were there.

I have a friend, Sue, who works for Hospice. She says she sees the amazingness of Spirit all the time. She told me about a time when she was with a patient who was very close to the end of her life, but she was still alert and talking. Sue was in this lady's room speaking with her. The lady, let's call her Ann, was looking above Sue's head and smiling. Sue could tell Ann was very distracted and not listening to what Sue was saying, so she asked her, "Do you see something behind me?"

Ann smiled and said, "Yes. Do you see them? Do you see the angels?"

Sue said it was a life-changing experience for her to know there were angels in the room with them. Even though Sue couldn't see anything, she had no doubt Ann could, and there were indeed angels in the room with them.

One might argue, "Well, that person was dying. The angels were just there to escort her to heaven. To the afterlife." But, I'm here to say I think these angels, this power, God, Bob, is here with us all the time; we just can't always see them.

Sometimes, we hear these things and think, wow. And then we move on with our boring lives, thinking we are doing this all on our own. I believe we could all benefit greatly if we entertain the idea that it's possible we're not alone. That, right there, is a magical, loving power surrounding us at all times. And we should tap into that BLEEP!

It didn't matter to Ann if Sue could see them or not. That wouldn't change the fact she saw them. We don't need to worry about how or if anyone else sees something or believes in something. I'm going to continue to return to this point. It doesn't matter what other people think. Don't let that get under your skin and change you.

Before I met my husband, I may have dated a guy or two or twenty. There was a guy I dated briefly in college. I didn't feel any huge spark with him and didn't see him as husband material, so I decided to end the relationship. When I talked with him about breaking up, I stated why I didn't see the relationship going any further. I said I didn't see it leading to my fairytale ending.

He said, "There are no such things as fairytales."

Ok. So, the fact that he just said that only *adds* to my list of reasons why that relationship wasn't going to go any further. I believe in happy endings, and I wasn't going to let anyone tell me they didn't exist. I refused to buy into that train of thought.

See ya, John.

Not everyone is on the same page. Not just about relationships, but about God, about beliefs, about miracles, about the magic of this universe. Some people think when they see something I would consider a magical sign from The Universe, it's just an ordinary coincidence. To believe something is of God rather than by chance would indicate there is first a belief in God. But it is like the "seeing is believing" saying. Coincidences give people a chance to see God, which can lead them to believe there could actually *be* a God.

The true faith or belief in God lies in believing without having to see it first. Then, that belief allows you to see God everywhere. The first recognitions are like baby steps in the belief, a belief in the magical existence of God. If one can first believe there's something other than just chance behind the coincidences they see in life, then that can lead to the next step in believing that God is, in fact, a powerful, magical force in our world. That force that's powered by the Love for all. All people, all things.

6

God is... Butterflies, Lyrics, and Lights! Oh My!

So, where can we see the magic? Where can we see the magical signs of The Universe? Well, let me tell you...they are everywhere. Literally. As I said before, my first couple of signs were the writing in the mirror and that little, yellow, dancing butterfly, but there are so many ways God can show face. This really is the fun part. It just makes me giddy when something new, jaw-dropping, and even hilariously funny happens. Like, tears running down my cheeks funny. We need to appreciate all that The Universe is willing to do for us.

DR. DOOLITTLE

Butterflies are, without a doubt, my God/Universe/Dad sign. It's totally amazed me the number of times and the ways butterflies have appeared in my life over the last twelve years. I've found great comfort and often awe in these sightings. I just know The Universe is giving me a hug, a nudge, or a laugh.

Many people I know have a connection with other forms of nature. Cardinals are a common one. There's an old folklore saying that when a cardinal appears in your yard, it's a visitor from heaven. Some say when we see a cardinal, we are to keep the faith in times that seem dark and bleak. If we can hold on to a message like that, it can do so much for our soul.

When I was working on the outline and book proposal for this book, I went to the cottage a couple of times for a few days each just so I could seclude myself and focus with fewer distractions. Each day, I would go for a walk on a trail through some trees and a small prairie. While I was in the prairie, I came across a caterpillar. I like to note all the little creatures I come across but knew that one day, that specific little guy would become a butterfly or moth, and I felt especially drawn to him. I stopped within a foot and a half of him. Even though we were headed in the same direction, he suddenly took a 90-degree turn toward me and crawled right up and onto my shoe, up my pant leg and jacket, to my shoulder. I was amazed. Before he made his way to my back, I carefully returned him to the path and told him to go and become a beautiful butterfly. Rather than chalking the travels of this little guy up to coincidence, I took it as a cheerleading moment to keep up the writing.

A friend of mine, Meredith, told me about her amazing experience with a different species of nature. She wrote in a message to me:

> Experiencing the loss of a child is the hardest thing a parent can experience. Our twins had been born at just twenty-six weeks. In 1987, Iowa City was just beginning to save babies at that gestation. So, to have survived all of

> that, only to lose our first twin, Jeremy, at 6 ½ years was heart-wrenching to us.
>
> Because his death was unexpected, we clung to our family for support. We had to decide where to bury our sweet boy. It made sense to us to bury him in a nearby town, near other family members.
>
> After the burial and luncheon, friends and family were invited back to our house. When we arrived home, there were two mallard ducks resting on our front steps. We had never had ducks on our steps before. The two ducks remained there even when we opened the front door and stared at them through the glass. As people began showing up, the ducks moved from the door.
>
> My mom and sister arrived a bit later than the other family members. When they got to our home, they shared with us that after they had changed clothes, they returned to the cemetery to Jeremy's gravesite. Upon their arrival, they noticed two mallard ducks sitting on the fresh grave. We, in turn, shared that we had two mallard ducks sitting by our front door at close to the same time. Since that day, we have never again seen ducks by our front door, but I believe that God was letting us know our sweet Jeremy was not alone.

Another friend, Julie, told me a Dalmatian dog walked with her on a beach for hours while she was walking with her newborn son in a carrier. This was her second-born son. Her first-born son had died soon after childbirth. That day of the walk on the beach was that first-born son's birthday. She knew without a doubt that that was her first-born child coming to comfort her.

Sometime later, while vacationing with her husband in Paris, she realized she needed to get a divorce. Shortly following the trip, on the day she moved into her new house, she went to an art fair going on in her new neighborhood. The first thing that caught her eye was a painting of a woman walking a Dalmatian dog on a street in Paris. She took this as a sign that she was doing the right thing.

DJ

I swear, sometimes, God really likes to play DJ. The timing of when certain songs have come on and the meaning in the lyrics has brought me to tears at times.

It has taken me many years to build up the courage to be vulnerable and write this book. Several years ago, I attended a conference for work. During the first day, I had mustered up the courage to tell the large room full of strangers about my fears of writing, but I knew I was to do it. On the second day, as I was driving to the conference, a song came on the radio that I have only ever heard that one time on the radio. It was called "What Are You Waiting For?" by Nickelback. The lyrics struck a chord with me.

A couple of years earlier, I walked into my next-door neighbors' house, and on the wall was a ginormous canvas that said in huge letters those same words, "What Are You Waiting For?" I remember staring at those huge words on the wall with utter shock. God is starting to yell at me now. I never asked her what the significance of those words was to her, but I knew without a doubt what those words meant to me. Obviously, "He's" a patient God because years later, he was still sending me the same message.

So, when I got home that day after hearing that song on the radio, I immediately bought it, downloaded it, and added it to my special playlist. I've collected several songs that have spoken to me over the years and made a playlist. I've listened to those songs too many times to count. I use it as my motivational pick me up playlist. Music and words have power.

Another song that has popped into my life at the most amazing times is "Brave" by Sara Bareilles. I've thought Miss Bareilles might have an idea in her head about why she wrote that song, but I was definitely at least part of the reason why she did. The lyrics and the song "You Say" by Lauren Daigle has also spoken to my heart. I believe there is such power in words, and when a song has impeccable timing, the words hit me even harder.

Several months ago, I thought, "I need to buckle down and get this book written already." I pulled some of my typed pages out so I could go over them. I then went into the kitchen to make some lunch. I told my Alexa speaker to play "Adult Pop," the playlist I listen to all the time. It's full of songs by Ed Sheeran, Adele, etc. After a usual Ed Sheeran song, the next song to play was a Willie Nelson song. Huh? Willie Nelson was Dad's all-time favorite musician. I definitely wouldn't consider Willie Nelson as Adult Pop. It was a song I had never heard of before. I asked Alexa, "What song is this?" She told me it was called "From Here to the Moon and Back"—I instantly had chills.

My cousin Amy told me about when her dad died of pancreatic cancer. He'd been sick for several months, and they knew it was incurable. Weeks before he died, she had started a slide show she knew they'd play at his funeral or visitation. The song she chose to play with the photos was "The Riddle" by Five for Fighting. This was about six years after the song was released, so it wasn't frequently played on the radio.

They thought he still had a few months left with him, but on Christmas Day, things took a bad turn, and he took his last breath. That night, her family stayed with her mom at her house. The next day, they went home to shower so they could start the funeral arrangements. As soon as they started their vehicle, you know what song was on. "The Riddle." The station had been playing only Christmas music all month and usually continued for several days after Christmas. Amy knew God was letting her know everything was ok.

Have you seen or heard of the TV show *Zoey's Extraordinary Playlist*? For some reason, I recently felt drawn to watch it. After the first two episodes, I was totally hooked. I watched all twelve episodes in forty-eight hours. This is the only time I've ever truly binged watched anything. In the show, the main character, Zoey, has a freak accident. Unbeknownst to the other characters, she can hear others sing songs that carry the message of how they are feeling.

... this was just another way The Universe was communicating with me.

Well, now this may seem really weird—because it is—but I sometimes feel like Zoey. Not quite in the same way. People around me don't start breaking out into song and dance, but I'll get a song stuck in my head that I haven't recently heard. Over and over, the song plays in my head. The first time it happened, I paid attention to the lyrics playing on repeat in my mind. They struck me. I looked up the rest of the lyrics and felt very strongly this was just another way The Universe was communicating with me. The messages often cheered me on to keep progressing with my book.

If you have a song that's significant to you, pay attention to the timing you hear it. The thoughts you were thinking, what else you can hear at the time, what is going on around you. I'm telling you, it's incredible.

ELECTRICIAN

I bet God was thrilled when man figured out how to harness electricity. That gave "Him" another avenue to wow us. Many times, I've experienced Godincidences when it comes to lighting or electricity. It started with the lights in the kitchen at the cottage, but it happens anywhere all the time now. It's usually the timing of what we're talking about or my thoughts at the time that makes it so noteworthy.

Recently, Larry and I were at the hospital with several of his cousins while his uncle was dying. We started talking about this book I was writing. One of his cousins had a daughter die unexpectedly at a young age. She told us how her electric can-opener randomly starts running by itself, and she knows it's a sign her daughter is still with her.

Another cousin of his has a rosary that lights up when someone is in need of prayer! What? She said it is just one of those cheap, plastic rosaries, and it glows like it's electric. Whenever this happens, she always soon finds out someone she knows needs prayer. Whoa!

Once, I read a story about a battery-operated candle that was going to be used at a loved one's visitation. It wouldn't light. They removed the batteries, and then it lit! With no batteries in it!

Clocks. I have had multiple people say they have experienced significant timing of a clock stopping. It's often at the same time that a loved one passes away. One family I know—who also holds a great significance to happy hour—told me when their dad passed away, the clock hands moved and stopped at 5:00. Get it? "It's Five-O-Clock Somewhere" by Jimmy Buffet. The Universe really does have a fantastic sense of humor!

VENTRILOQUIST

Sometimes, we hear things that are unexplainable, like when I said I could hear my dad singing behind me at his funeral. I also, more than once, swore I could hear Dad singing along to the UNI fight song right behind me. Mom and Dad's football season tickets were right behind Larry and me. I had heard Dad actually sing those words dozens of times over my left shoulder. That's why I know all the words. So, when I could hear him after he passed, it gave me chills. It sounds crazy and a little creepy. That's fine. You can call me a weirdo, but I heard what I heard, and I believe you're capable of hearing the same crazy, creepy, amazing things, too.

After Dad died, Mom shared with me that during the weeks before his death, she would often hear what sounded like choirs singing. Like church choirs, but she couldn't make out any actual words. She could just hear the Ah's being sung. It was beautiful singing. Each time she heard this, she would search to see where the singing was coming from—surely there was a radio or TV on somewhere.

But she would go to every TV and radio in the house, and every one of them was off. Nothing. No sound.

Some people might say maybe she just had some ringing in her ears, or maybe she was picking up a radio station through a filling in her tooth, like on that *Gilligan's Island* episode.

I don't know how to explain it, how she heard it, or why she was hearing it, but once Dad died, she didn't hear it anymore.

That was NOT a coincidence!

My dad's cousin, Kathy, told me one time after her husband, Jim, died, she had pulled her car into a driveway. It had recently snowed several inches, and the snowplow had just come by, so there was a mound of snow at the end of the driveway. If you live anywhere where it snows, you know what I am talking about. Kathy had remembered another errand she needed to do, so she was just pulling in the driveway far enough to turn around and venture back out. When she started backing up, she got stuck. It didn't matter if she tried to go forward or backward; the car didn't move. The tires just spun.

She sat there, wondering what she was going to do. Then, clear as day, she heard her husband's voice say, "Just straighten out your wheels, Kathy." It wasn't like she imagined what Jim might say. She actually heard his voice at that moment.

She straightened her wheels and backed right out.

My friend Michelle told me her younger cousin called her aunt by a nickname that only her grandma ever used for her aunt. The kicker was her grandma died long before her cousin was born.

Gloria, another friend of mine, told me about a time in her frequent drinking days when she heard God say her name in the middle of the night. She said it wasn't in an angry or condescending way. It was just matter-of-factly. And with hearing that, she knew what she needed to do. The next day, she checked herself into a rehab facility and hasn't had a drink since.

That is powerful.

Have you ever heard something you can only explain as God, The Universe, or a loved one trying to get a message to you?

Or maybe it's not a voice you hear. I've had more than one person tell me they heard a train whistle at the exact moment their loved one took their last breath, and they hadn't heard any trains for the hours or even days leading up to then. It was especially significant to one family because their grandpa had worked on the railroad.

SIXTH SENSE

Like Haley Joel Osment's character in *Sixth Sense*, some people say they have seen dead people...or angels. That movie creeped me out for years. Seriously. For years, I was scared to look down the hall in the middle of the night because I was just sure I would see a dead person standing there. But I don't think it has to be such a terrifying experience. Remember when I told you about my friend Sue, who works for Hospice, and the lady she was talking with who could see angels in the room? And she was elated about it. I've heard many stories like this.

I've had many times when I thought I saw my dad. Out of the corner of my eye, I will see someone who I swear was him. One time, when my aunt and uncle (my dad's brother) stopped by, I looked at him and was totally taken aback. I could've sworn I was looking into Dad's eyes.

My friend Michelle said after her dad died, the neighbors said they saw her dad in the backyard—not once, but twice!

My grandma just recently passed away at the age of 99 ½. She was in and out of the hospital, and several times, we thought she was going to die. I remember one of the times; a few of us were in the room with her. She was lucid one minute and not so much the next. Then, she started talking to people who weren't in the room. At least...as far as *we* could see. I don't remember what she said to make me believe she was talking with relatives who had already passed, but I could tell that was the case.

The next thing I knew, she was asking these departed people if there was a table or something where they could all sit around and take turns blowing out their candles. I thought, *Oh, no! Grandma is going to blow out her candle and die right now in front of us*. She didn't. This was several years before she passed.

I totally believe people who are dying see and are greeted by angels or past loved ones. I also believe the very young can do the same. My friend Deb told me about when her daughter was four years old and told Deb she had seen Grandma standing at the end of her bed. The thing is, Deb wasn't even sure how her daughter knew it was her grandma because she was an infant when Grandma died, too young to remember who Grandma was, but Deb believed 100% that that is indeed who she saw.

NUMEROLOGIST

I've talked with several people who have found significance with numbers and their departed loved ones. Sometimes, people are confronted with the same number over and over. It's kind of like when I see butterflies, but their sign is a particular number. When that number jumps out at them, they take it as a message from their dearly departed.

My friend Kris found significance in the date and time of her dad's death. Sometimes, there's a correlation between those numbers and maybe someone's birthday or anniversary, or some other significant date.

SANDMAN

I've always thought of dreams as very mysterious things. Sometimes, they're so vivid and real. Sometimes, they fill you full of clarity, and other times, you wake up lost in confusion. The memory of some disappears the second you wake up, and others, you can remember every detail for hours or even days.

I've always been fascinated by the meaning of dreams. Sometimes, I'll wake up and wonder, "Why did I dream about that?" I've Googled dream meanings many times, and sometimes, what's revealed makes perfect sense.

After Dad died, I *really* wanted him to come to me in a dream. I wanted him to give me words of wisdom or life guidance. It was several months after his death before Dad appeared in my dreams, but I remember when I was five or six years old, my great-grandma came to me in a dream soon after she died.

I was *freaked out*! It wasn't just that she was in my dream as a character, but it felt like she was actually there talking to me and giving me a message—a direct message meant just for me. I wish I hadn't been so overcome with the freakiness of the whole experience, so I could've really remembered the essence of the message.

My friend Meredith had a very vivid dream of her mom after she died. Meredith was really missing her; her mom had been such a huge support when her premature twins were born. She just wanted to know she was ok. Then Meredith had a dream with vivid colors and details. She was walking up the attic stairs of where she grew up. Each time she got to the next level, the surroundings changed. The colors were pleasant, and the rooms were bright. Eventually, her mom was standing right in front of her. She was wearing her big smile and glasses. The glasses really stood out to Meredith because her mom looked like she did before she was sick. Her mom looked at her, smiled, and said she was ok. She woke up feeling the peace she had prayed for.

When we wake up from a dream with such strong emotions attached to how it made us feel, I can't help but believe that sense of peace and love is a true gift from God.

While I was editing this book, I had a very vivid and weird dream. It was about some friends of ours. I'll call Fred and Ginger. In my dream, Ginger and I were going to be throwing some kind of surprise party. We were going to have it at Ginger's house, which didn't seem to make any sense since she lives about an hour and a half away, and all of the guests were from my area. So, I drove to Ginger's house to start prepping for the party. When I got there, I really had to go to the bathroom. I went into the bathroom, and while I was sitting there on the toilet, I notice the sound of running water. I thought to myself, *Wow! That water sounds really loud*. It was then I realize Fred was in the shower. Just then, Fred opened up the shower curtain without a care in the world, and I could see all of him. I quickly covered my eyes because I really didn't want to see any of that. It stood out to me that he didn't seem quite right. Right then, I woke up. It was 6:30 a.m.

Later that morning, I thought about my dream and felt I should get in touch with Ginger. I hadn't talked with her in months. I went about my day, and a little later, the thought came up again. I've learned (and I want you to learn) when something comes up repeatedly, we should pay attention and act on it, so I texted Ginger. I asked her how they were doing and if she was still working (this was during the 2020 pandemic). She replied she was not working and then wrote she had to take Fred to the E.R. that morning; they thought he had had a stroke.

I asked if I could call her. She said yes, and proceeded to tell me on the phone the details of that morning. Fred had gotten up that morning to go to his early morning workout class but didn't feel well, so he went back to bed. A while later, Fred got up to shower and go to work. She said he woke her up when he got out of the shower to tell her she needed to take him to the hospital. She said, "I was totally asleep. It was 6:30 a.m."

My jaw hit the floor! He got out of the shower at 6:30! That is the same time he got out of the shower in my dream.

We are more connected than we realize.

LIFE COACH/PRAYER ANSWERER

I met someone who lost his wife during the birth of his firstborn son. He was suddenly all alone with a newborn and seriously had no idea how he was going to survive. In those first days when he was at an all-time low as he was questioning it all, he suddenly had a switch go off and knew he would be ok. He had a sudden, mysterious sense of peace and knew he and his son were going to be just fine. He told me it was the most amazing, unexplainable thing. He had a shift in confidence and was no longer in his desperate state of despair. That's the peace that passeth understanding.

My friend Michelle was on her way home from her friend's husband's funeral. He had died way too young from complications of an organ transplant. She was driving to her home several hours away in a snowstorm. At one point, she could feel her car losing traction and started veering across the centerline toward the oncoming traffic. She said a quick prayer.

"God, you can't let anything happen to me right now. My friend would never be able to handle something happening to me on the way home from her husband's funeral."

She suddenly felt the steering wheel move in her hands, and her car returned immediately to the center of her lane and continued perfectly centered.

I think there are millions of angels working overtime on our roads and highways, like the two different times when we were heading up to Mayo when Dad was there. I know not every swerve of a vehicle ends so magically perfect, but when it does, the fact that no one's life was changed can be life-changing.

MAGICIAN

Have you ever experienced the mysterious appearance or disappearance of a particular object or thing? You have no idea how something got where it is or where it went when it was just there a minute ago. I'm telling you, God is a magician. Sometimes, there's just no explanation.

Many people have told me their sign is a particular coin: pennies, dimes, or quarters. They show up at very significant times, like when buying a new home, on the last day of work before retiring, or when longing for a hug from a loved one.

Coins mysteriously show up in places that just can't be logically explained.

One day at church during a sermon about not burying your talents (a form of money used in biblical times, but also I think a message in sharing our God-given talents with the world), I looked down to see a very shiny quarter under the chair in front of me. When I say very shiny, I mean it was like it was glowing. And it was under the chair in the shadow from the ceiling lights. So, how could it be so brilliantly reflecting the light? I kid you not. You can't make this stuff up.

Sometimes, a significant smell will appear where it doesn't seem to make any sense: the smell of a cigar or pipe, the scent of a rose, or a particular type of perfume. And like with most other signs or Godincidences, the timing is what makes it so jaw-dropping. While thinking of your grandpa and then suddenly smelling pipe smoke, but you're in your house where no one has ever smoked before. It's enough to give you chills.

While driving, sometimes, you take a different route than you'd normally take, and that different path leads to some life-changing event or encounter, or you just feel like you had someone watching out for you and your safety.

Some people chalk up an athlete having the game of their life right after a loved one dies to that loved one helping them out a little.

Or you find a piece of jewelry or a note from a loved one, and once again, the timing is impeccable. My cousin recently was going through an old jewelry box and came across a handwritten note from her dad who had passed about eight years earlier. The note was wishing her good luck at the district track meet back when she was in high school. She hadn't seen that note for nineteen years since he gave it to her. The timing could not have been better. She found it just a few days before she was going to take her team she coached to the district meet. The sentiment and seeing his handwriting brought tears to her eyes.

My friend Jan's sister died suddenly. After she died, Jan decided she would use her sister's devotional for that next year. Her sister would highlight things that spoke to her. Jan reached the day in December when her sister had died; it was the last day that was highlighted. On the next page for the day after she died, Psalm 23:6 was the scripture reference: "And I will live in the house of the Lord forever." Jan smiled; she felt peace.

Sometimes, we see things like when I saw the writing in the mirror. This same friend, Jan, said there was condensation that formed the shape of a heart on a window of her mother-in-law's house the week before she died. They all knew Love was near. A couple of days later, the heart changed shape and grew two long angel wings. Soon afterward, she passed.

MESSENGER

Like I've said repeatedly, the timing of things is enough to floor you at times. Sometimes, it lies in a message, a very well-timed message from someone. That someone can even be a total stranger. There was a day last fall when my friend Steff and I were at a coffee shop chipping away at our projects. We'd been meeting at this coffee shop once a week for over a year, so I could work on this book, and she could work on her grad classes. She was really just doing me a favor so I would dedicate time to writing the book.

On this particular day, a guy that kind of looked like a tall Ed Sheeran came and sat in one of the other club chairs near us. Steff had just finished telling me about a frustrating situation she was dealing with. She felt that something had to change; if it did, it would break her son, but it would break her if it didn't. We then sat there quietly working while "Mr. Sheeran" sat nearby, quietly reading a book. When it got closer to the time that Steff and I needed to leave to go to yoga class, "Mr. Sheeran" struck up a friendly conversation with us while we were packing up our things.

He started by just asking us how our day was going. When I returned the question to him, he proceeded to tell us in great detail about the book he had just finished reading. It wasn't just like a two-sentence summary, but a very detailed description that went on for over five minutes. Steff and I were floored. Everything he said related directly to either what was going on in her life at that time or with me and writing my book. We came away from it knowing Steff's son would be just fine, and I shouldn't worry about what other people would think of my book and just to let God speak.

It was crazy! Steff and I both left with this amazing and crazy warm, fuzzy feeling. We each got into our separate cars and drove to yoga. On the way there, I thought I should suggest to Steff to do "Freewriting" to see if any answers came up as to what she should do with the situation with her son. (I'll talk more about Freewriting in Part III of this book. But basically, it's a technique of writing without thinking about what you are writing. It may sound a little out there to some people, but it has yielded some amazing results for me.) Many people haven't even heard of it before, but I knew Steff was pretty open-minded, and I was going to suggest it to her.

After setting up my yoga mat, I walked over to Steff to talk more about the marvelous Ed Sheeran angel and his message. I asked her a couple of questions, and she immediately said to me, "You know what I think? I think you should try Freewriting. Have you ever heard of Freewriting?"

What?! Did she really just say that? She suggested to *me* to try the same technique I was going to recommend to *her*! It was such an obscure technique I knew most of my friends wouldn't have even heard of, let alone would suggest I give it a try. This was crazy!

When I think of that day of meeting our Ed Sheeran angel at our coffee shop, I can't help but smile from ear to ear and feel that same warm, fuzzy sensation. I wonder if he walked away that day wondering why he told us so many details about his book. I think he was nudged and just went with it.

Comedian

The Universe can be a hilarious comedian! Like, laugh until you're crying kind of comedian, and I'm not kidding. Early on in my writing process, I went to the cottage to sequester myself so I could make some progress on my book. Mainly, I needed to get away from my cat. Seriously. Anytime I sit at my desk, he thinks he needs to be on my lap. I love that he's so lovey, but I needed to make some serious progress.

My main goal at the cottage was to complete my book proposal. I needed to send it to my collaborative publisher for their review and a sample edit. It was glorious. I made progress. I got up when I wanted. I ate when I wanted. I had papers and notecards strewn about on most surfaces. And I didn't have anyone interrupting me for food or to do laundry or be pet. Ahhhh.

Once I completed my proposal, I e-mailed it to Larry and a few of my close friends to look over quickly and do a little proofreading. The next day, I drove back home. When I got out of yoga, I saw I had a text from my friend Jen who had a couple of questions about what I sent her. So, when I got home, I video-called her.

Jen's face was full of confusion. She said, "So... I just have some questions starting with the part with the recipes."

"Recipes?" What was she talking about? Part III was my how-to section. Is that what she was talking about?

"Yeah. The Jell-O shot recipes."

I practically fell out of my chair, laughing hysterically. "Jell-O shot recipes?"

"Yeah. You know. The seventy Jell-O shot recipes."

"Uhhhh... What are you talking about?!!!"

I was laughing so hard I could hardly breathe.

"Didn't you put in a bunch of Jell-O shot recipes?"

"NO!" I shouted between my gasps for air. "I did *not* put seventy Jell-O shot recipes in my book proposal!"

"Yeah. There are seventy different Jell-O shot recipes, and then a recipe for 'Oopsie Bread' repeated a whole bunch of times. It's repeated like eight times," Jen said.

"What?! Oopsie Bread?" I questioned.

My mind started spinning. How could this happen?

She flipped her camera so I could see the Jell-O shot recipes gleaming on her computer screen. Oh my!

Now, I really love good quality time with my friends and family. Quality time is one of my top two love languages. And Larry and I are rather social people. And what could make a social gathering better than a perfectly timed toast that's sometimes executed with a yummy Jell-O shot? So, yes. Yes, I have been known to collect Jell-O shot recipes. I just copy and paste them into a word document and save them for the future, just in case. You know, all for the sake of good quality time. So, that sounded like a document I would have. But I hadn't saved any Jell-O shot recipes for a long time.

I'd just gotten a new computer about four months earlier. Most of my document files from my old computer were saved in a separate folder on my new computer. I immediately started searching my computer for Jell-O shot recipes through tears of laughter. There were a couple of Word documents, but not one with seventy different recipes. Next, I searched for Oopsie Bread. Yes. I had a document for a low carb bread called Oopsie Bread. It was in that separate folder with all the other files from my old computer—a totally *different* folder than the one where my book proposal was saved.

Weird...

Somehow, when she opened the attachment, seventy Jell-O shot recipes and a recipe for Oopsie Bread (repeated eight times!) were inserted into the middle of the section with my sample chapters. She'd gone through the whole document in edit mode, making corrections, but when she went to save it, it wouldn't let her. It said the file was corrupt. Gee. You think? That's why she wanted me to video-call her, so she could show me what she was seeing. The hilarious thing is when she went back to the original e-mail and downloaded the attachment again...the recipes weren't there.

Riddle me that, Batman.

Funny, God or Dad or whoever! Very funny!

7

Big Things... Small Things

If you don't see big signs, it doesn't mean you're not seeing signs of God. Just because there isn't a giant billboard sign with your name at the top, a very profound message, and then God's signature at the bottom doesn't mean God isn't communicating with you. We need to find joy in all the little things, too. All those little things no one else would find any significance in—they all count. They're all ways The Universe is communicating with us. They all have value.

Let's say you found a dollar bill every day in a variety of different places. Some might be crumpled up in a ball, and others might look fresh-from-the-mint pristine. They're all worth a dollar. But you might look over and notice Joe Blow just found a hundred-dollar bill on the ground. And you are standing there, looking down at your measly little one-dollar bill, thinking it's worthless. But we need to remember if we are finding a dollar bill every day, then at the end of the year, we'll have 365 dollars. Woo! Party! That's more than Joe Blow's 100 dollars. They all add up, and we need to see the value in that.

Sometimes, the signs we see have very significant meanings, ones that make us cry or give us the chills. But sometimes, it's just God being our cheerleader saying, "I'm here. I'm aware of you. I'm paying attention. You matter. Let's have fun!"

Every June, our fabulous small city has a weekend celebration called Sturgis Falls. I love, love, love Sturgis Falls! There are multiple parks within walking distance of each other that have live music. I love, love, love live music! I dance like no one is watching, and I love it! There's food galore, and we see so many people we know and who I just can't get enough of.

A few years ago, we were at a live concert several days before the start of Sturgis Falls. We ran into some friends of ours, and we were all talking about how much we love Sturgis Falls. Our friend Kris talked about how much she loved all the food and listed off some of her favorites, including mini donuts. I love mini donuts, but if I ate a whole bag, I would be miserably on the edge of vomiting. So, I chimed in on how yes, they were delicious, but I really only ever just want one. I don't want a whole bag of them. Just one, and I would be thrilled. I just need to sample that delicious taste, and then I'd be done.

A few days later, during Sturgis Falls, Larry and I were at the park where the mini donuts were sold. We had to walk around the crazy, long lines of people waiting forever for their mini donuts. I scoured the line looking for someone I knew well enough who would maybe just give me *one* of their donuts. I just wanted *one* donut. No luck.

As we continued to our destination, I went on and on once again about how I just wanted one donut. As we walked down the sidewalk away from the masses, you'll never guess what was right in the middle of the sidewalk. Ok. So, maybe you can guess. Yes! It was the most perfectly round, pretty little donut that you ever did see. Usually, they are flattened and misshaped from being smooshed in a bag with twenty-three other little donuts, but this one was beautiful. It was perfect. I stopped right in front of that pretty little donut. I admired it. Then, no joke, I looked up at the sky and said, "Thanks, God. But next time, can you put it on a napkin?"

You may be thinking, "Michelle, what does this have to do with God?" The way I see it was God telling me "He" was paying attention. "He" knew the desires of my heart, even in a single donut. I didn't chalk that perfect donut up to coincidence. I took it as God is funny...and kind.

I took it as God is funny...and kind.

Sometimes, I've found God isn't so funny, like in a dad joke or a haha, very funny, not-so-funny kind of way. You know what I am talking about, right? My dad and now my husband sometimes think they were just so funny when, in fact, they were actually not. Sometimes, when Larry tells one of his not-so-funny, punny jokes, I groan and say something about having married my dad. It hurts, people.

And sometimes, The Universe displays this same kind of lack of humor. When this happens, just like with the donut, I look up and say, "Not funny." This would happen at times like when my kids were small and usually not very good at sleeping through the night, but they would be on a rare stint of sleeping well for two nights in a row, and I would say something to someone about how they had been sleeping through the night. And then, sure enough, they would be up all night for the next five nights in a row. Not funny. I think that's why so many of us knock on wood. Evidently, that stems back to some pagan beliefs of spirits in trees, but all I'm saying is don't try to be "funny," God.

A lot of signs God shows us go unnoticed. We haven't tapped into the language of The Universe. It's like "He" is playing charades with us. With a tug of the ear and two fingers tapped on the forearm, we're supposed to decipher what's being said. And we are over here like, "'Uhhh... I got nothing." It just takes a little practice, and then we can catch on. It's like God is creating our own little language we can have with "Him." This language will never be the same as someone else's, nor should it be. You've heard how some twins develop their own language no one else can understand, but these two-year-olds are going back and forth, carrying on a full-on conversation with each other.

I am a huge F•R•I•E•N•D•S fan! The TV show. I quote it *All. The. Time*. Many years ago, I was at my brother's house soon after buying a *Friends*-themed game. Mark, Amy, and I stayed up until the wee hours of the morning, acting out the charade scenes printed on the bottom of each of the question cards. By about three o'clock in the morning, we were very proficient at it. We had actions for each of the six main characters, so the other two players would immediately know who the card was about.

We'd point to my head if it was about Rachel because my hair was similar in color. We'd motion to Amy for Monica, again because of hair color. We'd act like we were pulling long hair in front of our shoulders for Phoebe. We'd do a small, quick throw back of the head with a "How you doin'?" look for Joey, *obviously.* We'd do a smirk while shooting both of our hands for Chandler. And we'd give a woe is me look for Ross. It was fantastic.

Several of the scenes referenced other characters from the show, so Mark came up with a new action to indicate this. He'd do a large, exaggerated "Wax Off" move (teens of the '80s will know what I mean) with one hand, then the other hand, and once again with the first hand. The first time he did this, Amy and I exchanged confused looks.

"What is *that* supposed to be?"

So, he told us, which was breaking the rules a little, but sometimes, you just gotta.

"This means Whole (while waving the first hand), New (with the second), Character (during the third swipe of the hand)."

"Oh... Ok."

Once we *knew* what it meant, it was very helpful. We all adopted this movement, and we continued to perfect the game and laughed hysterically for hours.

If only we could have an audible explanation of God's charades. God is patient, though, and will continue to show us our signs over and over until we get it. We need to be present and aware, so we can notice the signs. We can't be like Bruce in the movie *Bruce Almighty*. He even flat-out asked God for a sign, and God showed him sign after sign, but he was oblivious.

Sometimes, the signs are so blatantly obvious, and other times, they're barely recognizable. Both are equally awesome. Don't discount the small ones. Big and small, they're both great. We need to be able to find peace in the little things. We need to love and appreciate the things around us and notice the things where we are. If we can't appreciate all the things, big and small, how does The Universe know we'll be grateful for the desires of our heart when they show up? Nothing is for naught. It doesn't matter what the people around you think or believe. They don't have to be on the same bus as you. Your joy will multiply every time you notice all the little things.

The big and the small things are all part of the process. This process is a *feeling* process. When we feel the joy and the love in the little things, we are brought more tightly into this connection with the power of Love, with The Universe. So, rejoice in the butterflies, the caterpillars, the coins, and the Jell-O shot recipes. They're all a gift for our happiness. Seek them. Find them. Find more joy in the joy. God loves it when we do that.

I've said it, and I'm going to continue to say it: don't worry about how other people view this. If I've learned anything in fifty years, it's not all people see eye to eye. That's ok. People have different perspectives. It's like a kaleidoscope. When we look through one, we will continue to see a different sight with even the slightest turn of the knob. If we love what we see and then we hand it over to someone to see exactly what we do, in the handoff, the beads shift, and they end up looking at something completely different. It's all the same beads or gems inside we're looking at, but they are being viewed differently with every shift of perspective.

Let God develop your own unique language with you. Cherish it. See it here around us. God is creating a two-way form of communication with us. It's not just that we can talk to "Him" but that "He" also talks with us.

Be open to all the different ways "He" communicates with us. See each as a miracle. Know that God is not somewhere out there, far, far away, but right here with us, with you. Don't expect to know how God will show up. What fun is a surprise party without a surprise? Let God wow you in the most spectacular of ways.

The title of this book was going to be *God is...* Those three little dots at the end are very intentional. They are called an ellipsis. This is used to show when words are missing from a text, to show a pause in thought, or to indicate an incomplete thought.

The reason I wanted to use it in my title is two-fold. First, I wanted it to represent this list of things God is seen in goes on and on and on. There's no end to the description of all that God is. There's no end to the list. Second, because of all I've seen, I say all these things are proof, yes, there really is a God. God really does exist. And so, for that, I say, God is... Period. Period. Period.

Holy BLEEP! That was NOT a Coincidence

Discussion Questions

***This is a partial list of questions.
Make your discussion even better!
Go to https://www.michelleprohaska.com/free-resources/
for the full, downloadable, printable list.

Part II – God is...

1. Do you believe in a higher power?

   What do you prefer to call it?

2. Have your beliefs about "God" changed at all during your life?

3. Before reading this book, what were your beliefs about coincidences? Did you think of them as just a chance happening, or did you believe it to be orchestrated by a greater power? Do you feel different about these occurrences after reading this book?

4. Do you view The Universe as loving? Is life happening for you or to you?

5. How good are you at believing without seeing?

6. ACTION- Google "blue and black or white and gold dress" What do you see? Does everyone in the group see it the same way? Can you get yourself to see it both ways?

7. How have you experienced "Godincidences?" Nature? Animals? Music? Electricity? Hearing a voice? (It's ok. You're not crazy.) Sensing or seeing spirit? Numbers? Dreams? A scent? A message from a stranger?

   Have any of your experiences been funny?

PART III

How to...

In Part III, I will try my best to teach you how to see the magic in the world that I just described in Part II. To start, I'm going to say there's no right way or any one way to do this. I'll talk more about that in Chapter 9. I ask you to be open. Let anything that triggers something in you soak in—anything that doesn't resonate with you right now to slide on by. Maybe you'll come back to something someday. Just focus on the things that give you the warm fuzzies or trigger some kind of curiosity. Grab those things and run with them. You can always add on later.

1

How to… Seek and Be Open

Knowledge makes people humble.
Arrogance makes people ignorant.

—Anonymous

How do we see this magical Universe God stuff? Inquiring minds want to know.

Step one is needing to admit it's possible there *is* magic in the world. We need to be open to it. Being open-minded is the key, no matter who you are or where your beliefs currently lie. You may be new to this sort of belief, or you may be one who thinks you already have God and the whole Universe figured out. Or maybe you are somewhere in-between. I don't care where you fall on the spectrum; I invite you to be open-minded. We all need to realize and admit that none of us know all there is to know.

God is showing face in new and exciting ways every day. Just like our world is changing by the minute, God is adjusting and changing how "He" is seen too. Just a few short years ago, we didn't have Amazon Alexa devices, but God's figured out how to show up using these new-fangled devices.

We need to be willing to admit the thing that just happened that made our jaws drop on the floor, maybe, just maybe, wasn't a coincidence. Even if it wasn't jaw-dropping, the things disguising themselves as coincidences could be God, The Universe, our loved ones communicating with us.

People believe things in varying degrees. Most people don't always believe something 100% or not at all. So, for you doubters out there, I'm asking you to *just consider* the possibility of *maybe* believing it could *actually* be the case, that *perhaps*, maybe, *possibly* that thing was not a coincidence. Let's just start there. If you're leaning toward the doubting side, this is where we'll start. I'm not asking you to chop off your right arm or to give me your firstborn child. Just consider it's possible. That is my only job here. God will do the rest—if you let "Him."

We mustn't be like the unnamed protagonist in Dr. Seuss's *Green Eggs and Ham*. Man, was that guy stubborn. But Sam I Am didn't give up asking. He continued. He was persistent, and so is God. God will continue showing up. That's "His" gig. That's what he does. Day after day, he continues to show up in our lives, but some of us are just stubborn, oblivious, and doubters. But God will keep showing up whether we notice or not. The thing is, when that stubborn guy in the black hat finally gave in, he surprisingly liked the green eggs and ham. Now, isn't that fun. It is also very fun seeing God here, there, and everywhere. Try it; you might like it!

You have to believe it's possible, and if you're not quite there, you at least have to want to believe it is possible.

You have to believe it's possible, and if you're not quite

there, you at least have to want to believe it is possible. If you don't even want to think it's possible, well then, I bid you adieu. Literally. The meaning of bid you adieu actually comes from a French saying, "à dieu vous commant," which means I commend you to God.

As for the know-it-alls, first of all, they probably aren't reading this book, because in their mind, they have nothing to learn, but just in case...you don't know what you don't know. I also ask *you* to be open-minded. God could actually be bigger and more clever than you've ever imagined. Don't think you know the only ways to see "Him." You'll miss out on so much of the fun. And...nobody likes a know-it-all.

Be open to seeing more ways than just the way we think in our heads. The more ways we are willing to let God through, the more likely we are to hear "His" voice.

Once we start seeing and hearing God, we shift from believing it's a possibility to truly believing in the magic of The Universe. Once we start believing, we can't just hope to see it. We have to know we're going to see it. There are moments of grace when we're shown signs, even when we aren't sure if we believe. But the more we believe we'll see, the more we will see.

Let Grace ride with you on your journey. Invite "her" along. Grace is the knowledge we have in the now and in all that matters. If there's peace now despite what is going on around you, you've found Grace. Let Grace be your best friend.

Here comes the tricky part. We need to believe we'll see without trying too hard to see. The seeing happens with the belief of seeing, not in the trying to see. That makes perfect sense, right? It's like looking at those random-dot pictures called autostereograms. (I had to look that up.) They're also known as Magic Eye books. The best way to see the hidden picture is to relax your eyes and try not to focus too hard. Then, all of a sudden, it magically appears. Focus without focusing.

We need to practice patience and letting go. We've all heard it, "Let go and let God." Well, this is literally my case in point. Maybe it's a pie in the sky kind of concept, but there can be power in our feeling of certainty. It doesn't take a lot of effort if we know it's going to happen. Often, when we're trying too hard, it doesn't happen, but when we don't even try, it happens. Try without trying.

I know of multiple people who tried for months or even years to conceive a child. When they turn to Plan B and adopt a baby and are no longer trying to conceive, they wind up pregnant.

It's like the concept of if you grasp something too tightly, things can't flow. We need to adopt the mentality that it'll happen even without effort. This can take some practice and some trial and error, but eventually, you'll see what I mean.

This whole process is supposed to be fun, and when we are having fun, we have a *good* attitude. The good attitude makes it so much easier and even more fun.

Do you know someone who looks at the weather forecast and sees a 20% chance of rain for Friday, and all they can talk about is how horrible the weather is going to be? 20% is only 20%. There's an 80% chance it isn't going to rain. That's a four times higher chance it won't rain, but all they see is rain. We need to focus on the percent that's of a positive outcome.

I love quotes. I love words. Words have power and can be life-changing. Many years ago, I started collecting quotes that resonated with me. I printed several of these quotes out, framed them, and covered our bathroom walls with them. The positive phrases help keep me afloat and help to keep me in the right state of mind. A positive state. I believe we create our life with our words.

I think my all-time favorite quote is:

Whether you think you can, or you think you can't,
you are right.

—Henry Ford[5]

Basically, if you don't think you can do something, you won't be able to do it. So, if you don't believe you're capable or worthy of seeing signs from God, from The Universe, then you won't see them. Our state of mind and our beliefs is what allows things to happen.

God is always going to be there. Truth. Because God is God, and that's just how it is. But whether we can see and hear "Him" or not is up to us. We need to start with it is possible and let that lead to it happening. So, focus your heart on seeing, and you will see.

Once you see the magic in one way, don't expect that to be the only way you will ever see it. If I'd only focused on butterflies, I would've missed out on so many other things.

If I asked you to count the number of blue cars you see in a day and then the next day I ask you how many red cars you saw, you'd have no idea how many red cars went by. You were only focusing on blue cars. You might vaguely remember seeing a couple of red cars streak by, but you wouldn't be able to tell me how many. How about green cars? We need to take our blinders off and see all the cars, all the butterflies, all the birds... Be aware right where you are. Don't always expect to see the same signs.

Expect the unexpected.

Seek to be surprised.

Ponder anew what the almighty can do.

2

How to... Pray

I want to start by saying this isn't about the prayers taught by churches, the ones I call "canned prayers." It's about our own genuine connection and communication with God/The Universe. Once again, if you want to call prayer something else, go right ahead. I know it bothers other people, but it doesn't bother me.

Whatever you call it, how do you define prayer? People define it in different ways. Some people might consider it the conversation we have *with* God. The problem with that is a lot of people think they're talking *with* God when they're actually just talking *at* God. It's a one-way conversation. They are doing all the talking, and God can't get a word in edgewise.

We've all been there in a conversation that's totally one-sided. The other person is all about talking just about themselves. To truly connect, we need to interact with *two*-way conversations. We can miss out on so much, the whole point of life, if we don't participate in a fairly-weighted conversation and relationship with others and with God.

Someone who's all talk and no listen is like someone talking on a CB radio or a walkie-talkie, and they don't release their talk button to hear the other person respond. They need to let go of that button and listen for a response—more on this in the next chapter.

I think of prayer as *our* end of the conversation with God.

I think of prayer as *our* end of the conversation with God. It's us talking to God. Maybe it's a request for something or something we want to happen. It could be us thanking God for something. I've learned it's much more about our feelings and the level of those feelings than the actual words. The energy of our emotions in the space of love is what fuels our prayers.

So many of our prayers can come off as flippant. We really weren't even thinking about what we were saying. We put no emotion into it. I feel we need to put our intentional emotions and feelings with our words. The emotion behind it makes it so, and the emotions that really fuel our prayers are love and gratitude. There's so much energy in these two emotions.

We cannot come from a place of fear. Fear tells God that we don't trust in "His" abilities. Fear is the exact opposite of faith—not faith as in the definition of your religion, but faith as in your deep-down core beliefs. There is a huge difference there. The more we believe in the possibility of the outcome we're seeking, the more we can come up with the faith needed to drive our prayers to reality.

The space of peace is where the power of prayer flows. And if we can add the feeling of joy along with the sense of peace, even better! The problem with this is often when we feel the need to pray, it's when we're far from the space of peace.

We're hanging out with fear like it's our best bud. Or it may be we've been living in the space of fear for so long, we don't remember how to feel peace. In Chapter 9 of this section, we'll discuss practicing this feeling of peace and how to get there. For now, just know prayer is so much more effective when it comes from a place of peace.

If we can't find the feeling of peace, we must not despair. This is where that little thing called grace steps in. It's like the verse the first chaplain who visited with us read soon after we arrived at the Mayo Clinic: *Sometimes, we feel like we can't come up with the feelings or the words to pray, and all we can do is sigh. That's ok. Sigh it out. There is magic in that, too.*

I want to emphasize I totally believe in the power of prayer. When we pool our energy that's wrapped in Love (remember, that can be another word for God), that's even more powerful than when we're trying to pray for something without the feelings. There's even more energy there. It's like trying to push a stalled car. If we get out and try to move it alone, we're either not going to get anywhere, or we won't get very far, even with a lot of effort. If you have several other people helping you, it's so much easier to get it moving, and it may even feel as though there is something else assisting, like a tractor with a chain.

One very effective way to pray is to try your darnedest to be in a state of peace and certainty. Imagine your desired outcome. Picture it as clearly as you can. Then, feel the emotions you will feel when that outcome becomes a reality. The joy. The relief. Peace. Love. Wrap that result in those emotions. If someone you're praying for is sick, picture that person perfectly healthy and happy, laughing and smiling with their friends and family. If you are praying for an answer or solution to a problem, picture yourself once the issue is resolved and tap into the feelings you'll feel once that happens.

I know some people are very shy or private, and they don't feel comfortable asking others to pray for them. But I say the more prayers, the more Love power at work. And yes, even the more, the merrier because it just makes you feel better knowing you have other people pushing and pulling for you.

When my first pregnancy ended in miscarriage, I was broken. My heart was broken. The dreams of my future were broken. Everywhere I went, I saw pregnant women or newborn babies. Each time was like a punch in the gut and heart. It hurt, and I wasn't sure how I was going to get over it. I prayed, but I felt so defeated as I prayed, I felt like my prayers weren't getting off the ground. I knew I needed to change something because I felt horrible. I didn't feel like myself.

I was young, and I'm not sure I'd ever asked anyone to pray for me before. I struggled as a teen, but I never had the strength or the courage to reach out and ask anyone for help, for prayers. One day as I was looking through a little magazine, I saw in the back the answer. In bold print, it said, "In need of prayer? How can we pray for you?" All I had to do was send a letter in the mail (this was before the internet) to these people, and they would pray for me. I had confidence they would actually pray for me. They worked for a spiritual magazine, after all. And the best part is I could write out my request and never had to show my face or speak my words out loud.

A couple of months after sending the prayer request, I conceived my oldest daughter, Holly. I knew in my heart that prayer worked. Since that time, I've become a lot less shy about asking for prayers. I'll ask friends, family, even complete strangers to pray for my loved ones or me. It's kind of like inviting people to my Woo Hoo party. Prayer is a great gift, and it's one we can give to one another.

When we pray, we need to come from a place of sincerity—a place of sincere love and hope.

How many times have you seen on Facebook people comment on someone's post with the praying hands emoji or "Praying"? I often wonder how many of those people are actually praying for that person or their situation and how many are just saying and acting like they are. There's a difference, Miss Queen of Good Intentions. It doesn't matter if you're a pray-er; if you're not praying for that person right then and there and don't have intentions of actually continuing to pray for them, don't say you're praying. Instead, stop at that moment, block out all other distractions, and pray. "Send good love vibes." Like, really! There's power in them there actions. Focus on sending them love, light, peace, health, happiness—whatever it is—but send it to them with love right then. It only takes a few moments.

A shift happens when we pray—from mindless scrolling to a space of pure love. You direct that feeling, that palpable feeling of pure love to that person and their situation. Don't just send a sense of pity or empathy to them. Empathy, by itself, has no power without the honest action of prayer.

In prayer, we connect with the Love center within us that's of God. We tap into the loveness (Microsoft Word just tried to tell me that's not actually a word, but I like it, and I'm going to use it anyway.) of God and let it expand out into the world—into the world of that person.

Like I've said, this kind of love is palpable. You can feel it. And what's so magical is that the recipient can feel it, too. Have you ever felt it? Have you been on the receiving end of prayer and experienced a peace that surpasses all understanding even when you're enduring the worst days of your life? That is the power of prayer. I felt it when Dad was at Mayo, in the days after Dad died, and when Holly was at Mayo. There are those times when you realize that, yes, yes, you're going to be ok. You'll survive and get through it with the love sent to you in prayer. It's a moment of grace that's filled with Love and results from the beautiful gift of prayer all tied up in a bow.

The emotion behind the prayer is what's most important, not the words, or the format, or the time spent, or what you call it. I would highly recommend praying more than just once if you think of it, but most important is the love that accompanies it.

This love is what makes prayer palpable. Prayer, sending love, really can be felt. It can bring a sense of peace, whether big or small, and it can be felt. That's the thing I pray for the most when I pray for others: that sense of peace that doesn't even make sense given the circumstances they're experiencing. I'll pray for whatever they need—health, healing, forgiveness, answers—and then I tack on the feeling of peace because the more they can feel peace, the stronger their own prayers are.

One of the cool things about prayer is there isn't a limited radius in which it works. So many other things are limited in how far it can reach. Prayer isn't limited, like a Wi-Fi signal is. No matter the distance, it can get there. It sounds a little sci-fi when you think about it that way, but it's pretty AWEsome. You need not be present to win. Prayers enable the pray-er to be where they are not. In the mind and heart, that's where you truly are. Send out the love to The Universe and hand over control to God, to the angels, to love and watch love work.

3

How to... Meditate

People...sit down and be quiet.

—Ms. Bruns
My Junior High Home Ec. Teacher

Being Quiet

While writing this book, I've had many people ask me what I do with all my time. Instead of telling them all of the things I *actually* do to waste my time, I tell them I'm writing a book. Of course, they ask what it's about, so I give them the whole coincidence-when-dad-died scenario, and then I tell them how I teach people how to see the magic of the world and offer some tools to do this, like how to meditate. I've learned a lot of people in my circle in the middle of Iowa have heard of meditation, but they don't know much about it or how to do it.

I'd have to say one of the most valuable habits I've developed over the last couple of years is meditation.

You may be saying, "Okay, Michelle. Tell me more about this voodoo that you practice."

First of all, it's not voodoo. It's not anti-Christian. It's sitting. It's breathing. It's attempting not to think. That's basically it, but instead of stopping there and moving on, I need to tell you so much more: how I do it, why I do it, and why it's not a waste of time (because I know what some of you busybodies are thinking—"Sounds like a waste of time."). It may appear like that, but when you realize how much more efficient you are at doing the other things in your life, you'll see it is not a waste of time.

I feel like meditation is the other half of prayer. While prayer is our half of the conversation, us talking, meditation is the preparation and quieting of our minds, so we are able to hear God talking. It makes us more aware of our surroundings so we can notice the communication from The Universe, from Spirit.

I started meditating almost twenty years ago when I joined a yoga class and really didn't get it at first. Yeah, it felt great to just lay flat on my mat at the end of class and relax all my muscles. And for many years, that's all it was. But then I started noticing I was so much more aware of my body and how it felt. The yoga class was instructed to focus on different parts of the body and relax the muscles and everything else that resides in each area.

Fast forward several years, and I started going to hot yoga. I became even more aware of my body and how it felt: what felt tight, what needed relaxing, and that every single part of my body was so freaking hot I thought I might die. I'm not an iguana. I don't like to be hot. I don't like to be cold. I like to be just right, and 110 degrees is far from my "just right" zone. So, during hot yoga meditation, I focused more on survival than the meditation experience.

Imagine a smile without moving a muscle.

A few years later, I started doing yoga at the local university's wellness center. My friend Steff was the instructor. During a couple of classes at the beginning of meditation time, she told us while we were lying on the floor, relaxing all the different parts of our bodies, to imagine a smile without moving a muscle. This little thing, if you take nothing else away from this book, I want you to soak in, take away, and actually do this simple exercise! I'd love to put a million more exclamation points there, but I'm sure my editor wouldn't be too keen on that.

Imagine a smile without moving a muscle.

If It Comes Up Repeatedly

A couple of years ago, I noticed meditation kept coming up in my life. Many times, every week, I'd hear someone talking about it, or I'd read something about how meditation is life-changing and such an essential part of their life.

Whenever something comes up repeatedly, I take note. I'd learned, after all, there's no such thing as coincidence, and I know we are supposed to pay attention to these repeated things. So, I decided I would try a different way of meditation. I was going to be more intentional about it and came up with the routine I now do and have done five to seven days a week for over two years. Wow, oh wow, has it changed my life. Not in a brick-to-the-face kind of way, but in a very noticeable way.

So, Michelle, get on with it. How?

There's Not Just One Way

I need to start by saying there are many, many ways to meditate, and I'm sure some methods work better for some people than others. So, I'm just going to tell you what I do and what I know. I'm a big believer in not making something more complicated than it needs to be.

Most every morning, I walk to the loveseat in our living room and sit in the middle with a pillow behind my back (because I'm short and want my feet to actually reach the floor) and another pillow on either side of my legs. This allows my shoulders to relax fully. Some people lay on the floor, but I feel more connected and intentional when sitting up. Plus, it's a lot harder to fall asleep sitting up. Sleeping is not the goal here, people. If you tend to fall asleep at the drop of a hat, do *not* do it lying down! Duh. We are being intentional here. Other people sit cross-legged on the floor, but for me, there is absolutely no relaxing going on in that position, and I usually want to be able to walk that day—so, no floor for me.

Next, I grab my phone and hopefully remember to silence it. I open my clock app and set a timer for twenty minutes. Don't freak out! I'm sure there are plenty of you who just audibly shouted out, "Twenty minutes?" You don't have to start there. You can start with only five minutes, but the point of this whole process is to quiet our brains and bodies. The longer we practice, the better we'll be at it.

Using my free white noise app, I pick a calming sound—my favorite is running water, but some days I feel like a good ol' thunderstorm. I put my earbuds in or my headphones on and ready myself to meditate.

With my eyes closed, I take three deep, cleansing breaths. What's a cleansing breath, you ask? It's basically just a very deep breath in which you try to fill your whole body with air.

I know. The air we inhale really only goes into our lungs when we breathe in, but this is a visual to help you breathe deeper than you might otherwise. On the exhale, you just let everything go and try to feel every muscle in your body soften and relax. Let your brain, the little space between your eyebrows, and your jaw relax. Feel yourself sink deeper into whatever it is you are sitting on.

Feel the Smile

The next thing is my new most favorite thing! It's the smiling without moving a muscle thing I mentioned. When Steff told us to do this, I noted how fabulous that little "action" felt. I use quotes here because the crazy part of it is we aren't actually moving. There is no action. Well, technically, our muscles are firing just when we think about moving them, even though they aren't moving...much. But the point is, I was totally floored when I noticed the shift in how I felt when I did this. It felt peaceful, joyful, grateful, flippin' fabulous! And I wasn't really doing anything. *What*? That's crazy!

I could actually change how my body felt; my emotions and mood were better, more positive. And all I did was imagine a smile. I wasn't physically smiling. This was when I started to realize how much control we have over how we feel.

After practicing the smile shift for several months, I had the inspiration to try to shift the smile feeling to my heart space, and oh my! This is where it's at! The heart is our emotion command center, and when we can bring this space to a feeling of joy, love, gratitude, and peace, it can change our whole body. Literally. Our emotions change the chemistry in our bodies. When our chemistry is off because we have been sitting in fear, anger, regret, it affects our immune system and makes us more susceptible to disease and illness. Practicing the smile feeling in our hearts can actually make us healthier.

Try it! Try it right now! Close your eyes. Take three cleansing breaths. Then, right away, imagine the smile without moving a muscle. If you can't feel a difference while upright, try lying down. I sometimes feel the shift more when I'm lying down. The gravity effect on the muscles we smile with probably has something to do with it. With some practice, you'll get better at it.

If you need to think of something that brings you joy in order to feel the shift, then do that. But hopefully, eventually, you'll be able to feel it without associating it with any particular thing. You can go there just because you are breathing, feeling joy without any strings attached. The ultimate goal is to feel the shift without it being attached to anything in particular. (#feelthesmile. I really want this to be a thing that catches on. Tag me in your posts @micmopro and use the hashtag #feelthesmile. We can create a movement together!)

Don't Have Expectations

It's usually right about this point my cat, Rudy, walks into the room like he's reporting to a job he has to do. He usually looks like he's half-asleep, like his alarm just went off, and he just slid out of bed. He walks over to me, looks at me, meows, and jumps up on my lap.

In the beginning, this drove me crazy! Like really crazy. It would irritate me and make me mad, which was kind of defeating the whole point of meditating. In my head, meditation had to happen in a room all by myself with no distractions. No one, including animals, could be around, and they especially couldn't be touching me.

I tried to "train" him to leave me alone during my meditation time. Ha! Yeah, right. He's a cat. That wasn't going to happen, so I finally gave in. Now, nine times out of ten, I have a purring cat on my lap when I meditate. I figure what better way to add to this fabulous smile shift and the peace, joy, and warm, fuzzy feelings that go with it than to have a purring cat on my lap. The purring for him probably gives the same feeling as the imagined smile does for me. So, we sit there and "purr" together.

Conditioned Response

When we immediately create that smile shift within us right after our cleansing breaths, we generate a conditioned response within our bodies. It's like the Pavlovian response. That was when, over a hundred years ago, a physiologist from Russia was conducting an experiment where he would ring a bell just before giving a dog his food. The dog would salivate before eating the food. After repeatedly hearing the bell before receiving the food, the dog would salivate at the sound of the bell even when there was no food present.

I've experienced something very similar. Since our girls were very young, before we eat as a family, we go around the table and say things we're thankful for that particular day. Then the last person starts us all in one of our, what I call "canned prayers," or common prayers used by people before meals.

After doing this for a while, especially if I was starving, my mouth would start watering as soon as we began the canned prayer. My body had been conditioned and knew as soon as that prayer was finished, I would start eating.

That's what practicing the smile shift right after the cleansing breaths does. The more we practice this, we condition our body to go automatically into that blissful feeling right after a cleansing breath, which can also be disguised as a sigh. When we're so overwhelmed, and all we can do is sigh, we can still feel peace when we train our bodies to feel calm and relaxed with just a simple, deep breath. #feelthesmile (It's going to catch on.)

Don't Think About It

Next, I resume my normal breathing, sit still, and don't think. Move into the quiet that's already there deep inside you. Sounds so easy. But it's not. And that's okay! I believe this is the number one reason why people don't meditate. They sit and try not to think, but all they can do is think, so they assume they suck at it and quit. I suck at it, too! But I still make a point to do it almost every morning. It's okay. Some days, you'll be a little bit better at it than others. Each second you can sit and not think, feel the smile, and hold the joyful gratitude feeling is extremely beneficial to you.

There are some things you can do to try to stop—or at least slow down—the spinning in your mind. Many people use a mantra or saying while they meditate, and sometimes, I do that, too, but for me, it needs to be simple and meaningful. Some people repeat a Sanskrit word or phrase over and over. My problem is it takes too much concentration to remember the foreign words, which causes me not to be completely relaxed. Plus, I don't speak Sanskrit. The words mean nothing to me. Even if I'm told what the words mean, it just doesn't do anything for me. I need to use words or even just one word that means something to me and can resonate with my soul and emotions. I'm not saying using phrases in a foreign language will never be part of my meditation practice; it's just definitely not where I am right now.

I try not to use words or mantras. I only use them when my brain is exceptionally spinny. I use them when I can't stop thinking for even a few seconds. Then it's time to pull something out of my bag of tricks. I might use a single word like, love, connect, clear, thank you. Whatever resonates with me at that moment. If I am especially spinny, and my mind is acting like a monkey who desperately needs some Ritalin, I use a Hawaiian prayer called Ho'oponoono. It's basically just repeating four phrases over and over. The phrases are:

I'm sorry.
Please forgive me.
Thank you.
I love you.

There's no need to direct these thoughts and words toward anyone or anything in particular. I feel like that would only cause your brain to spin and think more. All you have to do is repeat the list as you breathe slowly and relax. I like to breathe in as I think each phrase and breathe out as I repeat that same phrase.

Inhale = *I'm sorry.*
Exhale = *I'm sorry.*
Inhale = *Please forgive me.*
Exhale = *Please forgive me.*
Etc.

Or instead of words, you can think about numbers. Pick a number, any number. Preferably, it's not a large number because the goal is not to think about anything. Let's say a number like twenty-one. Just like with the Hawaiian prayer above, you would think the same number with a set of inhaling and exhaling.

Inhale – *Twenty-one*
Exhale – *Twenty-one*
Inhale – *Twenty*
Exhale – *Twenty*

After you breathe out and think *one*, just continue with your breathing and try not thinking at all. Just focus on your breath.

Doing this gives your brain just enough to think about to distract it from all the other thoughts that are fighting for your attention. But like I said before, my goal is not to have to think at all. But if you do, that's ok. Let me repeat: *that's ok*. Do not beat yourself up about it. That would be defeating the purpose. Remember, we want to be in a calm, peaceful place.

Peace

If you're thinking, *I've never been calm or peaceful in my life. I'm not going to start now*. Well then, you, my friend, especially need to practice this. We need to be kind to ourselves, to our bodies, to our minds, to our souls. All the rushed activity and negativity of the world can be harmful to us. We need to offset that and bring our bodies back to peace so we can tap into more of what is loving and good in the world. Doesn't that just sound all warm and fuzzy? It is!

You can also imagine yourself floating in a space of nothingness. Not you as your body, but the part of you that is not of your body. Just float while focusing on and connecting with the void that's all around in all directions. Think of this nothingness as a force of love and feel the connection with it in your heart.

We need to quiet our loud thoughts to hear what The Universe is trying to say to us.

I like to think of meditating as cleaning your lantern. The flame inside the lantern naturally causes a tremendous buildup of filth and muck, and so does our everyday life. Meditation is like cleaning the inside of the glass of our lantern so the light can shine brighter. We need to quiet our loud thoughts to hear what The Universe is trying to say to us. Cheesy? Yeah, maybe. But it's true. And there's more than one way to clean a window. You need to do what works for you.

I just Googled meditation, and 415,000,000 results came up in a fraction of a second. And I bet they're all somewhat different. You just need to find what works for you. You might find that something works for a while, and then it doesn't. That's ok. Just try something else. My take on it, though, is it doesn't have to be rocket science. It doesn't have to be complicated. I say, the easier it is to do, the easier it is to get yourself to do it. Ha! I know, Captain Obvious again. But really, if something's too complicated, we're not going to do it. So, take it easy on yourself. Just breathe.

Why?

But why? What benefit is it to quiet our brains and thoughts? Since I've started meditating regularly, I've been able to hear God much more frequently. How do I know it is God? Because I hear things that don't sound anything even close to something I would say or think. It may sound crazy, but it is true. I'll talk more about this in the next chapter. I've been blown away at times.

You have a piece of God within you. Think of this piece of you as a treasure chest buried in your backyard. If you knew you had a treasure chest in your backyard, would you keep it buried, or would you dig it up? Think of meditation as digging up this treasure. This treasure has infinite value. Uncover it and reap benefits beyond your wildest dreams.

Another benefit is how I react to things that happen and to the world and people around me. For someone who used to get really worked up over a spilled glass of milk, for instance, I found it very noteworthy that when something spills, I will often just look at it and think, *Huh... Guess I'm going to clean this up now.* I'm not saying I have turned into a saint by any means! Golly, no. But if I've been meditating regularly, this is now my reaction more times than not. If I fly off the handle a little—or a lot—I usually realize I've skipped meditating for a couple of days in a row. If I have the time at that moment to sit and fix my attitude, even if it is just for five minutes, I'll do it right then and there. The practice doesn't have to be once a day for twenty minutes. It can be five minutes here and five minutes there. Twenty minutes is best for me, but five minutes can be just as effective. If I don't have even five minutes to spare, I practice the cleansing breath and then feel the smile method. It's amazing the shift that can occur. And the breath and the smile shift can even be done while driving a car.

The quote at the beginning of this chapter is in honor of my junior high home economics teacher, Ms. Bruns. We were a bunch of unruly, loud teenagers with raging hormones who were much more interested in the cute guy or girl in the kitchen next to us than we were in learning how to bake muffins. Looking back at it, I feel like we should all apologize to her. We would be loud, not listening, and I can't fathom to guess how many times she would say to us, "Peeeeo-pllle...(very long and drawn out), sit down and be quiii-eeet (also very long and drawn out)." So, that's what I'm going to tell you all now with hopefully much better responsiveness.

"People, sit down and be quiet..."

(Sorry, Ms. Bruns.)

4

How to... Freewrite

Whose Idea Was This?

I'm going to start this chapter by once again saying we need to be open-minded as to how God can show up in our lives and with how The Universe communicates with us. Some of the ways are jaw-dropping. We can't discount it just because it seems bizarre or foreign to us.

Remember when I told you the story of my friend Steff and me at Caribou Coffee and the tall Ed Sheeran angel who totally floored us with his weirdly detailed summary of the book he had just finished?

When Steff suggested I try it right when I was going to suggest she try it, I figured, alrighty then. Guess I better actually try this. When I got home after yoga that day, I went to the loveseat—my meditation spot—and did an abbreviated meditation. Then, I sat down at my desk with my pen in hand, took a few cleansing breaths to clear my mind, and started writing whatever came to mind. OMG!

I know this is going to sound crazy. I know! I think it sounds pretty dang crazy myself! But the things I wrote down that day did *not* come from me, from my conscious mind. It sounded like someone else was talking to me. The cadence and the wording were not how I speak or write. And the message! Wow! The answers! It's crazy. Like really crazy. I get it. It's so crazy that I've doubted many times whether I should even include this concept in this book.

Michelle, people are going to think you're a Fruit Loop.

But the effect it's had on me is incredible and is an exclamation point to the message I'm trying to convey to you in this book. God is magical! And AWEsome! And we all need to tap into this AWEsomeness.

What Does God Sound Like?

I must tell you this story of when Larry and I were at a local outdoor concert. I love live music. Did I say that already?

We ran into our friend Tim. I'm not sure how the conversation flowed to the topic of God, but it did. And not by my directing. I was just basically standing there, listening to Tim talk. Now Tim is not one who we talk to about deep subjects regularly. I wouldn't even say we even speak with Tim frequently. He's someone we run into from time to time, usually at a live music event of some sort.

So, there we were, standing by the beer tent, and Tim started talking about God. I wish I recorded this conversation. It was great. The thing he said I want to share with you is, "The funny thing is, God sounds a lot like me."

I loved it! I loved that we were standing in the middle of a crowd of people, by the beer tent, with loud music playing less than a hundred yards away, and we were talking to Tim about God.

Yes, sometimes, God can sound like you—that voice in your head. God doesn't always say things contradictory to your thoughts and beliefs; that's just how I started to recognize it. The message coming through didn't sound like something I'd say. The key is to practice differentiating between the two. Recognize whether you are starting to intervene and take over coming up with the words. As I've said, the key is getting out of your head and not fueling your thoughts. Let words flow without thinking them.

Don't Knock It 'Til You Try It

I realize not everyone has the same gifts and talents. Running, for instance. Some people love to run. Me? Not so much. I ran a 5K *once*. That's it. Done with that. Check that one off my list. Don't ever need to do that again. But there are a *lot* of people out there who *love* to run. I don't get it. I'm not going to argue that *they* love it. But I'm pretty sure it's never going to be *my* thing.

All I'm saying here is just give freewriting a try, a little test run. If it doesn't resonate with you, you can move on. I only ask that when you do try, you be open-minded about it. It's a great tool you can utilize when you're feeling stuck or have questions that need answers. And if you do it and discover it's not your thing, don't discount it forever. The same goes for all of the ideas and practices in this book. If it comes up again in the future, especially if it comes up repeatedly, don't ignore it! Give it another try.

How

So, how do you do it?

You need to set yourself up for success when you freewrite. Sometimes, I get so much more out of it than I do other times, and that's usually linked to what I did before freewriting, but not always.

I prefer to freewrite after meditating and maybe exercising, or when I just listened to my jam pick me up playlist—when my blood's pumping. I listen to a song that inspires me and moves me. I find a lot of meaning in lyrics. Words speak to me. Sometimes, we have to hear the same message over and over until it finally sinks in. That's ok. When it finally does, it may have a different, often deeper meaning than you originally thought.

If I have a period of time when a particular song is speaking to me, I'll listen to it over and over. I'll soak in the words and the meaning that move me to my core—sometimes, even to tears. This state, this euphoric, teary, joyful, woo hoo state, is a great place to be when sitting down to freewrite or auto-write.

The key is to get out of your head and try not to think, just like meditating. It's not always easy; in fact, it's rarely easy, but just like the song in Frozen, we need to just "let it go."

This is why I almost always freewrite immediately after meditating, when my mind is cleared of chatter clatter.

If any words come to you that you don't think are fueled by you, write them down. As soon as you feel yourself thinking thoughts, fueling words, and putting together full proper sentences, stop and clear your mind with your breath again.

I started doing it with a pen to paper, but now I type on my laptop with, get this, my eyes *closed*. I know not everyone's capable of this, but I highly suggest it if you can. I'm a decent typist. Not great, just decent. But I can type much faster than I can write by hand, which is beneficial because sometimes, the thoughts come much quicker than I could ever handwrite the words.

The key is not to worry about typos or grammar. Just get the words out. If you really must, you can edit when you are finished.

After my cleansing breaths and assuming the smile shift, I consciously think of not thinking. I try to clear my mind of everything. Sometimes, but not often, I start by posing a question. Other times, I just sit there until the words start coming to me.

I don't wait for a whole sentence to come. If I do that, then I find myself manipulating the words. The words often come out just one at a time. I have no idea what the sentence is going to end like when I type that first word. That's what is so crazy about this. It doesn't feel like it is coming from me when I do it this way.

And…get this! Crazy, I know! But I've even had to Google what something means! Really! Crazy right? It's usually a word I've heard of, but I'm not totally sure what it means. And then the message makes sense.

Floored. Floored, I tell you. I have been totally and completely amazed by what has come out. The words are very often a message of assurance to let me know I'm on the right path. Sometimes, I get a nudge on something I should do. Sometimes, I get an answer to a question.

Sometimes, I end up typing over 1,000 words! Other times it is only a hundred words. Not every experience yields the same results. I don't get caught up in that. I also don't freewrite every day. I do, however, find the more consistently I do it, the "better" it seems to work.

Quite often, when I go back and read a freewrite, I think, *Oh! I could put that in the book*! And that's why I stopped doing it as often. I was just getting too much good material. I don't want this book to end up being the size of an encyclopedia.

Not That Weird

I may have just freaked a whole bunch of you out. Like I'm talking about some woo woo stuff that has to do with a woman wearing a turban and heavy makeup, gazing wild-eyed into a crystal ball. That's not what I'm talking about, so drop that. But having said that, if you feel more comfortable gazing into a crystal ball or a glass vase, or your fingernails, then do that. Doesn't bother me. You do you.

I know this may seem very out there and too weird for any *normal* person to do. I get it. I *totally* get it. It's probably a completely new concept you've never heard of before. *What would other people think!? I am not going to do that because so and so would totally berate me. REALLY! I GET IT!* The voice in my head, the doubting one who always talks me out of things—even the good things—is saying I probably shouldn't include this in this book. Because really, what *will* people think?

But I have been completely floored at times when I read what I wrote or typed. It's often in a speech pattern I wouldn't use, or there's a message that didn't fall within my belief set. I don't mean belief set like religion, but in like "Wow, I've never thought of it that way before." Or I get that aha feeling that Oprah always talks about. Have you had one of those? Like when there's a new concept presented to you, and it totally and completely resonates with you and gives you a warm, fuzzy feeling. You wonder how or why you never thought of something that way because it resonates with your heart.

There's the kicker. It makes sense to your *heart*—your heart, not your brain. Your brain doesn't want you to grow. Growth occurs in your heart.

Your brain doesn't want you to grow. Growth occurs in your heart.

This practice of freewriting might not work for you. Or it at least might not work in the same way for you, but I encourage you to at least give it a try. If you're floored, too, please contact me and let me know. I love, love, love to hear other people's stories.

If nothing noteworthy happens, don't despair. Remember, God has endless ways to communicate with us.

5

How to... Be Grateful (or... Yell Woo Hoo!)

It's Not That Hard

We're taught from a very young age to say "thank you" when someone gives us something or does something for us.

I often hear it from parents on Halloween night when they bring their little ones up to the door. The little mermaids and pirates are all very rehearsed on the phrase "Trick-or-Treat." But sometimes, they're in too much of a hurry to move along and get to the next house, or they're too distracted by the treat they just received. Before they have even had a chance to examine and identify it, the parents pipe in with, "What do you say?" And right away, the wee one replies with a "Thank yooouu!" and a grin.

Most of us are taught this. We have it ingrained into us. It becomes an automatic response. And I think it's great. We're often offended when we don't get a thank you for holding the door open for someone or for letting someone go in front of us in line. Sometimes, we even make a point of it by saying, "You're welcome," when the person doesn't acknowledge the gesture.

"Come on, man. You could at least look at me and smile. You ungrateful little..."

Am I right?

So, why are we so bad at thanking The Universe for all it does and provides for us? Like is it really that hard?

Even the little kids have taught us that if we practice it, saying thank you can become an automatic response. It doesn't have to be hard.

But it does need to be sincere.

The feeling of gratitude is so much more important than the words themselves. You can usually see gratitude, love, joy, and excitement just by looking at someone who's sincerely thankful. We've all seen videos of people opening presents, and either by the shrieks of excitement or the tears of pure joy, you can see and feel their gratitude.

We need to be grateful for all things, big and small. When we can find joy in even the littlest of things, that's when God says, "You like that? Well, wait until you see what's next."

We also need to be grateful for the gift of gratitude. Not just the things we're thankful for are worthy of gratitude but also gratitude itself and the joy it brings. The feeling behind the gratitude. It becomes like a "vicious" circle that's not vicious in the least bit. The feeling of gratitude and the joy it brings in the body is what I am talking about when I talk about feeling the smile. The shift that occurs is like sincere gratitude. We need to tap into this. It's so AWEsome! I absolutely love it! #feelthesmile

Shouldn't Be a Chore

Gratitude doesn't have to and shouldn't feel like a job. That takes all the fun out of it. The feeling of gratitude is so much more powerful than the task of writing it down.

Multiple times in my life, the topic of gratitude journals, and the fact we all should keep one has come up—and keeps coming up. It all started back in the '90s when I was watching Oprah. She said something like, "We should keep a journal, and every day or every night, we should write down five things that we are grateful for."

Well, if Oprah says I should do it, then I should do it.

Guess what?

I suck at journaling.

Several years later, when it came up again, I thought, *Okay! I'm going to try that again. Let me find a journal so I can start right now.*

I looked in a cabinet where I knew some blank notebooks were. I grabbed a journal and flipped through it to make sure it was empty.

I stopped on one of the pages that had writing on it and read:

"I'm grateful for our great friends Jay and Aby."

It was my journal from the Oprah experiment—the one I wasn't very successful at.

Aby was the reason I was trying this practice again! I was taking an online class that my now distant friend, Aby, was teaching. That's why I was going to give it another whirl.

That, my friends, c'mon say it with me...was not a coincidence!

It was probably about ten years later, and I lived well over 300 miles away from where it all started.

Let's just say that attempt, and a few that came after, all yielded the same results. I've yet to keep up the practice for an extended period. I'm not giving up hope, though!

I think the problem was, it felt too much like a j-o-b, like something I was supposed to do. There wasn't any warm, fuzzy feeling attached to it. I'd be writing my list and just knew I had to come up with two more things to put on it. So, I'd look around the room and notice a lamp on the dresser and write "lightbulbs."

I wasn't truly feeling the feeling of gratitude inside. I was just fulfilling my obligation to write it down. Now, I totally understand the concept where if you have to write down five things, you'll spend your day looking for something to be grateful for. I get it. It makes sense...in theory.

But it's like telling a kid to hug his grandma and thank her for the pair of socks she gave him. So, the kid begrudgingly saunters over to his grandma's chair, musters up just barely enough energy to touch his hand to grandma's back, grumbles "thank you" to the ground, and walks away.

There's no feeling there, people. You know darn well he's not thankful for those socks.

This isn't the kind of gratitude I'm talking about.

Feel It

It's all about the feeling!

The feeling makes it so.

I'm not saying I'm totally against gratitude journals. Heavens no. I will continue to attempt to write down the things I'm truly grateful for. But I now have a better understanding of the importance of the practice—the feeling. And we can revisit these feelings when we write them down. (More on this in the next chapter.)

I encourage you to thank God for all. the. things. Have you seen the video online (I believe a church created it) that shows a guy waking up in bed and he's all wrapped up in wrapping paper? "I'm alive!" It's a gift. He looks over at his wife, and she's wrapped in wrapping paper, too. Then, his kids walk into the room, all wrapped up. The light switch has wrapping paper on it. The faucet has a bow on it. Wrapping paper covers his shoes. His breakfast is served in a gift box. His wife hands him his cup of coffee that is, you guessed it, wrapped in gift wrap. He walks outside to his car that's all wrapped up.[6]

Things to be thankful for are all around us. We just need to view them all as gifts and not just say thank you. Be like the guy in the video who's ecstatic about each gift he finds. By looking at him, you can *see* his pure joy in each discovery. You can tell he *feels* gratitude.

All The Things

Let's find joy and gratitude in all things big and small. It's God's great pleasure; when we're grateful, "He" just wants to show us more. When we ask The Universe for the desires in our heart, but we are not already thankful for the things around us, how is The Universe supposed to know we'll be genuinely grateful for the thing we're asking for?

If you give someone a small gift and they're not grateful, when they ask for something even larger, you won't be very gung-ho about giving them this even bigger thing or service. Gratitude is appropriate in all situations.

I even audibly say "Thank you!" or "Woo Hoo!" when I get a green arrow at the stoplight—especially a specific stoplight near my home. It's a particularly dangerous intersection. The speed limit is 55 mph, and if there's a car in the turning lane of the oncoming traffic, you can't tell if any other vehicles are coming. I often sit there through the whole light cycle because I don't want to risk it. So, when I get a green arrow, I am truly grateful, and I don't hesitate to verbalize it.

Give thanks for the sun when it is shining. Don't just miss it when it's not there. Be grateful for what's around you in the moment, every moment. Focus on the positive and see more of the positive.

There are things we can be thankful for that can be detected with all of our senses. Not just our "five" senses, but our sixth sense, too. It's that internal barometer we all have and can tap into it and be grateful for it.

Many years ago, Larry and I were in Jamaica for our tenth anniversary. We went to the same all-inclusive resort where we'd taken our honeymoon. Because we were returning guests, we were invited to be part of a special "Signature Guests" meal on the beach.

All of the "Signature Guests" were sitting at one long table, casually chatting with the people seated around. Once our meal was served, we began eating and continued talking. Our dinner included the most delicious lobster thermidor. It was amazing! Like really, really amazing, and as I sat there in awe of the party going on inside my mouth, I was equally amazed at the ability of the people around me to keep talking as if they were eating plain white rice.

So, I spoke up. "Are you people even noticing how amazingly delicious this food is?"

"Yeah, it's good," a couple of them replied and continued talking.

They didn't get it.

The more we focus on these things to be thankful for, the more we'll see. Gratitude is a talent. It's a talent; just like playing the piano or meditating, you must practice it to really be good. And just like meditation, not all days will yield the same results. Practice anyway.

There's a sense of peace in finding joy in even the small things. We can find things right where we are right now. Nothing is for naught. It's all in the process—a feeling process. Feeling is the connection. Love of simple pleasures brings it all to life. To find joy in sighting a butterfly...that's the bliss of the world. Rejoice in it and all the little things because they're a gift. God's gift is your happiness. Find it. Seek it. Find more joy in the joy. Every little thing is there for the taking. The Universe rejoices in the love—the love we have for things and each other.

Live into the joy. Lean into the joy.

6

How to... Record

Like I said before, the most important thing about experiencing a Godincidence is the feeling it gives you. It doesn't matter if the incident was big or small; if it stirred up a joyful feeling, that "woo hoo that was AWEsome feeling," then that's all that matters. The feeling will be in varying degrees, and we need to recognize them all.

There may be times when we feel disconnected and don't seem to be experiencing any woo hoo moments. These are the moments when all we can see are the clouds, and we can't see the sun that's just behind those clouds. That's the perfect time to revisit a previous Godincident and tap back into the feeling we had at that time. The best way to do this is to record all of these little occurrences.

Start with writing them all down. Big and small. Eventually, you might notice so many you start writing down only the ones that stir up the biggest reactions. But remember, they're all worthy of at least a "Thank You!".

... they're all worthy of at least a "Thank You!".

If you start to feel like you've hit a dry spell, go back to writing all of them down, no matter the size or the woo hoo level. The Universe loves recognition for its efforts, so the more you acknowledge them, the more you'll see.

Many of you might be thinking of writing them down in a journal of sorts, just like some people do in a gratitude journal. Since I personally suck at keeping a journal, I started to write the woo hoo moments on a small piece of paper. I put those slips into a large glass vase on a shelf in my living room.

I have a chalkboard label on the jar that currently says "Holy $#!+!" but could also say things like:

OMG!
Woo Hoo!
God is...
!
Wow!
What...?!?!
Holy BLEEP!
Butterfly moments

Pick something that resonates with you. Change it whenever you feel like it.

I have a stack of multi-colored paper near my jar, making it easy to walk over, write down as many details as I think it would take to remember the feeling, and toss it in the jar. But if I'm not at home, I use just any old piece of paper to jot it down before I forget. That's the key: write it down as soon as you're able.

Write things down on whatever you can find at the time. Use a napkin or the back of a receipt—it doesn't have to be pretty. If you prefer things to look pretty, you can copy it down onto the nice paper when you're home.

I love looking at the jar and seeing each piece of paper, knowing that each represents a time when Spirit was reaching out to me. Each is like a hug or someone saying, "You matter." All of those brightly colored pieces of paper were a message meant just for me. They represent a connection.

If you don't have a jar, you could keep them in a shoebox under your bed or in your closet. Just make sure it's accessible. Fill a drawer in your dresser. Toss them in your gym bag. Maybe even scatter them about in multiple locations.

There have been multiple times when I wrote something down and stuck it in a book or the console of my car, and many months, or even years later, I came across it. Sometimes, I don't even remember the incident, but it can still stir up those Holy BLEEP feelings. I love it!

If you're crafty, you could put all your woo hoo moments into a scrapbook. Or just stick them in a file box like a recipe card box. You could even decoupage them onto a wall.

If writing isn't your thing, you could use technology to record them digitally. Send yourself an e-mail and keep them in a special Godincidence folder. You could also send yourself a text or a voicemail. In a voicemail, you would be able to hear the enthusiasm in your voice. Or better yet, make a video of yourself recounting the incident. No one else ever has to see that video. But you can revisit it at any time.

Call someone and tell them so they can remind you later.

Take a picture if it is the kind of thing you can take a picture of. I wish I had a photo of the mirror in the hotel room at Mayo.

If you post it on Facebook, it'll come up on your memories year after year. I love this feature!

Create a digital calendar like a Google calendar. Make a separate calendar just for those "wow" moments and put a repeat setting on each event so it will come up every year.

The whole point is to record them somehow so you can revisit them again and again in the future. Revisiting your sensational moments is a great way to boost your mood or increase your energy when you feel a little sluggish.

It's all about the feeling and emotions. Everything is. That's what life is about. This is what fuels everything. And when we are excited about these things, they magically just keep happening.

7

How to... Do It the Right Way

Should

You should. How many times have you had someone say to you, "You should..."? I have to admit; I say this too. I say it to my daughters, to my friends. But I don't mean to say "you should" to you now.

I don't want to tell you how you should practice seeing God. I am *definitely* not going to tell you there's only one way to meditate or journal or pray or give thanks. I'm not.

But I *am* going to tell you about the way you *should* make a peanut butter and jelly sandwich. Yes, you read that right: a peanut butter and jelly sandwich. Well, it's at least the best way to make one, so it should be the only way anyone ever makes a peanut butter and jelly sandwich.

You start by getting everything you need to make your pb and j. It's a much better use of your time and definitely more efficient. Bread, peanut butter, jelly, a knife, a plate. Not a napkin! This is VERY important. If you make your pb and j on a napkin and some jelly falls out of the sandwich, then it's going to soak into the napkin and make a big mess. So, you must make your sandwich on a plate that's at least slightly bigger than a piece of bread.

Next, you put the jar of peanut butter to the right of the jar of jelly. Take out two slices of bread and separate them like you are opening a book so the sides of the pieces of bread that were originally together will be back together once you've put the peanut butter and jelly on them. This way, they fit together perfectly, and there's not a part of the bread that has exposed peanut butter on it and makes a mess all over your hands when you pick up the sandwich.

Get one to two tablespoons of peanut butter on the knife and apply it to the top side of the slice of bread on the righthand side. Once the peanut butter is evenly spread, wipe any excess peanut butter from the blade onto the clean slice of bread on the left. Now pick up the jar of jelly that's properly located on the left side of the peanut butter jar and apply the jelly to the left slice of bread using the same technique as the peanut butter.

Once you're done evenly spreading the jelly, immediately walk to the sink with the knife and rinse it off. Promptly place the knife into the dishwasher, so you don't get the sticky peanut butter and jelly on the counter. Return to your slices of bread and carefully pick up the piece of bread on the right with the peanut butter on it. Carefully flip it over on top of the slice with the jelly, so the peanut butter and jelly are in contact. Do not attempt to flip the piece of bread that has the jelly on it. The jelly could slide off of the bread and make a mess.

…

Now that we know the only way to make a peanut butter and jelly sandwich because it's the right way, everyone will always make pb and j sandwiches this way. It's obviously the best way. I even gave reasons—good reasons—why you have to do each step the way I said.

I'm sure you're all thinking, "This is ridiculous!"

There's no one way to make a peanut butter and jelly sandwich. There are probably like a million different ways. You could get out the loaf of bread, get your two slices…or even only one (gasp) slice of bread out.

Some people cut the crust off of the sandwich.

Some put the jelly on first.

Some put the peanut butter and the jelly on the *same* piece of bread!

What? No. That's crazy!

It's not crazy. You have got to do what works for you. There are many ways to do many things. If someone who's meditated for many years tells you how you should meditate, will their way work for you? Maybe. Is it the only way that would work? Probably not. Might there be a way that works better for you in the place you are now? Very possible.

Do What Works

My point is you do you. You do what works for you. If you're trying to do something one way and it is not working, maybe you could try another way. Yes, some methods may be more efficient or effective, but you have to figure out what works for you.

Here's a thought to ponder. You have an infection. You take penicillin. The infection goes away. You're healed. Someone else has an infection. They take penicillin. They're allergic to penicillin. Their body has an allergic reaction to the penicillin. They end up becoming sicker than they were. They take a different antibiotic and become well again.

Not everything that works for one person will work for everyone.

Your job is to figure out what works for you and do that. The key is to be continually assessing whether something works for you. Something that once worked might not be as effective anymore, and you may benefit from finding something new.

Journaling in a bound paper journal doesn't work for me. Does that mean I will never find journaling to be my jam, how I roll? No! A year from now, that could become my preferred method. Does it mean no one should write in a journal? Duh. No.

You SHOULD do what works for you.

Meditating while chanting Sanskrit mantras isn't my preferred method right now, but does that mean it won't ever be?

Again...

You SHOULD do what works for you.

And that goes for other people in your life, too. Sometimes, it is hard for us to relinquish control and let someone else figure it out for themselves.

You're doing it wrong.

How many times do I have to tell you?

Here give me that.

We all know someone who's like this, who thinks they have it all figured out and pressure people to do it the way they do. The "right way." Are there better and more efficient ways to do certain things? Absolutely. Some methods make some things more efficient, more effective, more complete, or more like the way someone else does it.

Do you know what I learned? There's more than one way to clean a house or to make a meal. There are probably as many ways as there are people. I'm not saying you can't and shouldn't learn from others. Absolutely do that! It can save you so much time, energy, frustration. But if you are the one who thinks they have something perfected, don't be alarmed when someone finds a different and better way to do that same thing. Heck, you could even learn from them. Or maybe the way you do something *is* the best way to do it...for you.

There are some things we, as a society, must do the same way for the good of all, like stopping at a red traffic light. If we think we shouldn't have to abide by that rule, we could be endangering others.

So, yes, there are societal norms and rules and ways we should do things, but this doesn't apply to meditation, praying, gratitude, etc.

We need to do what's right for us at that time where we are. But one thing you should do no matter what is to love and be kind to yourself and others. (I'll go into this at greater depth in Part IV.)

Be Consistent

No matter what way we find that works for us, I believe consistency is key. It's just like practicing anything. If we aren't consistent, we aren't as proficient or as good at it.

I have a minor in Spanish, but I haven't used it much since college. I don't remember squat. It's weird when I look in my Spanish/English dictionary and see the pages where I wrote down some conjugation rules and some conjugations of irregular verbs. It's my handwriting, but I have no idea what it says. Something I once knew is now playing hide and seek in my brain.

A popular saying is, "It's just like riding a bike." What I have found is there are very few skills that are like riding a bike. It takes a lot of practice to learn to ride a bike. But once you get the hang of it, you can go years without getting back on a bike, and when you do, you can still successfully ride it. With many skills, though, we need to practice maintaining them consistently.

8

How to... Practice

Most things we do require practice to be good at it. I couldn't wake up tomorrow morning and say I'm going to run a marathon today. (I would never do this because I hate to run.) But, let's say I didn't hate it and decided to try it. I couldn't just decide to do it and then do it that day. It would take consistent practice. It is called conditioning. You train your body to know what to do in certain circumstances.

Ask any runner, and they'll tell you some days when they run, they feel better than other days. When a runner has a run that doesn't feel as great as their previous run, do they quit running altogether? No, because they're a runner. They know some days will be better than others. But if they consistently practice, they know, overall, running will become easier.

Practicing these tools I've laid out for you will help you connect with The Universe's loving energy. There will be days when you don't feel as connected as others, but I promise the more consistent you are, the more you'll see, hear, and feel.

Someone can't simply read a book or take a class and then instantly master a new skill. You can't learn to ride a bike by reading a book. It takes practice.

It's like the slogan of the Powerball Lottery, "You can't win if you don't play." Or Wayne Gretzky's famous quote, "You miss 100% of the shots you don't take." You need to put yourself into this game of life day after day to experience it all.

And let me just point out, jealousy won't serve you well. If you're seeing how well someone can do the thing you want to do, don't become jealous and resentful. That is *not* going to help you. Instead of being jealous of that person, be inspired. Tell yourself if they can do it, so can you. Picture yourself being able to do the things they do and just as well, if not better.

Once you get into the swing of things, you can't consider it good and stop all practice. You have to keep moving. If you don't keep pedaling the bike, the bike will eventually fall over.

Who here has ever been on a diet? Ha! Most people I know have, at one point, been on a diet or at least have been more conscious about the quality and quantity of foods they put into their mouths. If you're consistently good about eating the right kind of nutritious food and eventually reach a place where you feel healthier, but then go right back to eating junk foods and not moving your body, that feel-good feeling isn't going to last.

Many years ago, when my kids were in elementary school, I wanted them to learn the piano because deep down, I wish I could play the piano. My mom had asked me when I was young if I wanted to take piano lessons, but because I was painfully shy and tried to avoid failure at any cost, I said no.

As an adult, I wished I could play. I imagined it would be fun to have a group of my friends standing around the piano and me fabulously playing "Piano Man." Everyone would be singing along at the top of their lungs, hoisting their beers in the air, and we'd all be having a gay old time.

Since I was no longer painfully shy, I decided to take piano lessons with my kids. I worked through the first couple of books, learned the basics, and then started playing some easy versions of contemporary music, rather than songs like "Twinkle Twinkle Little Star."

All along, I held the vision of playing "Piano Man" with my friends gathered around. I eventually told our piano teacher I would like to learn "Piano Man," and we found an "Easy Piano," dumbed-down version.

I practiced that baby every day, multiple times a day, and was nearing my goal. I was so happy and proud of myself. The joy of everyone in my vision was palpable.

Eventually, I got comfortable enough to think I could play the song with my friends gathered around. The next time we had our group of close friends over, I convinced them to gather around the piano so I could play my masterpiece.

It didn't quite go as I had envisioned, though. Everyone sang much louder and faster than I was capable of playing. It turned into an a cappella version without any piano playing at all. Oh well. So much for that.

Soon afterward, I discontinued taking lessons while my kids continued. My excuse? I was too busy to take lessons and continue practicing as I should.

Every so often, when I'd be walking past the piano, I'd stop and play the first part of "Piano Man." I'd never take the time to sit down and play the whole song or open a book or play any other songs. This went on for years.

Many years later, I decided to try to play more than just the beginning of the song. But when I tried, I'd get to the spot where I'd always quit playing, and I couldn't remember how to play the part that came next. I tried a few times and starting from the beginning every time because that's the only way I had ever practiced it.

Still nothing. After digging through all of our piano books to find the sheet music for "Piano Man," when I started to play, the musical notes looked so foreign to me. The right hand, or treble clef, looked a little familiar. I could at least count up the lines and spaces to figure out the notes using the old F-A-C-E trick for the spaces, and the Every Good Boy Does Fine trick for the lines—the tricks I learned way back when I was in elementary school.

But the base clef...nothing. Not a clue. I didn't even know a trick with cutesy words to figure it out. I felt a twinge in the base of my stomach. I'd lost it. I couldn't identify notes I once knew. I could no longer play the piano...only page one of "Piano Man." That's not a fun party.

Several lessons can be learned here from my "Piano Man" debacle.

Lesson #1 - Set a clear intention that will get you to where it is you *actually* want to go. If my intent was to be proficient enough at the piano to be able to play songs (not just one song) with my friends gathered around me singing, then my focus should've been on being able to play the piano and not just "Piano Man." What do you *really* want in the end? Don't cut the party short by only being able to play one song.

Lesson #2 - Don't quit when you think you've become proficient enough. Continue practicing. Continue eating the vegetables.

Continue meditating daily. Continue recording your woo hoo/ Godincidence moments. Continue. Don't be a quitter pants.

Lesson #3 - Don't quit when it doesn't go quite as planned. If I hadn't quit practicing, just think of the sing-along/piano bar parties I'd be having these days.

So, when you are practicing all the different ways, here are some things to remember:

- Be open
- Believe it is possible
- Be clear on your intention
- Don't limit yourself to one or two things
- Mix it up a bit
- Note what works for you now, but remember the other ways to try again later
- Regularly reevaluate your goals and intentions
- Remember what you focus on increases
- Set your focus on the positive

God doesn't always whisper. Once you focus on practicing, hearing, seeing, and communicating with The Universe, you'll notice God can sometimes be pretty loud. Regularly tuning in to God's "voice" is like turning up the volume.

... you'll notice God can sometimes be pretty loud.

9

How to... Hold on to the Feeling

Feel the Feelings

Feelings... Whoa whoa whoa... Feelings...

Feelings are a massive component of our lives, but did you know they're actually the most *important* thing in our lives. Our emotions are why we're here. They're why we're living our lives. We live to feel emotions. The key is to focus on the feel-good feelings.

I recently read an article about the chemicals in our tears. It explained that the chemicals changed depending on the emotion felt while shedding those tears. Different types of tears contain different molecules. The tears of different emotions look different under a microscope.

What!?

That is some high-tech stuff. Our bodies are amazing scientific machines.

The chemicals released depends on which chemicals *need* to be released from our bodies.

I am a crier. I can cry for about any emotion there is: I can cry if I'm happy or if I'm sad. I can cry when I'm angry, scared, etc. Like I said before, I can cry at the drop of a hat. Crying is my specialty. I'm an expert. I had no idea crying was actually good for me.

Have you ever noticed feeling better after a good cry? It's because our body got rid of the excess chemicals linked to a certain mood or emotion. If you can't shake a negative feeling, maybe you just need a good cry.

The complexity of our emotions is another miracle.

What we need to be aware of is what emotions we are feeling at any given moment. When we bathe in negative emotions, it leads to stress, and there's proof that stress is the leading cause of most diseases and illnesses.

We need to assess the feelings surrounding us all the time. Occasionally, evaluate your feelings and emotions. We can't do this every second of every day, but we can feel the shift, and when we feel the subtle change, we need to step back and determine how we feel about the shift in emotion. This is a very important action. Taking inventory of our current mood and asking ourselves if it makes us feel good or bad. Does it make us feel at peace or fearful?

When did this emotion start? What was happening right before you felt the shift? Did the thought of one word or name bring about the change? If the shift is toward the negative side of the emotion scale, can you reframe the situation to change your emotions to a positive? Can you build a story around it that creates a better feeling?

What do we *really* want in life? So many people would answer this question with "to be happy and healthy." And what will lead us to both of these things? Peace. Feeling at peace. We cannot feel truly happy when stress overcomes us. Feeling stress is only going to cause more stress. Feeling peace is what opens the door to experiencing happiness *and* being healthy. The state of our bodies and where we stand on the peace-to-stress scale has a tremendous effect on our health. Our emotions determine the chemistry in our bodies.

So, peace. How do we achieve peace? Peace is felt in the soul. It's a soul-level emotion and our ultimate goal. The way to experience this peace is to satiate its desire to be connected to its source. Its creator. Our soul's true and only desire is to feel connected to all that is of this source. When we're properly connected, we're at peace—connected to the higher power of creation, to each other, to nature.

Peace is the vibration that needs to be there for us to make a complete connection. If you're familiar with the law of attraction, you know it states like attracts like. Our frequency attracts things of the same frequency.

When we're on the frequency of stress, we can't completely connect with God, with Love, with the joys of The Universe. We might attempt it and achieve a weak signal. But to have no static on the line, we need to be in a state of peace. Most of us are not operating on a static-free line. If we're stressed, we might see glimpses of this pure connection, but that's only because of Grace. When we catch these glimpses, it's to whet our appetite, to make us crave more of that pure connection.

To be on the right frequency, we need to be humbly confident in our connection. Our confidence level is critical. Succumbing to fear puts us at a vibration that's too low. Our confidence can't be so high that we're cocky. It needs to be just right to achieve that pure connection.

To receive more of this pure connection, we need to practice the vibration of peace and joy.

How on earth do you practice that? By holding on to the feeling. Hold onto it as often as you can. Don't stop...believing... you're able to achieve this static-free connection. Practice being at a high vibration.

Don't Succumb to the Bully

Often when we're feeling bad, it's because we believe the lies the negative voice in our heads is telling us—that bully part of us who doesn't like change. Doesn't want us to grow. "You can't do that." "You don't have what it takes." Author Pam Grout calls this voice our "ass hat."[7] Ha! I love it! Our "ass hat" often causes our shift to feeling bad.

Our emotions are there to be our compass. They're there to let us know whether we're on or off course. If we feel bad, it's there to tell us to make a correction and change our course.

Since I've been regularly meditating, I'm much more aware of my current mood and able to feel when a shift happens.

When I'm going through my day, and I notice I'm suddenly feeling down or agitated, I back up and try to identify the moment when the yucky feeling butted in. I check in to see what may have triggered the bad feeling. Often, it's linked to some self-sabotaging or negative thinking. That's the bully doing what it does best—trying to make you continue to believe an unsubstantiated, limiting self-belief.

If it's stemming from the fact I just realized I forgot to do something or need to do something I don't want to do, then I make at least one step towards doing what needs to be done. I at least write it down or schedule a time to take an action step.

If it's negative self-talk—my bully talking—I try to replace the dialog with positive and affirming words.

If it's something that someone else has done or said, I try to remove myself from the equation. What other people say and do is more of a reflection on them than you. You've probably heard that before, but let it really sink in.

What other people say and do is more of a reflection on them than you.

Former First Lady Eleanor Roosevelt once said, "No one can make you feel inferior without your consent." This may be easier said than done but think about it. Why should someone else, especially if you don't like them or what they stand for, affect how you feel about yourself?

Take Action

If you're not happy with something you did or said, is there something you can do or say to at least begin to counteract it?

Once you've taken some action, then find a warm fuzzy that can put you in the right frame of mind. Pull something out of your bag of tricks: a memory, something to look forward to, or just immediately look around right where you are, and find something that brings you even a little ounce of joy. One thing might lead to another.

If watching a kitten video gives you the warm, fuzzy feeling, then do that. Watch one or two. Find the fuzzy. Feel the fuzzy.

Then move. You don't need to watch the cute kitties for an entire day. A little dab will do ya.

The point is, acknowledge the bad, take action if possible, and then move on to the positive. Keep focused on the good. Don't let the negative steal your life.

Feel the joy as often as possible.

The more we feel good, the more we see, hear, and feel the magic that exists in The Universe.

Feel good. Feel God.

Acknowledge

I'm in no way saying we should ignore or suppress our negative emotions. That would be unhealthy. We never want to disregard these emotions because we'll always return to it if we do. We need to acknowledge them and then determine if they are serving us or sabotaging us.

Is there something you have no control over that's bothering you? Being able to recognize what you can and can't control is a great benefit. Focus on the things you *have* control over.

Often, we have triggers that send us down a long, dark path, and we never make an effort to do an about-face and turn the other way. Usually, it's the part of us that doesn't like change—the bully. So it continues to tell us the negative story about how awful we are or how we deserve to feel terrible.

Some people might try to say, yeah but, look at my past. Look at what's happened to me and where I am because of it. I'm here to say no matter how much you live in your past, no amount of stress, anxiety, guilt, or grief will change the outcome of the past. We can't change that. But we can change our future. We can affect our future by how we feel today. Shift now in the present and know a pleasant future is a possibility. Don't let your past muck up your future.

Grief is a process that needs to be felt. It's different for everyone, but know God doesn't want us to stay in a hole. "He" wants us to feel joy. That's why "He" sends us all the signs, big and small. It's all for our joy. When you notice these, remember the feeling, that "wow" feeling you first had when it occurred.

We're not supposed to live in the past. We can't hold onto feelings attached to an event from our past. We're no longer there. We live in the present. If the same dangerous or damaging conditions from your past still exist in your present, then you may need to make a change in your present, so you don't continue to carry these emotions into your future.

Often these negative feelings stem from an untrue (and mean) story we continue to tell ourselves. We can be so mean and unfair to ourselves, and we need to stop that. Would you allow someone to say these same negative things to someone you love? No!

Loving ourselves right where we are is how we move forward into a better future.

Love is where it's at. Loving ourselves right where we are is how we move forward into a better future.

If it's in the past, we must see it there. The past event can't have ahold of us of its own accord. We have to allow it to have ahold of us, which makes us grow weary. Standing up to the hauntings of the past, to the fear and the doubt, gives us strength. The strength leads to a clearer vision of the possibilities in the future.

Fear is the enemy. It's the enemy of our joy, and we need to do what we can to take control of our happiness. We are all worthy of joy. We need to believe and want that. It's so much more pleasant and desirable than the codependence of fear, grief, and feelings of unworthiness.

Tackle the ghosts that haunt you. Move past the rubbish that lies behind you. Walk away from the thing that wants to handcuff you to misery.

This is on you. Don't expect someone else to fix you. We're the only ones who have that control. Someone else may be able to educate us and give us tools, but it's only us who can do the work to make the change in how we think and feel.

FEEL Your Future

Our feelings are very important. Not only do they affect our present, but they also affect our future. I'm a big believer of this.

You may have heard people say we should write down our future goals every day if we can. But I'm here to tell you I don't think that's good enough. It's all in the feelings we hold when we think about or visualize our goals, our future.

Visualizing can be a great tool, but only when it's coupled with the feelings that will accompany accomplishing the goal.

I've heard many times, most notedly, at a conference with Simon Sinek: when you have a goal, you should focus on your why. Why do you want to reach that goal?

There should be emotion behind the why, too.

I recently went to an Oprah 2020 Vision Your Life in Focus conference. It was A-mazing! Angela Manuel Davis was one of the speakers and said, "Your why should make you cry."[8] That's the emotion I'm talking about. Cry those happy, heartfelt tears!

So, go ahead and write down your future goals, but remember, what's most important is the *feeling* of that goal. If you see something in your mind, feel the sense of joy you'll experience when you get what you're dreaming about. The feeling is what gets you there, not just writing it down. Feel the woo hoo.

Laugh

Laughter is a tool that can bring us to a feeling of joy. It's a gift, a gift from above. How often do we acknowledge that? We rarely think it comes from somewhere other than ourselves or the person or thing who made us laugh. The wit, the humor, is all a gift from God, and we need to acknowledge that.

Often laughter turns into a memory that can last a lifetime. A memory that's filled with joy and can boost our mood over and over. I will forever love recollecting Dad laughing so hard, he couldn't even tell us what it was he was laughing about, which in turn, caused the rest of us to laugh. What a gift.

All of our gifts, where do they come from? That acknowledgment is what creates the fuel for more things to be grateful for. I'm so thankful every time I laugh. It's pretty much my favorite thing to do. Definitely in my top three, anyway.

Make Friends with Joy

Joy that's genuinely felt in the heart is a gift. Some things make us smile, but really, what's in that? What is in you? You can feel a shift within you, within your heart, within your cells when you feel pure joy. That's what we need to tap into. That right there is God, the love of God, which is to say the love of Love.

If we focus on that, the world unlocks to us. Focus on the joy. Feel it. That's the most important part—the *feeling* of the joy.

Sometimes, we need to talk ourselves into it. Joy doesn't always seem to be within our grasp. That's ok. Fake it until you make it—until you make it to joy. It *is* obtainable. Yes, bad things happen. There are things that happen all the time we can't understand or put meaning to. So, we always have two choices: we can move forward, or we can stay stuck in that moment. It's not going to change the fact that the bad thing has happened. It already happened. We must make the best with what we have right where we are. Joy is obtainable if that's our focus. Feel the shift in your smile and the shift in your heart. Close your eyes. Smile without moving a muscle. Feel that shift. That shift is Love and is what can pull you out of your hole, if you let it.

#Feelthesmile

Sometimes, our feelings may confuse us. We need to sit in silence more often and tap into that quiet space that is in each and every one of us. That space is the part of us that is of God. Tune into that space.

Meditation can calm and set our minds right to be in that space of love and joy, so when you're physically with your friends and loved ones, you aren't treating them like dirt or moping around with your pants on the ground. We need to hike them up and say woo hoo to all the moments we can. Not everyone is joyously joyous every minute of every day, but each day allows us to choose—to choose to be in that space of love. It's a practice. Practice the breath and practice the feeling of that joy in your heart space. *Within* your body, not just on it.

Sure, you can fake a smile, but the mojo is in the actual feeling of that smile. Practice from a space of silence. Do it a dozen times a day...or more! Do it as often as you think of it. Do it with your eyes open. Do it with your eyes closed. Move that smile feeling around to different parts of your body. This may take some practice but stick with it. It is worth it. #feelthesmile

Assess Your Feelings

Always take inventory of how you're feeling and set it right. It's natural to fall out of this space and not feel it. It's ok. Don't tear yourself up about it—just practice. Practice noticing when you feel a little or a lot off-kilter. Consider that acknowledgment as a blessing and work on shifting it. The *first* step is to walk away from the feeling that makes you feel bad and move into a space outside of that feeling. The *next* step is to move into the space of joy.

If you feel like you need a cheerleader, someone to give you a pep talk, try freewriting after meditating. So many times, when I do this, God does just that; "He" gives me a pep talk to convince me I'm worthy and can do the things I may be doubting I can do.

It can't always be all one way or the other. There *is* an in-between. The in-between is better than the bad spot, and the joy spot is so much better than the in-between spot. Notice, acknowledge, and move. Notice how you feel, acknowledge how you're feeling, and move to a space that feels even better.

Practice every day. Dive back into that feeling all day, every day, like a child who has just discovered the joy of jumping into a swimming pool and wants to keep jumping in repeatedly. Keep practicing that jumping-into-joy movement until it becomes second nature. Life will shift the more you practice.

Pause in the feeling of joy and visit it as often as possible. Then the joy of life unfolds in front of you, and heaven is experienced here on earth. Let it be open to you. How can you turn every situation into a positive? Practice that. If the breeze feels chilly, be thankful for the jacket you have to make you comfortable. Find joy in the rain that makes the fields and flowers grow. The rain in your life is *not* all bad. It's often bringing you respite, a chance to reexamine your focus and to set your sails for smooth sailing. Adjust your sails to the shift in the wind, and you may end up going so much farther than you ever imagined. You may end up in a different direction that far surpasses your original dream.

Assess. Assess your feelings. Fine-tune your sails. When driving a car, we're continually making minor corrections to keep us safely on our path. We're always making micro corrections we may not even notice anymore. It's all in the practicing of that. You didn't innately know how to do this the first time you drove. But after years of practicing, you do it automatically and keep yourself on your path.

That's the same as evaluating your emotions regularly, always practicing those micro corrections. With daily intentional practice, it'll become a habit and will become easier. The distractions won't ever totally go away, but you'll become practiced at making corrections to them, and you'll notice them less often.

That's the path God wants you on, that God wants to help you stay on. The Universe is always here to help you on your journey. Tap into the help of The Universe that's all around you. It can be very magical and crazy fun!

10

How to... Fill Your Bag of Tricks

Choose to Fly

It's in-flight when the bird feels free—free and in control. Barring any gusty wind, of course. But even when it's windy, once birds get off the ground and high enough, the wind works in their favor. It's like the wind is their respite. It carries them. All they need to do is soar. Lift yourself off the ground. Feel the power of the wind/The Universe and use its power. The power's strong enough to take you places you would have never dreamed of going. Just do the work to get high enough to soar.

Butterflies used to walk when they were caterpillars. But once they experience metamorphosis, they have wings and fly instead.

Be changed in your knowledge of your connection to The Universe. Know The Universe will lift you in flight as long as you don't insist on walking.

Come to the presence of tipping in favor of a God who loves you and will carry you far. You aren't alone. Take off in flight. I have no doubt the bird holds the shift of smile in its heart while soaring. Tap into the soaring feeling.

Have you ever been able to fly in a dream? Not in a plane, but just you in the air like a superhero. It's the most incredible feeling. In my dreams, I've been able to control when and how to fly. I feel the energy rise in me like a coffee percolator, and it lifts me off the ground. The feeling of flying is a euphoric, buzzing vibration throughout your body. That feeling is where we need to reside. Reside in the presence of the most powerful energy on Earth. When we go to this state of feeling, we're in vibration to receive and give love abundantly.

Dream of your life with the feeling of pleasant wonder. It's that feeling in the smile without moving a muscle. Hold on to the feeling. Like Journey sings, "Don't stop believing. Hold on to the feeling." Remember, it's the feeling that makes it so. The feeling leads to the believing. If you can feel it, you can believe it. If you can believe it, it can happen.

It's a beautiful life that doesn't have to be full of strife. Look at the negative or bad things around you and figure out how you can view them in the light of love. It's the dichotomy of the world. All feelings are either love or lack of love. Focus on the light. Where your focus is, is what you see.

You Get to Choose

Pick a card, any card. When a magician is doing a magic trick and says this line, it makes the trick so exciting because we feel like we have a little control of how things will go. Any card is for the taking; we get to choose. The magician is going to work their magic regardless. And no matter which card we choose, that's the card the magician reveals to us in the end.

Except in the game of life, when we pick our cards, we can see what is on each card's face. If we keep picking the eight of clubs, we wouldn't expect to see the seven of hearts in the end. If there's a particular card we want the magician to reveal, why would we pick a different card? Pick the card of joy and happiness, and that's what will be shown to you in the end. Pick that same card over and over. Make the card look well-loved.

Pick the card of joy and happiness, and that's what will be shown to you in the end.

When I was little, I *really* didn't like to lose. I blame my brother. (Not really. Love you, Mark. ☺) Anyway, we had an Old Maid© card game. For those of you who haven't played this game, you do *not* want to be stuck with the Old Maid card in the end. Well, one time when we were playing, my brother waited until the end to stick me with the Old Maid card. I got mad—really mad. I took that card and crumpled it up. Needless to say, it wasn't much fun to play with that deck anymore because it was very obvious which card was the Old Maid and which card to avoid.

Pick a card, any card. When you know which card is the Old Maid card, don't pick it. When you can tell which card is which, always pick the card you want in the end. Choose the feel-good card. Choose how you want your day, week, year, life to go. Picture it and feel it. Get excited about it.

Revisit that feel-good smile feeling repeatedly throughout your day and night. Live here and not in fear. Fear won't take you forward, and forward is the place to be. All the cool kids are doing it.

Find Love in Lyrics

Lyrics and the timing of hearing them have brought me to tears of joy. So many different messages are in the words that are written and sung by one obedient soul. Someone who lets the words that came to them become part of their message to the world. Not all lyricists realize their inspired words come from God. The words that are jammed packed with meaning and seem to come with such ease are the words that came to them when they were inspired or connected with God.

We can feel the connection to the power of Love when we hear these inspired words. The words may be in a song, a poem, a book, or even spoken in conversation. Find the words that resonate with you, with your soul, and revisit them often.

Make yourself a Pick-Me-Up Playlist. Pack it full of those songs that light your fire, bring a smile to your face, or make you bust a move. Music can have such power. Remember, many songs are created with inspiration, or you could say while in spirit and connection with God. Be inspired by someone else's inspiration.

Whenever I hear a song that really inspires me, I buy the mp3, download it, and add it to my feel-good playlist. Choose songs that don't just make you want to move but have meaning in their words. Consider this one of the tools you have in your Bag of Tricks of things that make you feel good.

Lean into Love

Joy can be contagious, just like a flame is from one candle to another. Find your sources of joy and lean into them. You must move and do the leaning in. Don't expect the flame of joy to jump over to you.

Just like we are instructed every year on Christmas Eve at the end of the candlelight service when we sing Silent Night, we are to tip (or lean) the unlit candle to the lit candle. When we lean our unlit candle into the flame, our candle is lit for someone else to light their candle from. We share our light with the ones around us, and this results in the once dark room suddenly glowing brightly.

If you can't see my analogy here, I'm trying to compare it to us spreading our joy in the world to those around us to make the world a brighter place.

Don't expect the light to come to you without you leaning in. Consider all these tools I've been spelling out for you as ways for you to lean into the light, into the joy, into the woo hoo of life.

We all want to look at life with a woo hoo attitude, not a wah-wah, crying, whining, complaining, bah humbug attitude.

If you're sitting in the corner, being a grump, and someone radiating joy makes you grumpier, take that as your sign to get your butt out of that hole you're sitting in. Maybe you don't like the way some people do things. That's fine. I understand that. Just move on and find inspiration somewhere else. Everyone's unique and driven by different things. Not everyone likes the same kind of music. Does that mean music you don't like should be banned from the world? No!

Why should the joy of someone else make you mad? It's not your right to try to ruin their joy.

My girls would come home from dance class, laughing and shouting while I was watching the one show I wanted to watch every week. This was when HDTV was new. I could no longer use my VCR to record shows, and we didn't yet have a DVR. It was so aggravating to me to miss part of the dialogue and lose grip on the plot. I would get frustrated every week. Why was I finding so much frustration in their joy?

Then we got a DVR! Alleluia! All I had to do was pause the show, and I could continue watching as soon as they ventured upstairs.

Figure out your DVR. What's the DVR in your bag of tricks to keep you even-keel and from going over the edge? Have tools, many different tools in your bag of tricks.

Service with a Smile

Have you ever noticed the effect a smile can have on people? Not just the person who's doing the smiling but to the people who are receiving the smile. Smiling is the simplest way to spread and receive joy and is one of the easiest ways we can serve others. Making even the smallest difference with one person *is* making a difference in the world. Helping others is an excellent trick to pull out of your bag of tricks and strengthens your connection to the power of Love.

I'm a smiler. Just like Buddy the Elf, I like smiling. It's my favorite. And I'm talking about genuine smiles. That's where there is the transfer of joyful energy. Not the kind of smile that just looks like someone is sending you pity. You know that smile, the one when someone smiles back, but they don't mean it. That kind of smile is pathetic, not sympathetic.

When we genuinely smile at someone, it's like we are saying Namaste. Do you know the meaning of Namaste? I *love* it! I learned the definition from my first yoga teacher about eighteen or nineteen years ago.

It means:

The God source within me
recognizes and acknowledges
the God source within you.

Nama means bow, as means I, and te means you. Therefore, namaste literally means "bow me you" or "I bow to you."[9]

Bowing in Eastern cultures is a sign of respect.

Most yoga classes end with saying namaste. I think it is one of the most respectful and loving things we can say to one another.

Think about it. We all have a part in us that is of God, whether we know it or not. When we tap into this part of us, we're operating on Love. When we notice that part in those around us, that's the epitome of love.

When we're mean or disrespectful to someone, it's like we're not acknowledging the God-part of them. I realize many people don't operate out of the part of them that is of God/Love, making it very hard to respect them. Some people don't even know it exists. Recognize this and don't allow their words and actions to affect how you feel. Remember, our feelings and emotions create the chemistry in our bodies. Bad chemistry can lead to a bad mood or even poor health. Don't let someone who doesn't operate from the part of them that's of love affect your well-being.

If someone sends you a genuine smile, take that as a reminder that you are to experience that smiling feeling in your heart, in your whole body, and move forward in love. And don't forget to smile genuinely back.

So, go out into the world and smile! Share and multiply the Love!

USE Your Bag of Tricks

Sometimes, we just don't feel right and don't feel like smiling. It's ok. We can't be *on* all the time. We just don't want to hang out in the off-position for too long. This is when we need to pull something out of our bag of tricks. It's not good enough to have the bag of tricks or the knowledge of what to do; you need to use it.

Remember all of the "How to's" I just spelled out for you.

Maybe you haven't experienced a coincidence, Godincidence, synchronicity, woo hoo moment in a while. That's when it'd be good to implement the O.M.G. and #feelthesmile methods.

O = Open	Be Open to how you can see, hear, feel, experience the magical synchronicities.
M = Meditate	Make sure you're regularly meditating—at least once a day. Maybe you could try meditating a few minutes longer or more than once a day.
G = Gratitude	Umph up on your gratitude practice. If you haven't been writing them down, give it a whirl. Maybe even sit down and make a list of a hundred things you're grateful for to give it a jump start.
#feelthesmile	Imagine a smile without moving a muscle. Move this feeling to your heart space. Do it twenty times a day if you need to. And remember to train your body by first doing that ever-important cleansing breath.

This is also when we can dig into our "Holy BLEEP" jar and reflect on a previous occurrence and revisit the feeling. That's why I advise recording your special, personal, woo hoo moments. Write them down, record a video, or do any of the ways I suggested earlier. Or maybe you have a better way that works for you. However you record it, do it right away, and include as best you can how it made you feel so you can revisit that feeling.

The only thing that matters is the way that thing made you feel.

Once again, it does not, I repeat, it does *not* matter what other people's reactions are to your story. The only thing that matters is the way that thing made you feel. That message was for *you*. It's easy to feel excited when everyone is also in awe of your story, but how special is the message that is personalized for you? That's your relationship with The Universe, with God. Your ah ha's fit in with your relationship. It is individualized for you. So, notice and recognize the joy that surrounds you. Be grateful. You'll see more.

And don't forget about another one of my favorites!

Play your Pick-Me-Up Playlist! Play it as often as needed. Continue to update your list. Maybe even have a separate list that just makes you want to boogie. Dancing and getting your blood pumping can make you feel so much better.

If dancing isn't your gig, do a different form of exercise. Maybe running brings you to that space of joy and feeling better. Perhaps you prefer to move your body differently. I love walking outside in nature while listening to an inspirational audiobook or podcast. Maybe it's Jazzercise or Zumba for you. Sometimes, we don't want to get started, but we feel so much better once we do.

Being out in nature, whether I'm walking or not, always has a good effect on me. Feel the peace when you're in nature. Feel alive and breathe in **connection** with it. Feel the abundance of The Universe in everything you see around you. You are the lens to The Universe. You need to see the things around you to recognize the power within you. You're strong in your power and must trust in The Universe around you. The Universe fuels your power to be free. Free from strife and fatigue. Your energy for life lies in your willingness to connect with God, with love, with nature, and with the people around you.

You can experience incredible joy by investing in connection with those around you. Don't be afraid to connect. Some people fear the pain felt by a broken heart, but there must be peace in the love and connection you find with others. That peace acts as a padlock to love. It goes back to that feeling of love and joy and peace in your heart that secures our love. Be grateful for the love in your connections. Feel peace in the time of love. Focus on what can go right rather than on what can go wrong.

Of course, I'm always going to be the one to recommend **meditation**. I think it's such an important, impactful tool. Like I said before, it has changed my life. Sit and connect to the space of love inside you. We've heard we need to love ourselves. Some people just can't wrap their brains around this. As I said, we all have a piece of God, a piece of Love within us. Maybe you can start with learning to love *that* part of you. It's there for all of us. Begin with that, and it will grow.

All of these how to's I've spelled out in this section are like polishing the glass of your lantern. It's like adding fuel to the fire—the flame of Love. Cleaning the gunk off the glass helps your light shine for others to see.

When we find our way to connect in this feeling of joy, we need to recognize there is a difference in the joy of the flesh and joy of the soul. Sometimes, they coincide, but sometimes, they don't. We need to distinguish the difference. Recognize the feeling in your heart that your soul desires. This is the place to visit often.

Like a ship sails on the ocean, there's rhythmic motion in the world. Feel joy in both the ebbs and the flows. Let the feeling move you like music. It's like getting a song stuck in your head. Let the feeling of joy get stuck in your heart. Feel the practiced movement and the free form flow. Move together in harmony. Be open to always moving in new ways.

Holy BLEEP! That was NOT a Coincidence

Discussion Questions

***This is a partial list of questions.
Make your discussion even better!
Go to https://www.michelleprohaska.com/free-resources/
for the full, downloadable, printable list.

Part III – How to...

1. Are you willing to admit that you could stand to learn a little bit more about God and how "He" can show up in your life and our modern world today? Do you believe that God can communicate with us through modern technology that didn't exist in biblical times?
2. ACTION – Write down this quote on a sticky note or piece of paper and stick it on your bathroom mirror or the dash of your car.

   Whether you think you can, or you think you can't,
   either way, you are right.

   -Henry Ford
3. Are you a pray-er? Do you ask The Universe for help throughout your day, or do you only pray in desperate times? Know that nothing is too big or small to be asked for. Do you follow your ask with silence? Sometimes we get our answers immediately. Don't miss the answer because you're too busy talking.
4. Are you too shy or private to ask others for prayers?
5. Have you ever intentionally meditated before? (deep breaths followed by clearing your thoughts)
6. ACTION – Have everyone try the #feelthesmile method.

7. When you attempt the #feelthesmile method, are you able to feel a shift within?

   If so, are you able to move this feeling to other parts of your body?
8. Are you ever able to clear, stop, or slow your thoughts?
9. Have you ever done any form of freewriting?
10. Have you ever received a profound message from God/ The Universe?
11. Do you have a gratitude practice? Are you consistent at it? Could you improve?
12. What would be your preferred method of recording Godincidences? Journal? Jar or box? Digitally?
13. Have you noticed a bully voice inside your head? What has it told you? Have you been able to tell it who is boss?
14. Do you have a bag of feel-good tricks? What is in your bag? Music? Acts of service? Movement? Gratitude?

PART IV

You. Are. Being. Nudged.

1

You. Are. Being. Nudged.

Read that chapter title again. You. Are. Being. Nudged. Those periods are there after each word to act as an emphasis or exclamation point to the statement.

You. Yes, you. No, I'm not talking about someone else. You. I am talking to you.

Are. You *are*... Not maybe. Not possibly. Not it could happen, but maybe not. Are. You. Are.

Being. The "ing" on the end of this tells you it is a *present* tense verb. So, I'm not talking about something that happened once in the past or might occur in the future. Being. Presently being. You. Are. Being.

Nudged. Meaning coaxed or gently encouraged. Some nudges are gentler than others. But nonetheless, they're being communicated; it's meant to get your attention.

You. Are. Being. Nudged.

My whole point of writing this book is to get this message across to you. See it. Recognize it. Do something about it.

Our Own Individual Language

My journey started with a small, yellow butterfly that then turned into hundreds, if not thousands of butterflies over the years. But doesn't everyone see butterflies all the time? Yes. We all see lots of things all the time. But what's in a symbol or sign? What is that sign supposed to mean to me...or to you? It could be very different.

You see, The Universe is talking to each of us individually, not collectively. That same sign may mean something totally different to me than it does to you. It may mean something different each time we see it or hear it or taste, touch, or smell it.

It's like The Universe is talking to us each in our own individual language.

Some of us are better-versed in our own language and are better at understanding and interpreting our language than other people are. Sometimes people try to understand someone else's language when that isn't their language. Those words and symbols were not meant for them, so they won't be able to understand what The Universe is saying to the other person. They cannot understand the ding, ding, ding, or Ah-Ha that happens when something is understood or realized for the first time.

The Universe wants to teach us the language it's speaking directly to us. You don't need to worry or get caught up with what other people think, feel, or say, no matter how close they are to you. It doesn't matter if they get it. It only matters that you get it.

Why

But *why* do these "coincidences" happen?

Sometimes these synchronicities or signs are there to let you know you're not alone

Sometimes these synchronicities or signs are there to let you know you're not alone. Whether we're grieving, suffering from anxiety or depression, or overwhelmed, we have all felt alone for some reason or another. Sometimes when we notice these coincidences, it's just to encourage us and help us feel supported, loved, and not alone. They are there to let us know Love is seeking us. We just need to be receptive to it.

I don't care who you are or what you've done or failed to do; *you* are worthy of this love. This love is patient and kind.

Other times, these nudges are to prod us along to do something in particular. When I first started seeing the butterflies, I felt like it was a loving hug from Dad, God, The Universe, telling me I was still surrounded by love: by Dad's love, by God's love, by the love of everything good and right in this world. It was like The Universe was throwing me a bone of hope and encouragement.

When I was probably around four years old, I was very shy and quiet and had crazy, wild, curly, frizzy hair. At night when we'd be watching T.V. as a family, I'd get it in my head I wanted popcorn. So, I'd start tapping my mom or my dad very gently on the arm and say, "Pa-torn." My mom or dad would act like they didn't hear me, so I would gently and quietly do it again. "Pa-torn."

I wouldn't say it as a question like I was asking. I would just state it over and over, all the while tapping them on the arm.

"Pa-torn."

"Pa-torn."

"Pa-torn."

Eventually, they would acknowledge me, and I would usually get the popcorn that I wanted. (It's probably because who could pass up such a cute, curly-headed little girl.)

When we see our sign or various signs repeatedly, that could be a sign that God is patiently and quietly asking us to do or say something.

Whether it's to surround you with a loving hug or to prod you to do something, it is The Universe acting as your cheer-leader—cheering you on to bring you to a higher vibration of love and support. Kind of like a loving pat on the head.

Is the nudge you're feeling loving and kind? Yes? Then it is of God. It is of Love. Embrace that. If it moves you to act with love and kindness to others, then we're not to question it. We are to move, act, and do. Acting on these momentous Love nudges is the natural state of Love. When we act without questioning, we tap into some kind of hidden magic. We tap into the power of Love. We tap into the power of God.

No Yeah But's

We are to act and not stand around, arguing why we shouldn't do it. No yeah, but's. Whenever we have this feeling, we should not ignore or question it. We need to act.

The big picture is *big*. It is much bigger than we know. We can't just let these nudges sail on by untouched. Acting and doing sets us free of those unsettled feelings. When we aren't doing something we know we should be doing, it creates an uneasiness in our bodies. Remember, our feelings create the chemistry of our bodies. Ignoring things doesn't make them go away; it only makes our uneasy feeling worse. Act and create a shift in how you feel.

When I knew I was to write this book, but I wasn't actually writing, I can't tell you how many people I know experienced the death of their dad. Every time I heard about another friend who was going through what I went through, I felt the tap—the "you need to write your book" message. I'm not saying these people's dads died just to get me to write my book, but it taught me God uses any and everything to move people.

Sometimes, we're driven to do things not for our benefit but for someone else's. This is the reason we're not supposed to question. It might not make sense to you, but the key is it might not have anything to do with us or our story, but it might actually be life-changing for someone else. You might be an essential part of someone else's Godincidence.

It doesn't have to make sense, so stop spending so much time trying to make sense of it all. The Infinite Power has knowledge beyond anything you could fathom. Just be glad you don't have to keep track of it all.

It doesn't matter if it makes any sense to us, just like it doesn't matter if nobody else understands our own "Holy BLEEP" moment. That moment is for us and us alone. Other people may be affected by it, but nobody else has to be influenced for it to be a life-changing moment for us.

The more we tune in, the more we can have and sense and feel and be. The more we do all of that, the more we bring peace to others, which helps them to have, sense, feel, and be.

Don't Overthink It

When I was in college, I started as an undeclared major. I later changed to Elementary Education. Then, during my junior year,

I switched from Elementary Education to a Finance major. My junior year! I wouldn't recommend this route. None of my major classes carried over, leading me to take multiple summer classes to play catch-up.

One summer day, as I sat in my first day of my first finance class, I had an idea. Our class met every day, Monday through Friday, for an hour. It was summer. I was in college, and I like to have fun. This class was really impeding on the fun to be had. So, I thought, *Hey, if we went to class for an extra fifteen minutes Monday through Thursday, maybe we wouldn't have to go to class on Fridays. That would make this a* much *better summer.*

So, right then and there, I did what most college students would *not* do. I raised my hand as my professor was going over the course syllabus and said, "I have a proposition to make."

Let me point out this was my first class with this professor. He didn't know me from Adam. What I didn't realize at the time was I would go on to have many more classes with this same professor. I gave no thought to what the repercussions could be to my suggestion. Now, knowing what they could've been actually floors me. If he had taken my suggestion badly, it could've drastically affected the remainder of my college career.

Long story short, he was intrigued by my suggestion. He quickly conducted an anonymous survey to ensure no one would have a scheduling conflict if we switched the schedule. And the next thing I knew, we only had to report to class four days a week instead of five.

Why am I telling you this abstract story? Two reasons.

One. I didn't overthink it. Which, to this day, totally shocks me. Like I said, I was a very shy and quiet kid.

There was one time when I was around five years old, and I was invited to a birthday party. I didn't want to go. It wasn't because I didn't like the birthday girl—she was one of my best friends. I didn't want to go because I didn't want to play games. I didn't want to lose or feel self-conscious about not being good at something. After a lot of pleading from my mom, she came up with a plan; I would just stand by the fence in the backyard and watch everyone else play the games. Then, I'd just join in on the present opening and cake eating. She ran this past the mom hosting the party, and I agreed to go. This was and often times is still who I am—a shy little girl, standing by the fence.

The fact that I could suggest such a radical change to my professor with not a bit of nervousness blows my mind. But I did it. I acted. I have often thought about this brave act, but I just recently made the connection that this act may have significantly affected someone else in that class.

This brings me to reason number two: My speaking up when nudged might not have *just* resulted in me being able to have a more chill summer, but it may have allowed someone else to be somewhere for a significant event. Maybe they went somewhere that first Friday and met their future spouse. Or perhaps someone who was struggling to find a way to pay tuition was able to work a full day on Fridays and pay for that summer class.

The point is, I don't know what kind of effect my suggestion may have had on someone else. And this is why I am telling you not to question why you should do something you feel nudged to do.

The really cool part is your nudge may have an effect on you *and* many other people too. I'm sure if you talked to any writer or lyricist, they would tell you there have been times when they felt like the words that came out of them felt like they were coming from somewhere else, from something bigger than them. Whether they call it God, The Universe, or don't even know what to call it, it's at these times they're acting out of inspiration. They were inspired, which means to be in Spirit. This means they had a direct line going with God, with Love, with the infinite power of The Universe.

Take the Nudge and Run

I've told you already, I love words. I feel they have power. I love to surround myself with meaningful, powerful words. When lyrics jump out of a song and grab me, at that moment, I don't care why they think they wrote that song; I know they wrote that song for me. Now, I realize I might not be the only reason they wrote it. Most popular songs with inspired lyrics touch many different people in different ways and with a different meaning. But that's when I jump up and yell, "This is my song!"

I'm in no way a saint at acting immediately on a nudge. This book, for instance, is over ten years in the making. Talk about the dragging of feet. Just the other day, I was in the checkout at the store. I'd never seen the guy working the register before, so I guessed him to be new. He was exceptionally friendly, even after my package of instant mashed potatoes sprung a leak and made a huge mess on the conveyor belt. I apologized, but he acted like that was the greatest thing to happen to him all day. All he needed to do was find some belt cleaner. I scooped up what I could with a couple of pieces of paper I found in my purse, and he happily cleaned up the rest of my mess.

Right before he handed me my receipt and sent me on my way, I was nudged to thank him, call him by name (Which is super easy! They wear name tags!), and to tell him he was awesome. So, I said, "Thanks so much, Alex." And that was it! I froze. How hard is it to say awesome? It's not! Awesome. Awesome. Awesome. It is a very easy word to say. I say it all the time.

Why didn't I just say it? It would have been no skin off my back. Why?

Some people think if they build someone up, they might push the other person up past themselves, but in actuality, when we boost someone up, we are also boosting ourselves up. And not just a little bit! We're boosting ourselves up just as much, if not more, than we're boosting the other person up. We won't get left in the dust when we help others. We'll also be helping ourselves. Just think of a world like that, one where everyone is getting boosted up.

When we can serve and build each other up and fill our own bucket at the same time, we need to act on those things. Trust me; the next time I'm nudged to tell someone they're awesome, I'm going to do it!

We shouldn't ignore The Universe's nudges. God didn't create you to ignore "Him." If you're a parent, you know how annoying it can be when your child doesn't do what you've repeatedly asked them to do. If only they would just do what you asked them to do the first time you ask them to do it. Am I right? If they would just do it, the whole household would be happier.

God didn't create you to ignore "Him."

Think about that one. Only you're the kid, and the house is the world. If we just did what we were being nudged/asked to do, the whole world would be a happier place.

Us being obedient isn't only a benefit for God. Well, technically, it is, but what I mean is it's not just a benefit for the part of God that's outside of us. It directly benefits our soul—our true self. That part of us that is of God. Whether we know it or not, we each have a part of us called our soul. Contained in our soul is God. It's our very own piece of the ruling power of Love.

Even if you're aware of the soul, you might not be aware of the soul's desire to connect with the divine power of Love. That is our true soul's desire—to have a connection with God. And God can be found everywhere. "He" is in everyone and everything. The connections made *with* and *through* the soul are the strongest kind of connections. These connections are the purpose of life.

2

Share. Your. Story.

Sharing is Caring

We all know it's nice to share the things we have with others. Sharing is caring. But we haven't always agreed this was a good idea.

"You should share your Halloween candy with your brother."

"Ummm. *No*. Why would I do that? It's my candy. What's in it for me?"

We can be stingy sometimes.

It's mine, mine, mine!

So, when we have these amazing, jaw-dropping, Holy BLEEP moments and we don't share them with anyone... I'm here to tell you that's being stingy. We need to share these AWEsome happenings with those around us.

But why...?

Remember when I talked about gratitude and said The Universe likes being acknowledged for those things it does for us and gives us? Sharing our Godincidence moments with others is another form of recognition and acknowledgment. Plus, it fuels the woo hoo fire. We are to share the love, share the excitement, and...share the joy.

We need to start the conversations. We need to spread the news that this magical force is with us...everywhere. We're not alone. So many people are desperate for this message: the lonely, the grieving, the sick, the anxious, the depressed, the doubter, the self-conscious. We can all stand to have a little more God in our lives. A little more woo hoo. A more loving view of The Universe. This is crazy fun stuff! Let's shout it from the rooftops.

God will show you opportunities to share your stories with others. Someone else may need to hear your story to see the magic in their own life. The more people share their stories, the more others will learn all the different ways The Universe can wow us. It can help to open up people's minds and inspire them.

We need to share these amazing occurrences with others so everyone can see the magic in this world, and everyone can feel hope and know we're not alone. We have the whole Universe on our side. If we can just set our minds to believe in this magic, we will see it everywhere. Notice these opportunities and act on them.

Boldness in belief can be the best tool in your shed.

And like I've said before—about a million times—if other people don't have the positive reaction you were hoping for, don't sweat it. Really. Don't fret. Not everyone speaks the same "Universal" language—kind of sounds like an oxymoron. But there is not a universal Universe language. It's like in Gary Zukav's book, *The Five Love Languages*. People show and receive love in different ways. There is more than one love language amongst us, person to person, and there is more than one Universal love language.

Some people are just straight-up deaf to God, period. Don't let their deafness be contagious to you. Don't let them put their noise-canceling or God-canceling headphones on you. Hold on to the feelings you felt when your Godincidence happened. Revisit that feeling and feel grateful for it.

It's Ok If They Don't Get It

A couple of years ago, when my oldest daughter graduated from college, we had a small gathering to celebrate at our house. We were sitting in the living room chatting away when my daughter looked at my Godincidence jar sitting on a shelf nearby and said, "Does that say Holy shit?"

I said, "No, it says Holy dollar sign, hashtag, exclamation point, plus sign, exclamation point."

Everyone laughed, and she said, "Whatever! That says Holy shit. What *is* that?"

So, I somewhat reluctantly said, "That's my jar where I put all the pieces of paper that have my coincidences-that-are n't-coincidences on them."

I was reluctant because I hadn't shared them with anyone else. I was afraid they would want to know what they said, and sure enough, several of them piped up and asked me to read some.

I went to the shelf, grabbed the large vase with both hands, took a deep breath, and returned to my seat.

Oh boy… *Please let it be a "good" one*, I thought.

I reached in and quickly glanced over what the first piece of paper I grabbed said. I smirked and explained how one day when I was walking through a parking lot and thinking about a personalized license plate a friend of ours has and the funny story that happened when he was telling us about his plan to get it. We interpreted it as something totally different (and inappropriate) than what he intended.

As I was walking, I chuckled to myself, recalling our thunderous laughter. I looked over about ten seconds later and saw a license plate that was almost identical to the one our friend had. Whoa! That was weird!

I got to my car and started driving home. About a mile later, I saw another personalized plate that said something along the same lines as our friends' plate's intended message. I was like, whoa! Really?

I continued driving, smiling to myself about the weird synchronicity The Universe threw my way. Another mile further down the road, while I was stopped at a stoplight, a car turned in front of me that was, I kid you not, covered from bumper to bumper with big, and I'm talking big, butterfly stickers. It was comically covered with huge butterflies all over it!

While telling my inquisitive audience about the incident, I smiled and felt a warm feeling inside, just like I did the day it happened. They all looked at me with raised, tilted eyebrows. Not in the "oh wow, I can't believe that" kind of way, but in the "really...you think that was The Universe talking to you? You're crazy," sort of way.

For a second, I was kind of taken aback. But then I quickly said, "I don't care what you think. I thought it was crazy, awesome."

I think someone actually said, "Whatever, Michelle."

Here's my point. When you share one of your favorite candy bars with someone, and they spit it out because they don't like nougat, that doesn't mean you should start questioning whether you should like nougat. Don't think, "Wow! They don't like nougat. Hmmm. Maybe nougat isn't actually good. Maybe I shouldn't like nougat either."

People! You can like the nougat! Different things can trip different people's triggers. Some things in the woo hoo zone will click with someone, and others will be sitting there like... uhhhhh. That's ok. If everything was the same for everyone, it would be a very boring world.

We Are Special Too

I should probably also mention the people who think God only showed "Himself" to and talked to people in biblical times, that "He" doesn't do that today in our current world. You know what I have to say to them, but I don't want to because I don't like conflict? "Wake up and smell the coffee!"

Why would God stop talking to people? "He" got tired? No! We're just as special. "He" is "talking" to and *with* us all the time, many times a day, all around us.

Sometimes when things happen to us, the message is actually meant for someone else, but they won't get that message unless you tell them.

Not Just For Us

A couple of years ago, I was at a bridal shower for my friend's daughter. The daughter's friend was hosting the shower. I'd met the hostess through work briefly but didn't really know her. We discovered I knew her mother and father-in-law, though. While we were eating, she asked me if I was still working at the school. I told her no, I was working on writing a book. At the time, I was only *intending* to write a book; not much actual writing was happening. She asked what the book was about, so I told her. She was very intrigued.

A couple of weeks later, her mother-in-law was tragically killed when she was hit by a car while out for a walk with her family.

As Larry and I were walking into the church for the visitation, a butterfly flew from behind me, circled right in front of me, and quickly flew back from the direction it came from. It was out of sight in an instant. My heart skipped a beat, and my eyes about popped out of my head.

"Whoa!"

When we reached the family, I told her about the butterfly I'd just seen outside. She looked at me and said, "Now, I *really* can't wait to read your book."

My butterfly sighting wasn't just for me.

Yet another validation.

Yes. I needed to write the book.

So, let me say it yet again, we need to share our stories with others.

So, let me say it yet again, we need to share our stories with others. We need to fuel this fire. We need to get other people on the bandwagon. Let's start the conversation. Let's make it commonplace. Let's not just start a conversation; let's start a movement—a movement of believing in the magic. #godincidence

You can also create your own opportunities. Have a party! I'm always open to any excuse to have a party! Get together with your friends, family, neighbors, coworkers, your small group, your mom's group, or total strangers. I don't care with whom.

Just do it! Get together with others and talk about the magic in the world. If you're half as geeked out about this topic as I am, it'll be grand fun!

Maybe you're still like I was when I was little: the shy girl standing by the fence who isn't quite ready to join the fun and games with your friends. You can send your stories to *me*. I'd love to hear them. Really! I'm getting excited right now just thinking about hearing all your stories.

My email and social media contact information are at the end of the book. Reach out to me!

Hey! You could even invite me to your little woo hoo party! Really! You just never know. I might just accept your invitation.

The opportunities to share your story will come up. I promise. Just pay attention. You'll get the little or big nudge from within, and you'll know. Then you'll say, "Whoa! Michelle knows what she's talking about."

3

Who. Am. I. To...

The Voice of Fear

Sometimes, The Universe nudges us to do something we don't think we can do. Fear kicks into overdrive, causing the nagging voice to start yapping away. This voice is the one we hate but have gotten so used to; we listen to whatever it has to say. It says all the negative, small belief stuff to us over and over. We weren't born with this voice talking to us, but as soon as we soaked in the negativity of others around us, this little (or big) voice started talking to us, telling us how unworthy we are to do anything grand.

We're not supposed to listen to this voice of fear. God wants us to hear the voice of Love instead. Trembling at the sound of fear only causes the sound of Love to go unheard. Fear lives in the present, representing the future. Paralyzing fear comes when we give presence to things that are not here. We need to be aware of what is around us, not get caught up in the imagination of the scary things that *could* happen.

It's like a child being afraid of the monster under the bed or in the closet. As adults, we know it's not there, but to that child living in the feeling of fear, they 100% believe it. They can see it in their mind's eye. We need to prove to them by showing them it's not there.

God wants to do that for us. "He" wants to show us there's nothing physically present to be afraid of. We're living in the present. We need to keep our focus here and not get caught up in our unloving imaginations of the future. We need to stand in the present moment in peace. Feel and act in that feeling of peace.

Your actions can only happen in the present, and we tend to focus on the future, which we can't see. We can't see what actually lives there. We need to view it in the positive light of love, joy, hope. We need to tackle the temptations that want to steer us astray. Give them a quick hip check and continue on our path.

We need to couple our intentions with joy—not fear. Fear doesn't belong. Let's make this fun. Let's cruise on down and ease on down the road.

Power in Your Belief

The message in this book is everywhere in children's literature and movies. The *Wizard of Oz* is just one example of many. Just believe. You've had it all along. Don't think you don't have a brain and aren't smart enough. Don't believe you have no courage. You have access to everything you need through this loving Universe. And your link to all of this is that piece of God's love that's *in* you.

The Universe is here for you. It's here to enhance your experience a thousand-fold. Tap into that $#!+ (otherwise known as stuff)! Like I said before, I don't swear very often, but I really want you to get this point. It's my exclamation point here!

There can be power in your words and actions, or you can take the power away. It's all up to you. You own this power. If you couple this power with your intentions and put it with your words and actions, you could be totally floored at the result.

Be a magnet for all you need and for all you want. It's there. It's there for the taking. Tap into the joyous feeling always. People will see it on you, and they will want a piece of that. Don't be afraid of that. This power of Love is limitless. The Universe is always very willing to fill you back up.

Be present. Take it in. Take it *all* in. Sift through it. Don't let the bad stuff, the negative energy in. Let the negativity end with you. It's not meant to be passed around. Spread the joy. Find it and spread it. If you are the recipient of someone else's joy, be sure to pay it forward.

Fear Likes to Grow

Have you ever noticed fear is amazingly good at growing? Do you know someone with a fear of bees? I'm speaking from experience here. I've gotten a lot better over the last several years, but I used to jump up and run—sometimes while screaming—at the sight of anything that might possibly be a bee.

What starts as a fear of bees because they might sting you and if they sting you, it'll hurt, turns into a fear of anything that flies, or a piece of grass tickling your leg, or a piece of your hair blowing in the breeze across your neck.

I might be guilty of all of the above. Here's the kicker. I have never even actually been stung. I have risked breaking my leg in a feat to run from something that may or may not be a bee. Breaking my leg would probably end up hurting more or at least hurt for longer than if I was actually stung.

The point here is we need to give our fears a reality check. Don't let them grow out of proportion.

You might be saying, "Yeah but...

> ...you have no idea what I did in my past."
>
> ...you don't know what happened to me."
>
> ...so and so won't let me do that."
>
> ...you can do that, but I can't do that."

I get it, really, I do. But I'm not any more special than you. We can all see, feel, hear the magic of The Universe. (Remember, replace the word with whatever you prefer to call it.) We can all tap into this because God is in all of us. It does not matter what country you're from or what language you speak. This is true for all.

I was in that place, though, when I thought I couldn't write this book.

Who am I to write a book about God?

I don't like conflict at all, and what are the two most controversial topics to talk about? Politics and religion. And that right there, the fact that God can be such a controversial subject is why it has taken me over ten years to write this book.

Who am I? I am a stay-at-home mom who never used her finance degree or minor in Spanish. I'm a former aerobics instructor who had a couple of other small jobs here and there.

I'm someone who loves Friday Happy Hour. I value quality time with friends and family. I love to laugh and dance like no one is watching and sing like no one is listening. But I'm also the one who was able to recognize the nudges, those persistent, "pesky" nudges I know were meant for me. I'm someone who is now very aware of our seemingly magical connection with this magnificent power.

So, here I am. I'm telling my story. Even though I constantly waver between the girl standing by the fence at the birthday party and the girl who wasn't afraid to raise her hand that first day of finance class. I am here. I'm telling and teaching my story. I'm being obedient to the nudges. I was so worried about writing a book about religion when that's not what God was nudging me to do at all. Quite the contrary. This book is to show people our connection to this grand power.

It has been a growing process, and I never doubted I would write the book. I just knew I had a lot of inner work to do to knock down the doubt and know I was worthy, that I could reveal my message in a way that people would actually get it. I finally realized not everyone will get it, and that's ok. The people who will get it will be the people who were supposed to get it. I learned it's selfish to hide these gifts and stories.

So, I get it. I get the "who am I" conundrum. When all the excuses pop up, we need to assess the resistance we feel and don't turn a molehill into a mountain. Realize when the stuff is actually small stuff and not the big monster under the bed we imagine. Don't sweat the small stuff. It's small stuff, people! It's so not worth sweating over. This focus on the small stuff is how we miss all the opportunities for the awesome, big stuff.

Convince yourself it's possible. Every day say:

> "It could happen. It could happen. It could happen."
> "It could be true. It could be true."

"Why not me? Why not me?"
"I am worthy. I am worthy."

Believe!

Remember, you have an unbelievable power within you!

Be open to receiving the nudges. If you believe you can receive them, then you can. And when you do, don't run and hide.

Oh No, You Di'int

I used to always say to people in my adult small group I wished God would send me a burning bush like "He" did for Moses. How can I really hear God? I don't ever seem to hear "Him." I need God to talk to me through a burning bush or something, so, I know without a doubt it's "Him." I'd heard there are people who hear God speak—like audibly. I wanted that. I wanted to be able to hear and to know.

That was my wish. That was what I asked before Dad died. That was before I started seeing and, yes, hearing God everywhere.

God believes we can do so much more than we think we can.

What I didn't realize was maybe I wouldn't like what God had to say. That maybe "He" would say things that were outside my comfort zone—*way* outside my comfort zone.

God believes we can do so much more than we think we can. It's true. "He's" dealing stuff out of "His" deck, like "Here, try this. It'll be great."

And we're like, "Oh, heck no! You're crazy, Dude. Mr. God, Sir. Sorry, but you don't know what you're talking about. I can't possibly do that!"

And "He's" like, "Yuh huh."

We got our first boat when our oldest child was about nine months old. So, our kids have grown up boating. Larry is a big water-skier, and much to his dismay, the girls and I do not waterski. But the girls would and still do go tubing. It makes Larry happy when people are willing to play on the water. So, he tries to make it extra fun. And by fun, I mean fun for him.

He doesn't believe in driving in a straight line when someone is tubing because...what's the fun in that? Instead, he swerves from side to side like a drunkard so the people on the tubes will go flying outside the wake and pick up speed. It can be terrifying to fly over the wake. Sometimes, it's going so fast, the tube leans. The next thing you know, you're being flung off the tube and are skidding across the top of the water.

He's gotten better about not making the tube actually flip, but...he still likes to use his evil laugh and scare the riders out of their shorts and make them *think* they are going to go flying.

So, when Brooke, our youngest, was somewhere around eight years old, and she'd be perched atop a tube, Larry, of course, would go into his zigzag driving pattern. She would look at the approaching wake with wide eyes and then at Larry, and she'd put her little pointer finger up in the air and wag it side to side with a little waggle of her head. The first time she did this, Holly started laughing hysterically.

I'm like, "What is she doing?"

Holly puts her pointer finger in the air and does the same wag and waggle that Brooke had and says, "Oh no, you di'int!"

We all laughed, and that became our running joke for years. Brooke would tell Larry he needed to be nice. He'd say with an evil chuckle, "I'm always nice." And as soon as he sent her toward the wake, she'd stick that finger in the air and wave it, "Oh no, you di'int!"

That's what we often do when God sends us toward the wake. God says, "Ok, now do this..." And we're throwing our finger in the air, wagging it with sass, and saying, "Oh no, you di'int! No. I can't do that. I'm not qualified to do that. I don't want to do that. I'll suck at that. That does not sound like any fun."

Yes, You Can

Do you know what the number one fear is? Seriously. The number one fear is public speaking. So, when God gave me the knowledge I would be on a stage telling my story, I was more than a little reluctant. I was like, "Oh no, you di'int! I'm not doing that! I am not, I repeat, *not* a public speaker. I trip over my tongue all the time. How the heck would I stand on a stage and talk to a large group of people about the most emotional time in my life? Uh... I think not. Thanks, but no thanks."

But God is persistent and kept encouraging me in "His" own little ways. So, when our youth director put the call out to us adult leaders to share our faith story during an upcoming large-group time at confirmation, I knew the timing of the request was of no coincidence. I had learned that by this point, so I thought, *Ok. Fine! I'll do it and get it over with, ok? Then will you leave me alone? Sheesh.*

I'd been picturing myself up on that stage for months, telling people about my awesome experiences. I knew I was supposed to do it, but I didn't know how to go about it. I mean, really...it didn't sound like much fun. Talking in front of a large group of people never really has been my thing.

Plus, I can cry at the drop of a hat. So, I couldn't believe I was supposed to get up in front of dozens of people and talk about the single most emotional event of my life. How could I get through that? Could I keep from crying enough so the people would be able to understand the words I was trying to get out?

Whose idea was this anyway?

Pretty sure it wasn't mine. But what was I to do...sit around and wait for an invitation?

Oh, wait! I got that too. This was God's invitation addressed directly to me, that I'd been expecting all along.

So, I very hesitantly e-mailed our youth director back and said I would do it. I warned her about my finely honed crying skills.

I wrote it all out, highlighted keywords, and wrote those words out on notecards. There was even a PowerPoint presentation. I was going to try my best and give it all I had. And get it over with. I knew I "had" to do it, so I just wanted to do it and get it over with.

A couple of weeks later, just two days before I was supposed to do my big talk, I was scrolling through my news feed on Facebook. Suddenly, right in front of me on my computer screen was a picture of Dad giving a thumbs up. I couldn't believe what I was seeing. Dad was smiling, looking right at me, giving me a thumbs up!

My cousin had posted the picture of Dad with the caption "R.I.P. Uncle Bernie." She had taken it the day before Father's Day 2008—the day before his aneurysm at Grandma's b-day party. It is probably the last picture ever taken of him, and I received it two days before my talk!

And it's not just a picture. It's a picture of Dad giving a thumbs up.

It was like he was giving me his approval and encouragement.

That was *not* a coincidence. I'm sure there are many people out there who would say that's all it is—a coincidence. But I 100% believe in my heart this was *not* a coincidence. God wanted me to see that, and "He" wanted me to see it at that time.

The weirdest part... My cousin posted the picture in 2008. I saw it for the first time on my newsfeed in November of 2010.

When that picture of Dad giving the thumbs up showed up on Facebook, I knew I was on the right path. *Yep. I'm going to do it. Thanks for the encouragement. Now let's get this over with.*

Two days later, when I started giving the talk, I could hear my voice quivering. My heart was racing, my palms were sweating, and my hands were shaking.

See, God. I told you. I can't do this. I'm not a speaker.

I even looked over at Deb, our youth leader, and said, "I don't think I can do this."

I'm a crier. I'm a crier. I'm a crier.

See, I told her too, God. I'm not good at this kind of thing. Really. Now, do you believe me? I didn't say this out loud, but this, I'm sure, was conveyed in the pathetic look on my face as I looked at Deb with grief-stricken fear.

She just gave me a warm, small smile and said, "You're ok," and nodded her head.

I took in a deep breath and let it out slowly. Things improved after that. I was able to speak, and even in a way people could understand what I was saying. Yay me! I thought for sure I'd be up there sobbing, or my voice would be quivering so bad that no one would be able to understand a word I was saying. But... I did it. I made it to the end.

People clapped. I returned to my seat.

Was I breathing? *Why can't I seem to get my breath? It's over—time to resume normal breathing.* I wasn't sure what would happen if I dared to take a deep breath. I would probably start sobbing uncontrollably. *Ok, fine. We'll just stick with short, shallow breaths for now.*

After our large-group time had ended, several adult leaders came and hugged me. As the first leader came to me, I hugged her and felt a sense of relief, a very brief sense of relief followed immediately by that same constriction in my breathing.

This resulted in...a snort. A very. Loud. Snort.

Oh geez! Really? Let's add some insult to injury here. I didn't even really know this person, and I just snorted louder than I've probably ever snorted in my life...right in her ear.

Then, it finally happened. The tears started coming, and I was gasping for air.

When I went in for that first hug, I finally let my body relax and felt the slightest bit of relief; that's when I heard God again.

"That was a nice start, but you're not done."

Really?! Come on now! That was hard! That took a lot out of me. You're telling me I have to do that again? Or just what are you saying, God? Wait a minute. I don't think I want to know.

When I said I wanted to hear God talk, I didn't mean I wanted "Him" to tell me to do *hard* things. I just wanted "Him" to give me encouragement for the things I wanted to do. Or I wanted him to tell me something to do that I would think is fun, nothing but fun. That. That right there, the standing on stage shaking with my voice quivering. That was not my idea of fun, God. It hurt. It hurt my heart. I didn't *want* to do that again. I wanted to stamp my foot on the ground and protest like a little kid. When I agreed to do that, I didn't realize it would turn into more. That's not fair!

What's really interesting about this story is that's how I remembered it for years. My voice was quivering, and I was on the verge of tears the whole time. But when I dug out the video of that talk just a few months ago, I realized it wasn't nearly as bad as I had remembered it for all those years. I had actually done a much better job than I thought.

We need to understand that The Universe thinks a lot more of us than most of us do about ourselves. The Universe expects those things out of us because The Universe doesn't view the things we think are big as big. They're just things.

Is It Actually Hard?

There's a saying out there that has become trendy lately.

> "I can do hard things."

Now, I understand the purpose of saying this to ourselves. Yes, we can do hard things, but I think a lot of us have started using this for all things—things we maybe don't want to do or we might think will be hard. We have to be careful not to overuse this term. Some of the things aren't actually hard.

Running a marathon. Now I would think of that as hard. Climbing the world's tallest mountain, hard. These would be hard for people, like me, who aren't physically fit enough.

But some things just need some practice—consistent practice.

Meditation isn't that hard. It's just sitting and breathing, people. We do that all the time. We just need to practice stopping the thoughts from ruling our minds. You have a thought. You brush it off. You start again. No sweating. No strenuous muscle strain.

Writing a book. Wow! That would be hard. But there are millions of books written every year! Just because you don't know how to do something doesn't make it hard. Most things just need to be taken one step at a time.

I fear if we call everything we don't want to do hard, it will be our excuse not to do it.

The thing about the things, people, is we don't have to do these so-called "hard" things all alone. No! I was not on the stage alone. I didn't know it at the time, but I was not. As soon as I took that deep, I-can-do-this breath, The Universe/God joined me and got me through it. Yes, God, too, was saying, "Let's get this over with." Only "He" was saying it in a much different tone than I.

For the Love

Now don't let this change your mind about wanting to see and hear God. Please, for the love of God... (Ha! See what I did there?) No *really*, for the love of God, don't let this change your mind. These things—these "hard" things—are why we're here. We just need a little shift to occur in our minds to realize these hard things aren't as difficult as we think they are. That voice in our mind telling us it's so hard is the same voice that won't just be quiet for a minute so we can hear God. That's the voice we need to learn how to shush so we can get on with getting on.

That chatter voice is what can get in your way. Don't let it interfere with The Universe's plan. Don't be that teenage kid who won't just do what you're told. Just move forward. Don't get too focused on the how's.

Have you ever overthought something? Ha! We all do, but we're called to act, not to overthink. Remember, The Universe will help us along the way.

There is a famous quote that has come up a lot for me lately.

"The cave you fear to enter holds the treasure that you seek."
—Joseph Campbell

Read that again. Let it sink in.

"The cave you fear to enter holds the treasure that you seek."

We say we want something, but we aren't willing to take the steps required to get it. Don't let fear keep you from entering the space of what it is you really want.

We might say it's better to be safe than sorry. But I think we might be even more sorry for not trying than we would be sorry for the thing we fear.

What if I told you your joy is on the other side of comfort? God wants you to know just because where you are may feel comfortable, it's not where you belong. Comfort can just mean easy, which can be lazy. Action is usually required. And as long as we don't let some action scare us away, we can be led to our dreams.

If we can block out our fears and preconceived notions, we can be shown things we don't yet see. The more we quiet our fears, the more these things will shine, and this will help us focus on them.

Tune In

What we put importance on isn't what's always important. We may truly believe it is, but our bodies can know the difference if we increase our awareness. We just need to tune in to how our bodies are feeling. The vibration that's held with every thought and idea has deep significance.

There is a difference between the space in us that is of Love and that of the ego. The ego is a scaredy-cat and cannot withstand the pressures of what's to come in the unknown. It can be confusing to decipher it all, but we must ask ourselves when the negative feelings, emotions, and vibrations surface, do we really want to be held hostage by the power of fear?

Love, not fear, is our natural state.

What we need to get through our thick skulls is we are dreaming so much smaller than The Universe is. God knows we're capable of so much more than we can even fathom. So, we need to start dreaming bigger.

Talent is in the hands of everyone if only we would see that. We all need to find our goal contained in our superpower. It doesn't have to be of earth-shaking proportions. We all don't and shouldn't have the same goal. Not everyone is supposed to write a book or start a non-profit. Not everyone is supposed to build houses for the poor. We all have different talents and gifts that should be expressed in different ways.

We need to be content with the dreams and vibrations within our souls. It's all within you. Everything you would ever want to do and can do with the help of The Universe is in you. The power is willing and ready. We just need to put forth a little effort, and we, too, can overcome our obstacles, move mountains, and succeed.

Your superpower was planted in you at the time of your creation. You instantly had everything you needed to do that you wished to do. You need to step up to the fountain of youthful thinking. We're born with that creative belief, but somewhere between birth and seven years old, most of us lost it.

You Are Creative

This space of creative belief is where we're comforted and expanded. We're truly able to feel the joy we're meant to feel. This space is where things are to be shared with one another in a template of curiosity and wisdom. With every breath, step into alignment with creativity and notice the feeling of love and assurance.

We are to be co-creators with The Universe.

Your identity lies in the eyes of God and not in your own or with those around you. Knowing this can bring us to a place of security, peace, and infinite wisdom. The peace that passes all understanding is only found in the spot within you that is of Love. We are to keep shedding light on this part of us. In this space, continue to glow. Our growth is in this space. We are to be co-creators with The Universe. When we stand in the space of doubt, we're outside of the space of Love. The Universe is always inviting us back into the space of Love.

Why do you think you can't do something or you're unworthy? You are the worthiest. That's why God picked you. Yes, *you*. Feel this. Feel the vibration. It's a good one. Let it warm your soul and fuel your fire—the fire this world needs. This fuel can spark peace and understanding. We have the chance to act on behalf of The Universe, to be the antennae to Its signal.

Embrace this knowledge. Stand there in confidence like Wonder Woman or Superman with your hands on your hips, your head held high, proudly showing off that emblem on your chest.

We need to recognize this power within us and know we have the potential to be spectacular. Butterflies cannot see their own wings, but they still fly. They don't continue to crawl as they did as a caterpillar. Butterflies fly even though they can't see what is making them take flight. Those tiny creatures are equipped, and so are you, even if you don't know it yet. God has equipped you to fly.

4

Do. Your. Part.

Act

If I've learned anything on my journey of discovering the loving magic of the world, it's if I'm being nudged to do something, I need to do it. I've learned I shouldn't question any of it. I should just do my part and act. It's all part of the process, the bigger picture. We are *all* part of the process.

The not questioning part can be challenging. I know that. But often, our rebuttal is more exhausting than actually doing the thing we know we need to do. Suck it up, Buttercup. Even when you think you can't do it or don't understand why or how you could do it, do it anyway.

I've been telling people all along, even though I've known I was supposed to write this book for ten years, I haven't always been actively writing. But I've never doubted I would actually write the book. The reason is I don't want to get to heaven at the end of my life and be a disappointment, knowing I didn't do my part I knew deep down I was supposed to do.

Les Brown talks about this. He said, "The graveyard is the richest place on earth, because it is here that you will find all the hopes and dreams that were never fulfilled, the books that were never written, the songs that were never sung, the inventions that were never shared, the cures that were never discovered, all because someone was too afraid to take that first step, keep with the problem, or determined to carry out their dream."[10]

While I knew I would write this book, I also knew I needed to do a lot of inner work to get my deep down beliefs to match up with the idea I could actually do something so vulnerable and be ok with it. So, I've jammed packed myself with as much personal development information I could get my hands, ears, and eyes on.

If you want to accomplish something, you must first expect it from yourself. The way to get to this point is to realize if God puts you up to something, it's because "He" already believes you can do it. And "He" doesn't expect or even want you to do it on your own. The Universe is here to help us do whatever it is we are nudged to do. We just need to tap into that.

Just like Fitz and the Tantrums, God is singing, "I can make your hands clap." And if we're playing along as we should, we would clap on cue to the beat, not stand there and argue. It's way more fun to clap along.

Like a horse, The Universe is leading us to the water, but It can't make us drink. We are thirsty for all to be right with the world, but we are stubborn, and frankly, rather stupid and not drinking. I'm sure it has to be quite frustrating to The Universe to keep leading all these horses to the water they refuse to drink.

Let me just put this out there to you: if something continues to come up for you—no matter where you are in this process—be open, believe there's something to this, and act on a nudge if it continues to show up. (Remember, nudges are a sign you're supposed to pay attention to.) Put it to the test. Is it loving and kind for you, for others, for the world? Then do it!

There can be freedom in your action. Practical and safe is not the way of the free. Don't play it safe and find comfort in the mundane. Venture out into your community and the world. Be bold in living. You won't regret that. There's strife in the things left undone. Find peace in your movement.

Peace

Stay in that state of joy and peace, knowing you are not alone. It can feel lonely in this physical world. But if we find comfort and connectedness in the things we see around us, we can then move on to the joy of connection with all that is good in Love. It's there and available to you. Know your love and peace don't depend on any one person. Love is in the togetherness of all. It's in our connections. Find peace in that knowledge first, appreciate it, and everything else will fall into place. Don't stay in a state of despair. Peace is available for all who are willing to seek it.

Move forward in confidence and know other's actions aren't on your shoulders. Each person has an individual and personal link to The Universe. Move forward in *your space* and find comfort in knowing your actions are all that matter to you. Don't get distracted by the actions of others. Stay in your *own* lane. Do *your* thing.

So, move and act in love today, tomorrow, and always. It's a space you can always return to when you feel lost and off-kilter.

Proclaim there's good in your life, and so it shall be. Seek the good and create together with The Universe.

You can think of yourself as one of many puppets of The Universe. Each of us is playing our unique part.

Don't Put it Off

Top 10 reasons to procrastinate:

#1 ...

Some of us are really good at procrastinating. I'm not innocent, but I've learned if you just get moving, it's so much easier to keep moving. We need to know in continual movement, things are not as difficult.

To get momentum to move, there will always be more resistance and friction. When you're starting from a standstill, there's resistance. It's like pushing a stalled car. To *get* it moving takes a lot more oomph than it does to *keep* it moving. Know once your momentum builds after the initial effort, the movement gets easier.

Our momentum is there when we keep moving and accomplishing. It doesn't matter if everything we do is huge or profound. Just keep spitting things out. Don't expect perfection. Perfection is a curse that kills dreams and accomplishments.

Move. Produce. Be fruitful. Provide and more will be provided to you. Keep producing, and the world will give you success. Just knock, and the door will open.

Forward progress is always where your peace lies. There's a restless feeling in not producing and not doing what you know you ought. A rolling stone gathers no moss. We don't want moss growing on us. Our souls desire a different type of growth. So, keep the stone rolling and move forth.

Progress doesn't have to be at a sprinting pace. Haste can make waste, after all. Just continue at a rate that won't require you to keep starting over with all that extra effort needed to overcome the standstill.

Surrendering to the temptation of anything other than our ultimate goal gets in the way of not producing. Even if what we are doing is being productive, it's not helping us if it's not related to our ultimate goal. It may be something that needs to be done—cleaning out closets, organizing those piles of papers that have sat on your desk for months—but is it moving us in the direction of our ultimate goal? If not, then it's just like standing still.

This lack of forward movement is a different kind of being still than what we seek in meditation. Meditation stillness makes us more efficient, as does movement and productivity. Sit in the stillness of meditation, then move. Sit in the stillness to connect and be led, then follow those leadings.

Act. Do your part. If we would all do this, there would be harmony in the flow of the world. Don't second guess or ask, "What's in it for me?". Acting makes the gears of The Universe turn, and it's then when the conveyor belt moves things to you. We must continue to move the gears.

It's like a bicycle built for two. You can tell when the other person isn't pedaling. When one person isn't pedaling, there's too much effort required by the one left pedaling. They might not reach their destination because the momentum isn't there. Or if they somehow do, it's a struggle. If both people do their part, the momentum builds, and less effort is required. They get places in a fraction of the time, and no one is burned out and tired. So, rather than taking many times longer to get somewhere and maybe risk pissing someone off, do your part and pedal. You don't even have to worry about steering or figuring out which way to go. The Universe will be upfront steering. Pedal together with The Universe and get things done.

Once we know we are to act and move, we can't hesitate. Hesitating can be dangerous. A few years ago, we went to Mexico for spring break with several other families. One day, we went on an excursion off of the resort. At one point, we had the option of climbing up some rocks up to a cliff that stood next to a small river. The river at this spot was deep—deep enough for people to jump off the cliff into the water.

I can be adventurous, but on that day, I wasn't feeling it. Larry and the girls decided to do the jump. I waited in the water at the bottom with a camera in hand. When it was Brooke's turn to jump, I anxiously watched while recording all the action. She started several steps back from the edge of the cliff. She took several small, quick steps, and at the moment when she was supposed to jump, she thought she heard the guide say "no" (he most likely said "go"). She hesitated and tried to stop. If our guide hadn't been there to grab her arm, she probably would've slipped and hit her head on the rock as she fell off the cliff into the water. My heart raced. If she hadn't hesitated, all would have been just fine.

She couldn't see the water from where she was. But sometimes you can't see the water before you jump. It was there. She knew it was. She just couldn't see it.

It's like the famous quote from Martin Luther King, Jr.: "Faith is taking the first step even when you don't see the whole staircase."

So, when you get that nudge, you don't have to know exactly how to do it; you just have to take that first step in faith, knowing and trusting the next step will be shown to you. It can be a process to live in the space of trust and faith—faith in knowing

God will show you what to do next if you just take the first step.

When coincidences blow your mind, that's just a small peek into what God can do with and through you. We are to be creators along with The Universe. We are the hands and feet of God. We need to be the doers, the makers, and the shakers and rattle this world back to Love.

So, go be the doers and not just thinkers. Don't be queens or kings of good intentions. Intentions are good, but only as a start to the action. Don't let the nudges be for naught. Bring them to fruition and see what happens after that.

When we're nudged, it's like The Universe is giving us a car that's all fueled up and running. We can't just sit there in the car and leave it idling, burning gas, and not going anywhere. We need to move when the car shows up. You never know what might come out of your joyride.

You're here to make a difference for someone—for the world. Recognize when you make a difference to one person, you make a difference to the world because we're all connected. Write the letter, make the phone call, write the song or the book. Take that leap that's meant for only you to take. Trust that the water is there. Don't just take up space. That is not your purpose. There's a reason you're here. Just move. You may feel you need to move with grace, confidence, and perfection, but all you really need to do is just move.

Take the first step. Then, take the next first step. Don't even try to figure out how many steps you'll have to take. Just keep taking the next first step; that's all you need to do at this moment, which leads to the next step and next moment.

It's ok to wobble and feel off-kilter. It's ok if it ends up looking different than you think it should. You are strong, and you can move. Let God and this magical Universe move you. Know you're never alone, even when you feel like you are. The saying "If God brought you to it, 'He'll' bring you through it" sounds cliché. But seriously, people! Take the nudge seriously. Big or small, it doesn't matter. Just move in the direction of it.

Don't focus on all the squirrels that can distract you. It's easy. I know! For almost *ten years,* I've been focusing on all the squirrels. Hey! Maybe I'll start an online business. Now I'm going to get a full-time job. I knew full well these things weren't going to help me get to the place I knew I needed to go. I know all about the squirrels, but I don't want to be a squirrel specialist. I want to be a connection specialist. I want to move in the direction that God is pointing me. I want to do the thing. And you know what? I don't even know what the thing is.

I know I am supposed to write this book. I know that's the first step, but I know it's going to lead to something else. I've spent time—too much time—thinking about what could be next. But that's not my job. My job right now, my intention, is just to write the flippin' book and then see where I'm pointed after that. It might be something I can't even fathom right now. It might be something bigger, much bigger than I think I'm capable of. Or it might just be leading to making a difference in one person's life.

All I have to keep telling myself is just to do the thing. Geesh. I am so crazy stubborn. But finally, I'm catching the fire I've been fueling for almost ten years. As I said, I've never doubted I would write the book; I just let too many things get in the way. I let the voice that is not of Love take over. It's stupid!

I could be really ashamed that I've been so incredibly stubborn and affected by fear, but what good would that do me? Shame has no place in the forward progress. Look to the future. Look in front of you and not behind. Looking behind you or even at nothing can be so dangerous. Just look forward to that first step and move.

When we get the idea or nudge, we need to act. Many ideas get passed by while they are being presented. Sometimes things make no sense, but that's where trust needs to come into play. To trust is to have faith The Universe is guiding you and will continue to do so. Trust, and it will be given unto you. Trust, believe, be inspired, and feel the feelings within. When you trust and move, you are moving together with The Universe.

Continued action brings continued ideas. The Universe likes movers and shakers. It likes action. Many people think their idea is just that: *their* idea. But the idea doesn't belong to them. It was only loaned to them, and they need to act on it in partnership with The Universe.

I recently listened to the book *Big Magic* by Elizabeth Gilbert. In it, she talks about this very idea, that the ideas we have or receive do not belong to us, and if we don't act on them in a timely fashion, they might move on and take up residence with someone else. She tells of a book she had an idea for but never actually got around to writing. She later met someone who received that same idea for a book, and that person actually wrote it. It was a very obscure plot, so Elizabeth didn't doubt her inspiration moved on to someone else.

Being present is essential. We need to notice all the things and ideas that surround us. Keep your notebook or notecards handy. These ideas can fly at us at the speed of light. We need to be ready to catch them and act.

If you're not moving your ideas to fruition, they will move on.

When we slow down our action, the ideas slow down. They can't stay still. If you're not moving your ideas to fruition, they will move on. Be grateful for what you receive and know more will always continue to come as long as you act. Don't dawdle. Dawdling is the dulling of the knife that cuts through the forest. To make it through the forest, you need to keep your blade sharp. It's how you continue to pass through the briar and the bush, the weeds and the thistles. The undergrowth can overtake you if you don't keep moving and keep your knife sharp.

Trusting your path exists and that you'll find it is essential to finding the path. Know the path is there to be found.

I love the title of Elizabeth Gilbert's book. *Big Magic*. Because it is big, and it is magic. Google defines magic as: *the power of apparently influencing the course of events by using mysterious or supernatural forces.*[11] That's what this whole book is about. It's about the supernatural forces at work in the world, and we can connect with this. It can be crazy fun!

Don't just sit on the wings of life. Take center stage and believe in your magic—in *the* magic.

Sometimes it feels like we don't have the time to do the things we're nudged to do. Time and oomph are measured differently. Time is very valuable because you can't buy it. You can't create it. You can only manage it. Time needs to be spent on a day to day budget. There are days when it seems as though we have all the time in the world and others—most days—when we feel like we're drowning in our lack of time. Time can seem very elusive, but it doesn't have to be.

We just need to sit our butts down and prioritize. Prioritize what really matters. Do the important things that make up your dreams and goals—the things you know God would be saying to you, "Atta Girl" or "Atta Boy."

Think about your first moments when you're no longer physically on this earth. What will be the things that stand out to you that you did right? Will you regret the time spent with your children, your spouse, all your friends, and your family? No! Will you regret the time you spent to better other people's lives? That's our most precious gift: time spent in Love. In love and joy.

Time can be a burden if you let it. Don't fall into the temptation of all the distractions that can occupy your attention. Just walk past the first temptation and do what you need to do. Focus is a practice, just like in meditation. Distractions come easily and are a dime a dozen, but focus is the key and just takes practice. Move forward with intent. Set an intention every time for progress. That will be your guide.

Move forward. Just keep moving forward. Push the play button. Why are we so fixated on all the other buttons? The pause button, the stop button, the rewind button, or even the fast-forward button. Those buttons aren't going to benefit us. Those buttons take us away from what God knows we can do.

We get paralyzed with fear and push the pause button. We don't seem to be able to move forward to act on the things we know we should act on. We just sit there and stare at it—stare at it in fear. And the longer we stare at it, the bigger the fear grows.

Or we push the stop button. There's no action with the stop button, and there's no acknowledgment of where we are. We can't face up to the facts of our reality. If we just push the stop button, we act like we can't see what's right in front of us. The thing is, we can't get anywhere while stopped. We can't get to the big plot twist that's awaiting us. We can see the plot twist if we just push the play button and move forward. The plot twist will take us to that big wow we're capable of but refuse to consider.

Some of us are so hung up on something that happened to us, we can't stop making ourselves relive it day after day. We push the rewind button and keep viewing what was in our past and never move beyond that. It doesn't matter if what happened in your past was something good or bad; it's in the past, and if we focus only on the past event, we'll never progress to our future. Our future holds such amazing potentials. We need to move forward and keep living. Keep keeping on.

Now, when I say move forward, we need to move that way at life speed, not at a fast-forward pace. So often, we wish away time. We just want to fast forward past a particular event. I get that. I totally get that. Just get past the funeral. Just get past the grief. Just get past the pain. Past the surgery. Past the test. Past the...whatever. There are things in life that suck. There's that fancy word again. They suck, suck, suck, but they're necessary. We just need to keep breathing through these times. These times, these experiences can be soul-sucking and painful beyond belief. But people, we're not alone during these times.

Sometimes, we're so terrified, and we have no idea what to do. We just need to start by breathing. Breathing is our band-aid. Breathing is our guide. It's when we breathe that we can hear that gentle guidance and feel that gentle nudge. If we just sit and hyperventilate, it'll only lead to more hyperventilation. God is present in that slow, calming breath. God is waiting for you to take that slow, calming breath. Just breathe. Sometimes it's our only defense.

And after that breath, we need to move past that moment. It's like when you're in the throes of birthing a child. If you've ever given birth to a child without the glorious assistance of an epidural or some other numbing drugs, you might know the pain that makes you feel like you can't go on, that you're going to die before you ever successfully push that baby out.

I was there with the birth of our first daughter. I literally thought I was going to die if I had one more contraction. So, at that point, would it have been best for me just to lie there and dwell on the pain surging through my body? No. If I didn't push through that pain, I might have been in excruciating pain for hours longer than I needed to. I just told myself the pain was never going to end unless I pushed through it.

Move forward.

Now, I'm not saying this analogy can directly relate to all situations. I'm just saying to keep moving. Don't just sit there in your pain. Feel the pain. Notice how bad it hurts and decide to move anyway. I'm not saying you have to sprint; just move. Sometimes running away is good, but it is not always possible. That's ok. Just move.

So, when God gives you that nudge, stand up and say, "Put me in, Coach. I'm ready to play." Step up to the plate and see how far out of the park you can hit it...with some magical help.

5

God. Will. Steer.

As I said before, we don't have to know how to do what we're trying to do. We don't have to know all the steps or to have it all figured out and do it alone. When you believe The Universe is on your side, it'll be sure to show you the ropes and guide you.

Have you ever noticed some of us are complete control freaks? We have to control every little detail. We stress out about all the little things. Why do we have to feel like we need to control everything?

Like the Serenity Prayer says:

God, grant me the serenity to accept the things
I cannot change...[12]

We need to accept we can't control everything. We don't have to. There are things and will always be things we cannot control. God is happy to be in charge of control. We can just sit back, relax, and enjoy the glorious, beautiful ride without worries.

There's victory in the surrender.

When we're confident in knowing something, there is an assuredness there. But when we feel like we don't know something, self-doubt creeps in. It's then when we're no longer in the land of the sure and safe-footed. But when we acknowledge the peace of Love is always within grasp, we tap into that safe space within us. Keep shedding light on *that* part of you. We can glow in this space that's on the other side of doubt. When we're doubting, we're standing outside the space within us that's of God. We can choose to step back into that space at any and every moment.

God is not elusive; "He" is always present—just like your breath. As long as you're alive, your breath is there.

Most of the time, we're so reluctant because we think what we have to do will require a lot of hard work. But all we really have to do is flow with the current of The Universe. Allow it to move you along. When you're doing your part, you contribute to the flow that's carrying you along. You may not see how this works, but the power is there. Don't fight the power. Don't try to paddle upstream. If you do all your little parts, it's like rowing your boat merrily down the stream.

While you're merrily paddling away, God will nudge you as to which fork in the river to take. Don't see the fork and panic. Don't turn your boat around and try to paddle against the current. Move with the flow. God is providing the current to make your journey more pleasant.

It's like the bicycle built for two analogy I used earlier. You need to do your part with the pedaling, but you can leave the steering up to The Universe.

Have you ever been white water rafting? Think of your guide in the raft as God. "He" yells out whenever you're supposed to do something. "He" tells you when to paddle and when not to paddle. "He" never makes you steer the raft all by yourself. "He'll" let you know when to paddle on the left and when to switch to the right. You just have to do as instructed, and all is fine and dandy.

All you have to do is believe you have a guide in the boat helping you. You're not manning it alone.

I used to tell my confirmation girls having faith and believing in God doesn't just mean you believe there is a God; it means you believe in what God can and will do for you. Have that kind of faith.

I love the T.V. show F•R•I•E•N•D•S. I know I already said that, but I quote it all the time. Here's one for you. In the one where Ross is trying to teach Rachel and Phoebe about self-defense and unagi, Ross attempts to explain to them about this state of total awareness. Later, when they have him pinned to the floor, they say, "Tell us we are unagi." And he says with his face pressed up against the floor, "It's not something you are; it's something you have."

What I'm telling you is you have this. You have this within you, within your reach. It's the love and power of God. Let this power help you.

You don't have to take off in flight from a hole in the ground. You can take off from much higher up. It's much easier to fly this way.

Remember, God is in that calm, loving feeling of joy. Everything feels so much better and easier when we operate in this state. Practice it often. Feel the smile. This feeling of joy lifts you higher and makes your take off much easier. When we're not feeling good, we're at a low point. It's possible to take off from this low point, but it's a lot more work. Tap into the calm, loving feeling of joy, feel uplifted, and ease into your flight.

Don't overthink things. We're capable of so much when we work together with The Universe. The powers are all around you, not just in you. Many people think all they have to work with is what's within them. But God has dominion. "He" has staff.

God isn't just the creator, but "He" wants to co-create with you. If we were all as obedient as nature, there would be no doubt in Love. Ask for help and use it when it shows up. Don't expect to know how it will show up. Recognize the many ways.

Don't be like the guy sitting on his roof during a flood.

> A fellow was stuck on his rooftop in a flood. He was praying to God for help.
>
> Soon a man in a rowboat came by and the fellow shouted to the man on the roof, "Jump in, I can save you."
>
> The stranded fellow shouted back, "No, it's OK, I'm praying to God and he is going to save me."
>
> So, the rowboat went on.
>
> Then a motorboat came by. The fellow in the motorboat shouted, "Jump in, I can save you."
>
> To this the stranded man said, "No thanks, I'm praying to God and he is going to save me. I have faith."
>
> So, the motorboat went on.
>
> Then a helicopter came by and the pilot shouted down, "Grab this rope and I will lift you to safety."
>
> To this the stranded man again replied, "No thanks, I'm praying to God and he is going to save me. I have faith."

So, the helicopter reluctantly flew away.

Soon the water rose above the rooftop and the man drowned. He went to Heaven. He finally got his chance to discuss this whole situation with God, at which point he exclaimed, "I had faith in you, but you didn't save me, you let me drown. I don't understand why!"

To this God replied, "I sent you a rowboat and a motorboat and a helicopter, what more did you expect?"[13]

We need to be open as to how God will show up and help.

We need to be open as to how God will show up and help.

Let me throw a couple of cheesy analogies your way.

God gives you a box with a puzzle in it. You know you're supposed to put it together. You sit and stare at the box. You notice it has a lot of the same colors in the picture. You know it will be really hard and take a very long time.

You look closer at the box. It has 4,000 pieces!

OMG! No way!

This puzzle is way too hard!

I can't do it!

I'm not going to do it!

This will take way too long!

I'm getting a headache just thinking about it.

I think I'd rather do this other puzzle over here, this one of a cute little puppy dog that only has five pieces. It looks nice and easy. I know *I can do this one. I could even do this one in the dark.*

If we would just open the box of the big, scary puzzle and ask, "How do I do this, God?", "He'll" hand you a baggie with all of the edge pieces, and there will be a note on the bag that says "START HERE."

And after you have the edges all put together, you ask, "Now what?"

He hands you another bag and says, "I've sorted out all of the sky pieces for you."

Don't expect to know what your puzzle will look like when it's finished. Let God help you put it together. "He" drew the picture.

The puzzle you hold is not yours to put together on your own. We're not alone. Want help? All you gotta do is ask. Figure out the now and be shown the how.

Or here's another one.

You have a pile of rocks you're supposed to move from point A to point B. They're big, heavy rocks. You groan, but one by one, you start picking them up and carrying them to their destination.

Meanwhile, God is standing beside you with the handle of a wagon in "His" hand. But it's like you have blinders on, and you don't even know "He" is there.

God starts whistling to try to get your attention, but you can't hear "Him" because you're too busy mumbling to yourself how not fun this is.

You get a bright idea that it'll go faster if you carry two rocks at a time. You start this new and improved method.

Now, God starts pulling the wagon back and forth right across your path, but you're just agitated that this wagon is in your way. Every time you cross that spot in your path, you have to wait for that stupid wagon to move out of your way.

After a couple of trips, you start to get tired and dirty from the rocks. As you wait for the wagon to move out of the way yet again, you get the idea to put the rocks in the wagon. That way you won't get so dirty.

What a great idea! *I'm so smart to have found this wagon all by myself.*

So, you put several rocks in the wagon. You'll be able to move more than two rocks at a time this way! You get excited about your new plan.

You pick up the wagon and carry it to point B.

THE WAGON HAS WHEELS, Ding-a-ling!

If you had simply asked before you ever started, God would've shown you "His" fancy, red wagon with wheels. And you wouldn't be dirty and tired.

God is more than willing to help us out. We just need to trust "He" will. Often, we don't see our answer immediately, so we come up with our own way of doing things. Our ultimate success lies in our trust. Allow God to steer and to guide you on your journey. You may not know where the path will lead you, but you must trust God and The Universe to guide you to love, happiness, and good things. That joyous feeling I keep talking about, that tingling feeling of joy, can work tremendously for the good of your future.

A while back, I heard the story of Charles Blondin. He was a tightrope walker. In the summer of 1859, he walked several times back and forth on a tightrope stretched between the United States and Canada, 160 feet above Niagara Falls, while huge crowds of people watched in awe.

> Once he crossed in a sack, once on stilts, another time on a bicycle, and once he even carried a stove and cooked an omelet.
>
> On July 15, Blondin walked backward across the tightrope to Canada and returned pushing a wheelbarrow.
>
> The Blondin story is told that it was after pushing a wheelbarrow across while blindfolded that Blondin asked for some audience participation. The crowds had watched and "Ooooohed" and "Aaaaahed!" He had proven that he could do it; of that, there was no doubt. But now he was asking for a volunteer to get into the wheelbarrow and take a ride across the Falls with him!
>
> It is said that he asked his audience, "Do you believe I can carry a person across in this wheelbarrow?" Of course, the crowd shouted that yes, they believed!
>
> It was then that Blondin posed the question - "Who will get in the wheelbarrow?"
>
> Of course...none did.[14]

Even if we believe God can do great things and believe in the magic, we don't always trust it'll work for us. We let fear take over. That's not faith.

Remember what I said about faith: "Believing in God doesn't just mean you believe there is a God; it means you believe in what God can and will do for you." There is *such* a big difference. That's the *true* definition of having faith.

The love and "magic" of God surrounds you and is in you to guide you forward. Connect and trust.

When Larry and I were engaged, we decided it might be good to take dance lessons since all eyes would be on us at our wedding. So, we used the yellow pages—yes, I'm that old—and found a dance studio that would give us private lessons. We just wanted to learn enough not to look stupid during our first dance as husband and wife.

We learned we have a style all our own that doesn't follow any formal rules or steps. We took away one thing, though, that we still apply today after being married for twenty-seven years: the finger in the back trick.

This method is only applicable when we're slow dancing, which isn't very often. Basically, when Larry is leading, and we're doing our usual swaying back and forth while slowly spinning clockwise, if he wants to be crazy and mix it up a little, to have me move toward him, he'll take one finger and press it into my back ever so slightly. This signals me to know I'm to move toward him.

It works! That's why we still use it after all these years. Well, that little finger in the back can be how God nudges us. It may be ever so slight, but once we become accustomed to it, we know when it happens, that's our cue to move, to change direction. Don't be afraid to dance with The Universe. It's really good at leading and won't steer you wrong.

The Universe is like your GPS. Instead of calling it a global positioning system, think of it as your very own God Positioning System. God chooses the best route for you to get where you want or where "He" wants you to go.

"He'll" direct you every step of the way. Even when you take a wrong turn and go a different way than the way "He" told you to go, "He's" continually recalculating. "He" will tell you to make a legal and safe U-turn if you're off track.

God is always willing and ready to tell us which way to turn, but we constantly ignore "Him." We're continually putting The Universe into recalculation mode.

"Recalculating. Recalculating."

We have the ability to tap into the greatest navigational system in the world. The most direct path is to listen to God first and do what "He's" telling us to do. It's not rocket science; it just needs to be in our awareness. When we know where we are and think we know where we want to go, all we seem to be able to focus on is the destination.

There's a path in-between we continue to ignore. We can't just teleport ourselves to the final destination. We need to follow the kind, loving voice that is directing us and trust it'll get us there.

Unlike the navigation systems in our phones or cars that sometimes lead us astray or is uninformed of road closures and new roads, The Universe is always in the know. It knows all there is to know, and we don't have to worry. We just need to trust.

"Turn left."

"But why on Earth would I ever want to turn left? Clearly, I should be turning right. I can see my destination just over the horizon to the right."

But what the GPS knows and we don't is going left is actually the more direct way to get there.

Why do we ignore it? It's all-knowing. Do you really think you know more than the All-Knowing? Psshh. Wake up and smell the jumbo grande caramel macchiato!

It doesn't have to be our job to figure it all out. So many of us think we have to have every single step mapped out before we even begin to move. It's only the first step we need to know. What we think are steps two, three, and four may be something totally different. We just can't see the real step two until we are well-planted into step one. And like Brooke jumping off the cliff, we might not be able to see it until we've already jumped.

Trusting is hard. Trust me, I know. We feel doubtful. We reflect on previous regrets we have, and we tend to live in that space. That space is full of fear. *Oh, but I can't do it that way. Remember what happened before?* Chances are, whatever steps you took to land in that spot of regret happened when you ignored the GPS, and you were going on your own ideas.

Let your God Positioning System call the steps one by one. If you aren't sure how to go about the first step, ask. Ask and be aware. When we ask, God is really good at answering. We usually can't come up with the right answers by ourselves. The unknown can often seem larger than the terrifying present.

Your way is your path and for you alone. It might not look like anyone else's path.

Don't let other people's paths or routes throw you off. Your way is your path and for you alone. It might not look like anyone else's path. So, when you see someone taking a different way as you stroll merrily along, have no worries. They are on their own path.

And if your road gets a little bumpy, don't assume you're off course or your GPS is broken. It might just be a short cut.

6

All. For. Love.

This thing we're doing here on planet Earth, this thing called life, is All. For. Love.

We're here to love and care for one another. The meaning of the word "love" is so much deeper than most people think.

Love is our only fluid emotion. It flows through us at all times, whether it's of lack or plenty. Love is a connection—a warming of the soul. The soul cannot be touched by any other way than Love; it's the language of the soul and what the soul craves.

Sometimes, when we're not connected to the Love of The Universe, we try to fill this craving with something else that often turns into addictions: shopping, gambling, drugs, alcohol, etc. We get a rush, but the thrill is short-lived, so we need more. It doesn't matter how much we take in; it'll never fill the spot in the soul that craves that loving connection with The Universe. We're looking for love in all the wrong places.

The soul sings at the sound of Love. The caringness of humanity lives in the song of Love.

Love cannot come from anything other than our beingness of God—being one with God. Our soul is the part of us that will never die and is the part of us that is God. Since God is Love, our soul only understands the language of Love. All other emotions are either rooted in love or are a lack of love.

What drives you? The thing that drives you will either help you thrive or force you into the ground. Thriving is flying in all that is Love. It includes all. All people. If your thriving runs on any single person's suffering, it's actually driving you into the ground.

Review your actions. What are you doing for others? Are you holding others in the space of Love? Can you try harder? We can never love too much.

Love is like a less-than sign. <. It starts small and only grows larger as it moves forward. There's no cap as to how much it can grow. Growing in kindness and love is the key to life. There's always room for growth. Growth always shows in love.

Bitterness because of lack of love isn't going to grow you. The focus cannot be on your bitterness toward others. Love is the only thing that can overcome bitterness.

The field of Love is impenetrable. As long as love continues to grow and doesn't stagnate, it becomes an unwavering force that grows people. Other people need your love. Never hide it somewhere it can't be seen. Let your light shine among others.

Be shiny and sparkly and magical.

I once heard glitter is the herpes of the crafting world because you can never get rid of it. That's also true of the authentic light of Love. Love never fails because it always overcomes anything less than it. If you always error on the side of Love, you will always come out safe.

Caution doesn't mean to sit still in silence because of fear. I want to be clear on that. It doesn't mean to be silent and avoid conflict. If your silence leads to someone else's pain, then you're doing it wrong. Stand up for Love, even in the face of fear. Love will always be on your side.

The truest form of love is the love God has for us because God is Love. He's going to get it right.

Love never needs to be held in a stranglehold. That isn't true love. Like 38 Special sings, "Hold on loosely, but don't let go." True love is free-flowing. When people interpret love in their own skewed way, you get a mumbled up, jumbled up mess.

To love as it's intended is to love all. Love each other despite—and actually more accurately, *because of*—your differences. If people can appreciate that, then they can grasp Love.

Interpretations that differ can really muck things up. It's like playing the telephone game or having three different eyewitness accounts of an incident. The end story can be very, very different. Only a clear mind can account for the truth—a mind that isn't cluttered.

Clearing our minds of those other voices, whether it's your own voice that's living in fear or that of others, is the way to hear the voice of Love that matters.

Some people try to take the love of The Universe, of God, and turn that against others. That isn't God's love. That doesn't resemble God's love in any way, shape, or form. Universal Love is for all. We need to find peace in that. Why would God distribute love differently to pit people against each other? That's not how it works. Love is for the togetherness of all.

In this day and age, where transportation and technology are so advanced, you would think that would bring the world together. Instead, it's destroying humanity because of the twisting and maiming of what people call God's love. Humanity is a connectedness amongst us all—God included. God is in you as "He" is in everyone. We need to love that part of everyone.

It's like the saying: no tree would be so foolish as for the branches to fight amongst themselves. That would only be killing itself. In order to thrive, the branches must create space for each other. Nurture each other. Live in harmony amongst each other. There cannot be Love in any other state.

So many think they're doing it right and believe they're being just. But often, the love they think is there is not because they're not being fair to all. They're not being just in a together fashion, as it should be. Instead, they're contributing to the wrongness of love. We see glimpses of people getting it right. Some get it much right-er than others. But the love is fleeting and is quickly shoved out and replaced with judgment.

It's understandable. There can be frustrations. It's a difficult thing to try to navigate. People are stubborn. They're uncompromising in their differences when they need to be stubborn in Love. Love is what conquers it all.

The epitome of love lives in an unconditional state.

Just try to imagine it.

Try to feel it.

Have you ever felt a love in you that has brought you to tears?

Like I've said before, I am a crier. Any other criers in the house?

A love that brings you to tears is an awesome feeling. This is the space I've been traveling to ever since I've been on this journey of viewing The Universe differently. This love is expansive. It is ginormous, people! And even if you feel just a small fraction of this love whenever you experience a coincidence-that-isn't-a-coincidence (a Godincidence), you will know you're not alone.

This love is seeking you. You just need to be receptive to it.

I don't care who you are or what you've done or failed to do; you are worthy of this love.

Whatever you would want for those you love most, want it for all. Want the love in you for all creation. Creation is life and love in the fullest form.

Feel the love inside you and be present in that feeling. The feeling of love is where it's at—rejoice in the presence of that moment. Don't ever feel your best days are behind you. Always know there's an opportunity for growth and compassion. Compassion expands the world. It expands creation.

There are many ways to connect to this love. Find your Universal love language. Feel it and find joy in it. But always continue to explore the possibilities of connection. Learn and explore. Never stop learning and seeking and finding Love in all forms. Feel it in the presence of every moment.

Let every moment shine with the love and feel it deep down, bubbling up like a percolator. Experience the bubbles rising and explode into happiness beyond measure. Share it with the world and continue to grow; it's a gift. It'll multiply like a flame, spreading over the oceans and into the stratosphere. There are no boundaries for this love. Let it seep out and ignite someone's fire that has gone out.

Always, always share the love and feel the presence of the love of The Universe everywhere that can be imagined and know it extends far beyond your reach.

Find comfort in knowing Love knows no bounds. Share it with one, share it with the masses. Don't pass over anyone. Where there is enough for one, there is enough for all.

Things flow in and out of our lives constantly. It's happening day and night, whether you notice it or not. People continually flow in and out of our lives too. Be ok with that. Know there's a time and a reason for everything. Some departures hurt way more than others. It wouldn't hurt if, at first, you didn't love. Love is the gift.

Sometimes, you just need to walk away. Avoid. Not partake. It's all a part of life, and the beauty of it is we always have a choice. Choosing with a loving and kind mindset is a gift. Loving and kind. To ourselves and all others affected.

The earth is included in our realm of relationships. Everything's connected and tied together with the realm of Love. How you treat the earth is directly related to how you treat your loved ones. How you treat the earth determines how future generations will live their lives and pursue their purpose. Let's make it easier for the world to love everyone in it.

Always, always, always error on the side of Love. Love is a quantitative thing. It grows and multiplies with every little act. It grows and blossoms wherever you go. Fertilize that Love planted by other people. Work together in harmony in Love. It's like from the '80s song "Ebony and Ivory." I'm not talking just as black and whites, but as humanity, nature, and the universe as a whole.

We need to love like it's our only job. Everything else just falls into place when you focus on Love. If you see anything other than Love, don't fuel it. Always continue to focus on Love. It's like when we are practicing meditation; we're trying to silence and not fuel the chatter. Like we try to fuel the silence in meditation, we need to focus on only fueling the Love in life.

Martin Luther King Jr. wrote, "Hate cannot drive out hate; only love can do that."[15] What an awesome quote. There's great power in those words. Think about it; if you and someone don't agree on something, do you think if they continue to get angrier, you will finally come around to see it their way? No. No one can learn in that state. Anger can only fuel people not to want to buy into that way of thinking or being.

Love is to light as hate is to darkness. If it's too dark to see, can you see better by adding more darkness? No. Only light overcomes the darkness, and only Love overcomes the hate. They say darkness isn't a thing but is the absence of light. Could that be true for hate and love also?

Hate, many say, is a powerful word. But hatred is just the absence of love. Some people also say apathy is worse than hate. Hate is the absence of love, and apathy is the absence of both love and hate. Love is the only way to overcome them both. It's the solution for the world, but we continue to focus on other things. On control. Maybe if we focused on love, there would be no need for control.

If there's someone you think you could never agree with or love as they are, know you can always send love their way. Send them love in thought and prayer. Love is the only thing that will change or better a situation or relationship. They don't even have to know about it. Just quietly, peacefully, and genuinely send love in their direction.

No one will ever always be on the same page about everything. Never. But adding in hate is never going to bring anyone together. Some might say, "Well, I don't want to be brought together with them. They don't feel the same way I do." And believe me, no one understands that more than I do. But really, you know how they ask beauty pageant contestants the question of what is most important in the world, and the cliché answer is world peace? Really. World peace would organically fix so many of the other issues in the world. Love and peace. Ah. "Imagine" by John Lennon. Really. Just imagine.

Titles and labels don't serve us. They only create more divisiveness. People assume too much when there are titles or labels. Politics and religion are two very pointed examples. If you claim a title of sorts for either of these, most people will assume they now know how you stand, what you think, and how you believe. How can that be? How can people and all of their beliefs fall either into this category or that category? How? It just baffles me. People might even adopt an opinion that's not actually in their belief set simply because it goes along with the label they have adopted.

Imagine there're no labels, no assuming of beliefs. Imagine we just loved and accepted humanity.

The energy of love and compassion is contagious. It spreads like wildfire.

The magic of Love around us can be magical beyond belief. That's what makes it so fun. That shock and awe factor. In awe, not fear. Awe. AWEsomeness. There is immense feeling in it. Use this feeling to determine your "why" in everything you do. Let your "why" be because of Love.

When I was going through the dragging-my-feet stage of writing this book, I had a shift when I focused not just on the act of getting the book written, but I started focusing on you, the reader, and how I truly want to better everyone's life who reads this book. I want everyone to shift how they view the world.

Wow! Holy BLEEP! omG! The expansive Universe is here to shock and awe us—to serve us.

The Universe is willing and ready to help and serve us, especially when our goal is to love, serve, and connect.

Connections are the root of life, and the roots give you life. I don't mean roots as in your background or heritage. I'm talking about connections. Connections with God, nature, people. Family, friends, strangers. There is nothing better than feeling connected. Connections give us fuel. It's why we're here. We're not created to be hermits who live in the woods and never interact with others.

There's an interdependence in our connections with people. We have more needs than food, shelter, and clothing. Love. Love is one of our greatest needs. Love is needed not just to thrive but to survive. That's what God is. God is that love and the feeling of that love. God isn't just a noun. God is also a verb. God is the giving of and receiving of love between one another.

Love doesn't have to come from an intimate relationship. It can come from the smallest of interactions with a stranger: a smile or assisting someone in opening a door. Really put feeling into these actions and feel a difference in appreciation. The more you appreciate, the more you receive. Giving and receiving is the flow of life.

It doesn't make one noble to give, give, give of themselves, and never receive. Receiving is just as important. When someone does something for you, accept it, receive it. When they say something positive to you, take it in. Soak it into the part of you that's dependent on these connections. It's the part of you that grows in our oneness. It's a connection to the oneness, the namaste of us.

Namaste is the love we are supposed to have for one another—to see our similarities, not our differences.

Namaste is the love we are supposed to have for one another—to see our similarities, not our differences. The differences are not the parts that matter. It's the love in the similarities that matter the most. Love it. Accept it. Flow with it. It's always there between us, but society, the world, the patterns we create have pushed us away from this.

A life that's lived in Love is not competitive. There's way too much focus in this world on competing. It's the togetherness in peace and love that's the jam in this world.

I'm going to tell you something about me that's going to sound awful. Really awful. But hear me out. When tragedy strikes in the world, I get excited. Massive destruction, tornados, 9/11. Yes, 9/11. As in September 11, 2001.

Why? How could I possibly feel excitement in someone else's tragedy? It's because of the connectedness that happens at such times: the shared empathy, the prayers that happen, the helping that occurs. And the healing that eventually occurs.

Even when you feel helpless in such a tragic moment because of logistics, resources, and physical abilities, you can pray. You can feel. You can empathize. That's Love, people. That is God. God is in that love of every single exchange that happens.

So, no. I don't like tragedy or seeing people suffer. Like I've said, I'm a crier. I'm a feeler. I am empathetic to a fault, but in these times, I see love. I see people functioning as God intended. And it's AWEsome.

This is how we do it right. I've talked a lot about how some people like to tell us we're doing something wrong and how I don't want to tell someone how they should do something because there are many different ways of doing things, and what works for one person may not work for someone else, but...

> <u>If you hate someone because of your religion, you're doing it wrong.</u>

I've known from square one I didn't want this book to be about religion. I want it to be about God/The Universe and the magic around us. But the two tend to go hand in hand.

I have to say this, though. This statement of hate in the name of religion. If this is the case for you...

<u>You're doing it wrong.</u>

I love the scene from the movie *Mr. Mom* when Michael Keaton's character is dropping off his kids at school for the first time. It's pouring rain, and the kids are telling him he's doing it wrong. All the other cars are honking at him. He asks why they are all honking, and his son tells him once again, "Because you're doing it wrong." Then the crossing guard, in her yellow rain suit, comes up to his window and says, "You're doing it wrong."

So, I was joking before when I told you there's only one way to make a peanut butter and jelly sandwich, but I'm not joking when I say if your religion teaches you to hate others, you are doing it wrong.

We are to love one another.

Your love for others is your shine.

It is imperative to keep shining. People need to see your God-light. This abundant love needs to be shared—shared and enjoyed by all. Everyone shines differently. Everyone needs to see different kinds of love. As individually unique as it may be, it's always there inside everyone. They just need to find a way to let it out.

This little light of mine... I'm gonna let it shine.

One year when I was a teenager, I was at Christmas Eve service with my family. And one of the most awesome things about Christmas Eve service is the candles. Not just the candles up front and by the altar, but they actually trust everyone to hold an actual real-life lit candle. Open flame! Crazy, isn't it?

But this particular year, they encouraged everyone to carry their lit candles out into the world—into the night. I don't recall how this worked since this was Iowa. We surely had to wear coats. How did we put on our coats holding lit candles? This, along with a myriad of other reasons, is probably why this was the only year I ever remember doing that. Anyway... My brother, Mark, and I were walking out into the night with our lit candles, and we started singing "This Little Light of Mine." So, I'm singing away.

"Put it under a bushel? No! I'm going to let it shine....

Don't let Satan blow it out..."

And I swear we did not blow out our candles, but both of our candles were extinguished with a gust of wind at the same time. My mouth dropped open in utter shock!

"Oh, no! Satan blew out my candle! How am I supposed to let it shine?"

I'm telling you now. What some people call Satan—or what I like to call self-doubt or fear—is blowing candles out left and right. "He" LOVES blowing out people's light.

Fear and doubt are the voice in my head who talked all the negative talk. It's the one who incessantly tried to talk me out of writing this book. It was the voice inside my head who wasn't God. Just like darkness isn't actually a thing. Darkness is the absence of light; Satan is what can happen in the absence of God/Love. We need to focus and hang on with all our might to the love in the world and within us.

Let's share it and point it out to each other. Be the light for others when they need it. It's like on Christmas Eve when the flame of one candle lights all the other candles in the church. If one candle goes out, all you have to do is tip it back to a lit candle, and it shines again. So, when "Satan" blows out your candle, you just have to relight it.

People need to focus on Love. Hate and fear can't exist in the presence of Love. Darkness can't exist when a light is shining. Ignite the light in your soul, and Love prevails. That's why noticing all the signs all around you every day is what will grow the love and diminish the hate and fear. FOCUS.

Plan. Plan ahead for when things can creep in. Have tools to arm yourself with to ward off the negativity in your head and the world. It'll change you, and it'll change the world.

We need to hone in on the things that should be done, not focus on the things that are and have always been done. Peace is in the space of doing things for love. Love is a template for all actions to be taken. It is a privilege to be on the planet, let alone be able to influence and change it. We need to stand tall in the fight against hate and corruption.

We need to do what is in the heart. Sometimes, something might not make sense financially, but it won't matter if things are done from the heart through love. The Universe will find a way to make it happen. All the things done in love need to be done.

The force is a power so strong, and when something is done in conjunction with Love, it is AWEsome. It can be mind-blowing. When some of your Godincidences blow your mind, that's just a small peek at what God can do for you, with you, *and through you*!

Succumb to the pressures of love. The opportunities surround you. Open your eyes and your heart to see and feel the love.

Tremendous joy will move you. Spread the love like the movement of a butterfly. It's like a dance. Presence with love and each other can find great liberation.

Love all people where they are, where they stand—broken or whole. Everyone needs to be loved as they are. That's what will help them to get to where they would rather be. Love wholeheartedly. Love as we are loved.

I've told you song lyrics really speak to me at times. What blows my mind is when I hear a song I've known for years or even decades, and I hear the words I thought I knew but didn't.

For the last several years, we've gone with friends to a cabin in Michigan. The lake the cabin is on is the most beautiful water I've seen that wasn't the ocean or the gulf. While we're there, we spend most of our time out on our friends' boat. They have the kind of boat that can throw a wake you can surf on. Once you find the sweet spot, you can toss the tow rope back into the boat and just surf away. I haven't found the sweet spot yet, but I think this is my year!

Many of us have a surfing song we prefer to listen to when it's our turn to surf. A couple of years ago, Larry, who's a stud at surfing, chose "Higher Love" by Steve Winwood. It's a song from the mid-'80s, so I've probably heard it about a thousand times. I've heard it repeatedly the last couple of years since Larry chose it to be his song. I purchased the song to have it in my playlist, in case I'm spinning the tunes on the boat.

A couple of weeks ago, it came on the radio (which was no coincidence), and a couple of lyrics jumped out at me. So, when I got home, I Googled the lyrics. OMG! I'm not sure what I thought this song was about, but it's clearly about the love I've been talking about here. I originally thought it was about romantic love and finding a better someone to be his soulmate.

Wrong!

Look up the words! Seriously!

I'd put the lyrics here, but...copyright laws.

Without love, life is nothing more than wasted time. We walk blindly, trying to see yet failing to comprehend what could be.

Without tapping into this love and magic in the world, we're wasting our time. There is so much power we can connect with if we see it and try. The Universe is here to love, support, and help us. If we don't tap into it, we'll fall behind in what could be.

This kind of stuff just makes me giddy!

7

Join. The. Party.

Join the party! Join this magical party. Let this book be your invitation to the party. It's an invitation from me to you. Better yet, an invitation from The Universe, from God to you. It's the best party ever! Complete with party hats and horns, cake and ice cream, and even magical pixie dust floating through the air.

I'm writing this chapter while riding in the car. Larry is driving, but while I was driving on this bright, sunshiny February day, I noticed little dots of rainbow light on the speedometer. It took me a second to figure it out, but I realized those beautiful dots of light were coming from the sun bouncing off of my ring.

I love rainbows. It's not just that I think they are super pretty, but I'm actually in awe of the magic of them.

I remember as a kid in elementary school when we learned about rainbows in science class. We had little three-inch prisms. Our teacher told us that light—white light—has all the colors of the rainbow in it. What? How could that be?

When the white light hits the prism, it bends and reveals all of its true colors. The concept still fascinates me. All the different colors are there, but we just can't see them until the light is bent and BOOM! Suddenly, all the different colors are revealed.

This is kind of like how this journey of mine of bending how I view the world has changed how everything looks. A renewing of the mind has led me to see shiny, bright "rainbows" everywhere. Some are small, and some take up the whole sky. And now, I know they've been there all along; I just couldn't always see them. Even now, when I think I can't see any rainbows, they're still there.

For us to see things, there has to be light and within that light is the potential to see rainbows. It's always been there and will continue to be there. It's all in how you view it. So, let's all take our prisms out of our pockets and let the rainbow light shine through.

Sounds like a party to me. One with fireworks and sparkles in the air, cascading all around like magic pixie dust. There is magic all around. Expect it, and see it.

It's like Dorothy at the end of *Wizard of Oz* when Glinda the Good Witch tells her she always had the power. Or when Austin Powers figures out at the end of *The Spy Who Shagged Me,* he had his mojo all along. You have the power to tap into the magic; you just need to believe it. You need to believe there's magic in the air, and it will be. You'll see it.

Live in that place of joy. Think happy thoughts like Peter Pan, and you can fly.

Believe. It is a powerful word.

I'm going to throw another song at you: "Hot, Hot, Hot" by Buster Poindexter. It's a fun one I've recently added to my Pick-Me-Up playlist.

People who come to the party of life knowing what they've got? They're hot, hot, hot!

Come to the party and know what you've got.

Just jump in!

It's like hopping on the spinning merry-go-round or jumping into the spinning jump rope. Eventually, you just have to jump and shoot the gap, as my dad would always say. Shoot the gap into silencing your fears. Fears are continually coming at you like the bars on that merry-go-round. The spaces between the bars are where you're trying to land. When you get in rhythm with the spin, you'll be in sync with the bars that keep passing by. That's what all this work—these practices—do for you. They get you in sync with The Universe that will keep spinning whether you grab on or not.

You don't want to sit the ride out and then listen to everyone else talking about how great and fun the ride was. It's like not wanting to ride the roller coaster because you're so scared of what might and probably won't happen. Then you sit there while your friends go on the roller coaster. Your friends get off the ride, and they're giddy, talking a mile a minute about how exhilarating that ride was. They are walking faster. They are talking faster. And you struggle just to keep up as they trot along to the next ride. Join the group. Take the ride. Get in sync and enjoy the ride. Join the conversation. Be a part of the "Woo Hoo's" and the "Oh my God's" and the "That was soooo AWEsome's!"

There may be times when it doesn't seem as fun as I am making it sound, but remember, before you take the plunge on the roller coaster or jump on the sled at the top of the snowy hill, there's the trudge to the top. As with the roller coaster, your emotions may be continually up and down. But it's all worth the exhilarating ride!

But it's all worth the exhilarating ride!

It's more fun than you can imagine!

Be a super soul on fire and...

Join! The! Party!

Don't forget to share with me all your woo hoo, AWEsome moments.

Email me!

mystory@michelleprohaska.com

Or you can submit them on our website:

www.michelleprohaska.com

Holy BLEEP! That was NOT a Coincidence

Discussion Questions

***This is a partial list of questions.
Make your discussion even better!
Go to https://www.michelleprohaska.com/free-resources/
for the full, downloadable, printable list.

Part IV – You. Are. Being. Nudged

1. Have you felt nudges from The Universe to do something?
2. Do you think God "talks" to you?
3. Do you think The Universe will guide you if you ask?
4. ACTION – Share. Your. Story. – Do you have a Godincidence story that you could share now with the group? Send it in an e-mail to Michelle? Please! We really do want to hear your story. mystory@michelleprohaska.com
5. Do you believe your thoughts create your reality?
6. ACTION STEP – Write "IT COULD HAPPEN!" (notice the exclamation point) on a sticky note or piece of paper. Stick or tape it up somewhere you will see it multiple times in a day.
7. ACTION STEP – Write an oath to yourself stating how you will move when you are nudged.
8. Have you ever ignored God before?
9. Is there someone that you "hate"? How can you put them in a different light so that you can send them love?
10. Namaste – The next time you pass a stranger, think "Namaste. The part of me that is of God/Love recognizes and honors the God part in you.

Discussion Questions?

There is a partial list of questions
at the end of each part.

For a full, **pretty**, downloadable list of questions, visit:

https://www.michelleprohaska.com/free-resources/

-Or-

Get the
Interactive Video Book Club Experience at

www.michelleprohaska.com/courses

To read is one thing.
To do is another.

Apply what you have learned.
Start with one of the How To's from Part III.

Connect with me. - Let's be friends!

Follow me on **social media.**
@micmopro on Facebook, Instagram, Pinterest.

Join my **free private Facebook group**, Not a Coincidence,
for community and action steps.
https://www.facebook.com/groups/notacoincidence

Sign up for my **newsletter**
to hear about all the latest offerings.
www.michelleprohaska.com/newsletter

E-mail me.
hello@michelleprohaska.com

Share YOUR story.
mystory@michelleprohaska.com

Take a class with me. 

For the latest fun learning opportunities, visit:
www.michelleprohaska.com/courses

Take the quiz.

Are you getting the most out of life?
Take the quiz at www.michelleprohaska.com/quiz

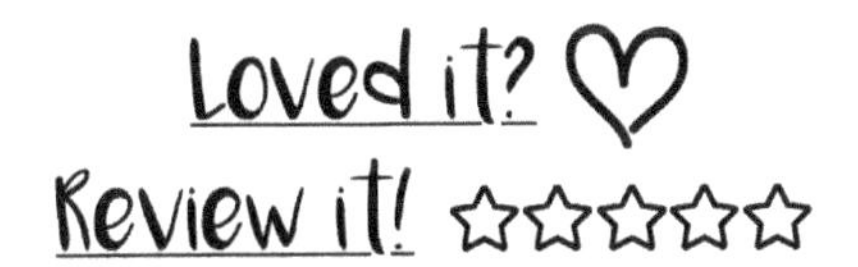

If you loved the book,
please give it a 5-star review on Amazon and Goodreads.
This will help get this AWEsome message
in the hands of more people.

Life is meant to be FUN!

I am an author, speaker, coach
who helps others, at any place in life, find happiness
by connecting with the supernatural
so they can feel nudged
and respond in joyful action.

Let's practice
living a
fun, full, fabulous life
TOGETHER!

Acknowledgments

Larry, it sounds so cliché, but you truly are my rock! Your support for everything I do means everything to me. I love how our love has grown with each new adventure and learning curve. Just when I think my love for you couldn't be greater, the way you love me makes me love you even more.

My daughters, Holly and Brooke. Being your mom has taught me so much about love. You both amaze me with your caring hearts! Never lose your love for humanity. It will take you places you've never dreamed. Don't let the world harden you, and always, always, always believe you can do BIG things!

My mom, Barb. I once made you a cross-stitch wall hanging that said, "Mother by chance, friend by choice." That still rings true today. Thank you for always supporting and being there for me. I miss our weekly happy hours, shopping excursions, and Sunday suppers. Always looking forward to summer and sunset cruises.

Aby, you were one of, if not the first person to know I was going to write this book. You were such an awesome encourager in the beginning when I still wasn't confident that I could do this. Thank you! I appreciate you and miss you fiercely!

Traci, my personal development buddy, I am so fortunate to have you by my side through this journey. You have always been willing to help me see my potential and to grow into the vision. Thank you!

Aleta, your willingness to help and coach me through the last several months has been above and beyond anything I expected. Your assurance has helped me know that I can and will get there. Thank you from the bottom of my heart for all your kindness and wisdom.

Chris, your friendship is that old, comfy, worn to threads sweatshirt. The thing I go to when I want to feel better and ok with where I am. I value the validation you've given me time and time again, and I cherish the times that we've laughed until we cried. Oh, so many.

Steff, I can't thank you enough for your willingness to be my first accountability partner. Your consistency is exactly what I needed to keep moving, even if it was only at a snail's pace. I love that your open-mindedness exceeds mine and that you've never thought of me as a fruit loop.

Andrea, your willingness to help a friend in need is what the world needs more of! I could tell you thank you every hour until I die, and it still would not be enough. I appreciate you and value your insights. I value our new friendship.

Bill, you have a heart of gold and would literally give anyone the shirt off your back or take off your shirt with your belly painted and sing to me to give me a birthday laugh. You always go above and beyond to make people feel loved. Thanks for being a gem.

Jenny, I knew from that first playdate that this friendship was going to be gold. Many miles between us and sometimes months between visits can't tarnish this friendship. You and Mark are a constant I don't ever have to worry about fading away. Thanks for being real. We need to get together more often and maybe do some Jell-o shots.

Jodi, even though I knew you were going to move away when we met, our friendship has followed you around the globe. You are a golden friend with a servant's heart. I cherish all the memories we have made and look forward to always making a memory with you.

Jill, I am so glad I found you! I needed someone with which I could be me, and I was led to you. Thank you, God! I appreciate your patience, gentleness, and willingness to help. It has been such a comfort to bounce things off of you. To see the grace with which you are traversing life is a true inspiration.

ISC tribe, the guidance of traversing this foreign journey was much needed. Thank you for the map to bring this book into the world. I am especially grateful for the heartfelt relationships created around the world. Connection is my key, and I have found many in this positive tribe.

Notes

1 Yogi Berra, "Yogi Berra Quote: 'That's Too Coincidental to Be a Coincidence.'," Quotefancy, accessed February 1, 2020, https://quotefancy.com/quote/941712/Yogi-Berra-That-s-too-coincidental-to-be-a-coincidence.

2 Merriam-Webster, s.v. "coincidence," accessed February 1, 2020, https://www.merriam-webster.com/dictionary/coincidence

3 Oliver Wendell Holmes, "Quote from Oliver Wendell Holmes," The Quotations Page, 2018, accessed July 1, 2020, http://www.quotationspage.com/quote/26186.html

4 Albert Einstein, "A Quote by Albert Einstein," Goodreads, 2020, accessed July 1, 2020, https://www.goodreads.com/quotes/987-there-are-only-two-ways-to-live-your-life-one

5 Henry Ford, "Find Quotes," Goodreads (Goodreads), accessed July 28, 2020, https://www.goodreads.com/quotes/search?q=Whether+you+think+you+can%2C+or+you+think+you+FORD.

6 Ben Andrews and Mary Andrews, "What If We Saw Everything As The Gift ~ That It Is?," YouTube (YouTube, December 7, 2016), https://www.youtube.com/watch?v=BZKg6N10OBo.

7 Pam Grout, "Transcending the Chatty Asshat in Your Head," Pam Grout, January 10, 2018, https://pamgrout.com/2018/01/10/transcending-the-chatty-asshat-in-you r-head/.

8 Angela Manuel Davis, "Oprah 2020 Vision Tour Talk w/ Angela Manuel Davis - Super Soul Sitdown," AfterBuzz TV Network, April 28, 2020, https://www.afterbuzztv.com/oprah-2020-vision-tour-talk-w-angela-manuel-davis-super-soul-sitdown/.

9 Rita Geno, "The Meaning of 'Namaste'," Yoga Journal, Pocket Outdoor Media Inc, Updated November 12, 2018, https://www.yogajournal.com/practice/the-meaning-of-quot-namaste-quot

10 Les Brown, "A Quote by Les Brown," Goodreads, 2020, accessed February 1, 2020, https://www.goodreads.com/quotes/884712-the-graveyard-is-the-richest-place-on-earth-because-it

11 Google Definition (Oxford Languages), s.v. "Magic," accessed February 1, 2020, https://www.google.com/search?rlz=1C1CHBF_enUS832US832%2Cmagic+definition.

12 Faith B, "The Serenity Prayer: Learning to Let Go," Alcoholics Anonymous, October 4, 2020, https://www.aanoc.org/breaking-down-the-serenity-prayer/.

13 Truthbook, "The Drowning Man," The Urantia Book and the Life of Jesus, accessed February 1, 2020, https://truthbook.com/stories/funny-god/the-drowning-man.

14 "Charles Blondin Story - Faith on a Tightrope," CreativeBibleStudy.com, accessed February 1, 2020, https://www.creativebiblestudy.com/Blondin-story.html.

15 Martin Luther King, "Black Power," in *Where Do We Go From Here; Chaos or Community?* (Tokyo: Simul Press, 1968), pp. 65.

CPSIA information can be obtained
at www.ICGtesting.com
Printed in the USA
BVHW091032230421
605637BV00003B/688